# AUSTRALIA'S IMPRESSIONISTS

National Gallery Company, London
Distributed by Yale University Press

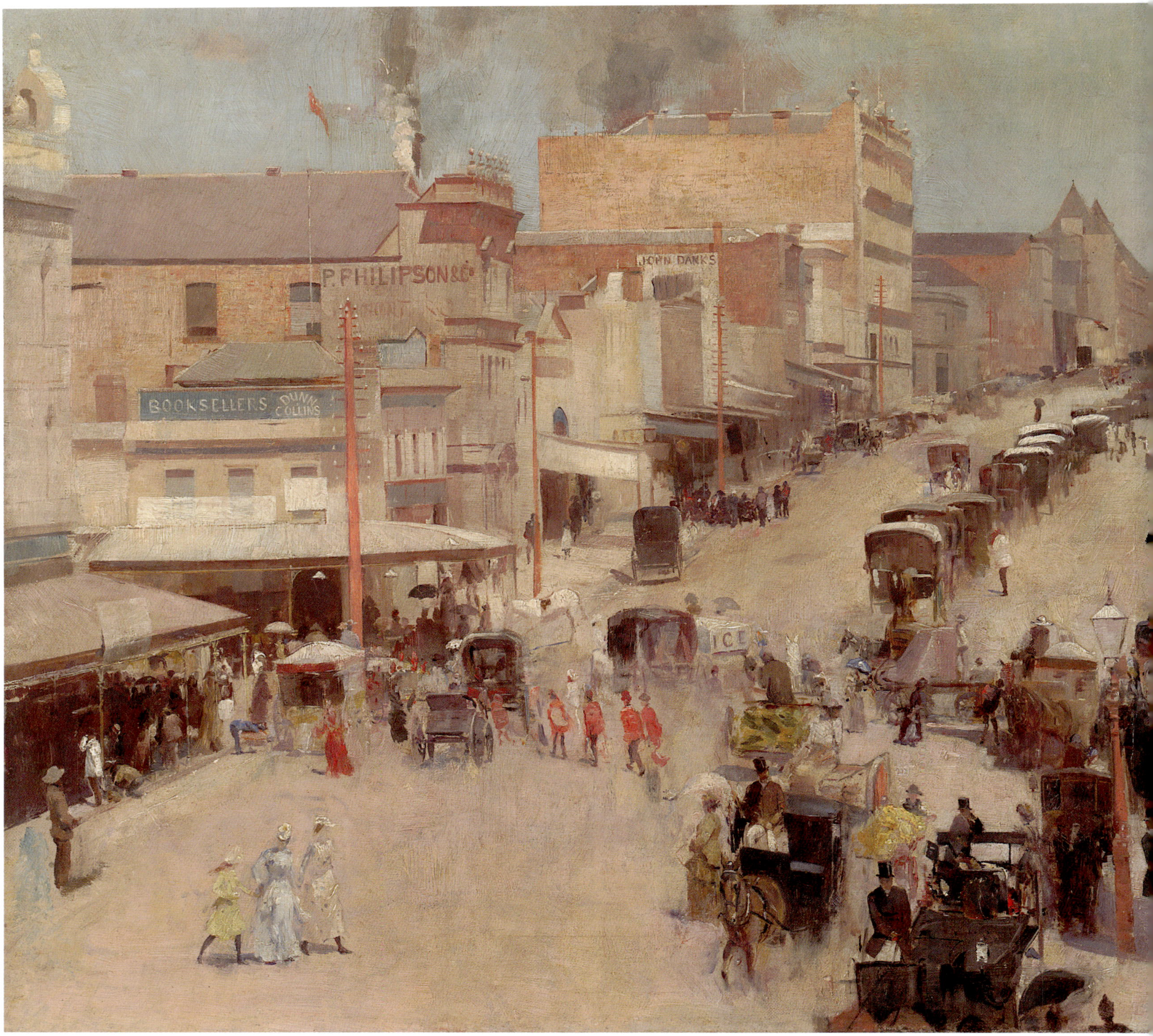
P. PHILIPSON & Co
JOHN DANKS
BOOKSELLERS

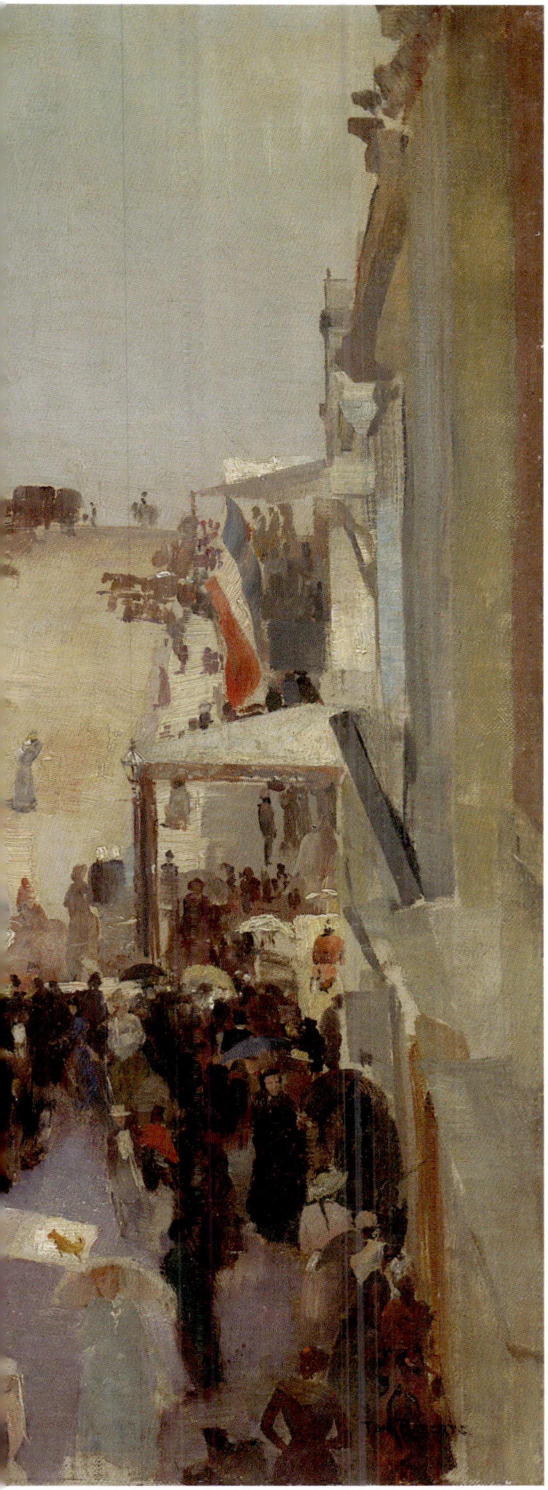

# AUSTRALIA'S IMPRESSIONISTS

Edited by Christopher Riopelle

Tim Bonyhady, Allison Goudie,
Sarah Thomas and Wayne Tunnicliffe
with contributions from Alex J. Taylor

Published to accompany the exhibition

**AUSTRALIA'S**
IMPRESSIONISTS

The National Gallery, London
7 December 2016 to 26 March 2017

Exhibition organised by the National Gallery, in collaboration with Art Gallery of New South Wales, Sydney

Curated by Christopher Riopelle and Allison Goudie, with Wayne Tunnicliffe

Catalogue has been supported by

Australian Capital Equity Pty Limited

Mr Kerry Stokes AC
& Mrs Christine Simpson Stokes

The Kerry Stokes Collection,
Perth, Western Australia

Exhibition has been supported by

Packer Family Foundation

and members of the Australia's Impressionists Exhibition Supporters Circle

The Sunley Room exhibition programme is supported by the Bernard Sunley Charitable Foundation

This exhibition has been made possible by the provision of insurance through the Government Indemnity Scheme. The National Gallery would like to thank HM Government for providing Government Indemnity and the Department for Culture, Media and Sport and Arts Council England for arranging the indemnity.

AUTHORS:

*Tim Bonyhady* is a cultural historian and environmental lawyer. He is Director of the Centre for Climate Law and Policy at the Australian National University, Canberra

*Allison Goudie* is Harry M. Weinrebe Curatorial Assistant at the National Gallery, London

*Christopher Riopelle* is Curator of Post-1800 Paintings at the National Gallery, London

*Alex J. Taylor* is Assistant Professor of History of Art and Architecture at University of Pittsburgh

*Sarah Thomas* is Lecturer in the Art of the Nineteenth Century, Birkbeck College, University of London

*Wayne Tunnicliffe* is Head Curator, Australian Art, at Art Gallery of New South Wales, Sydney

# Contents

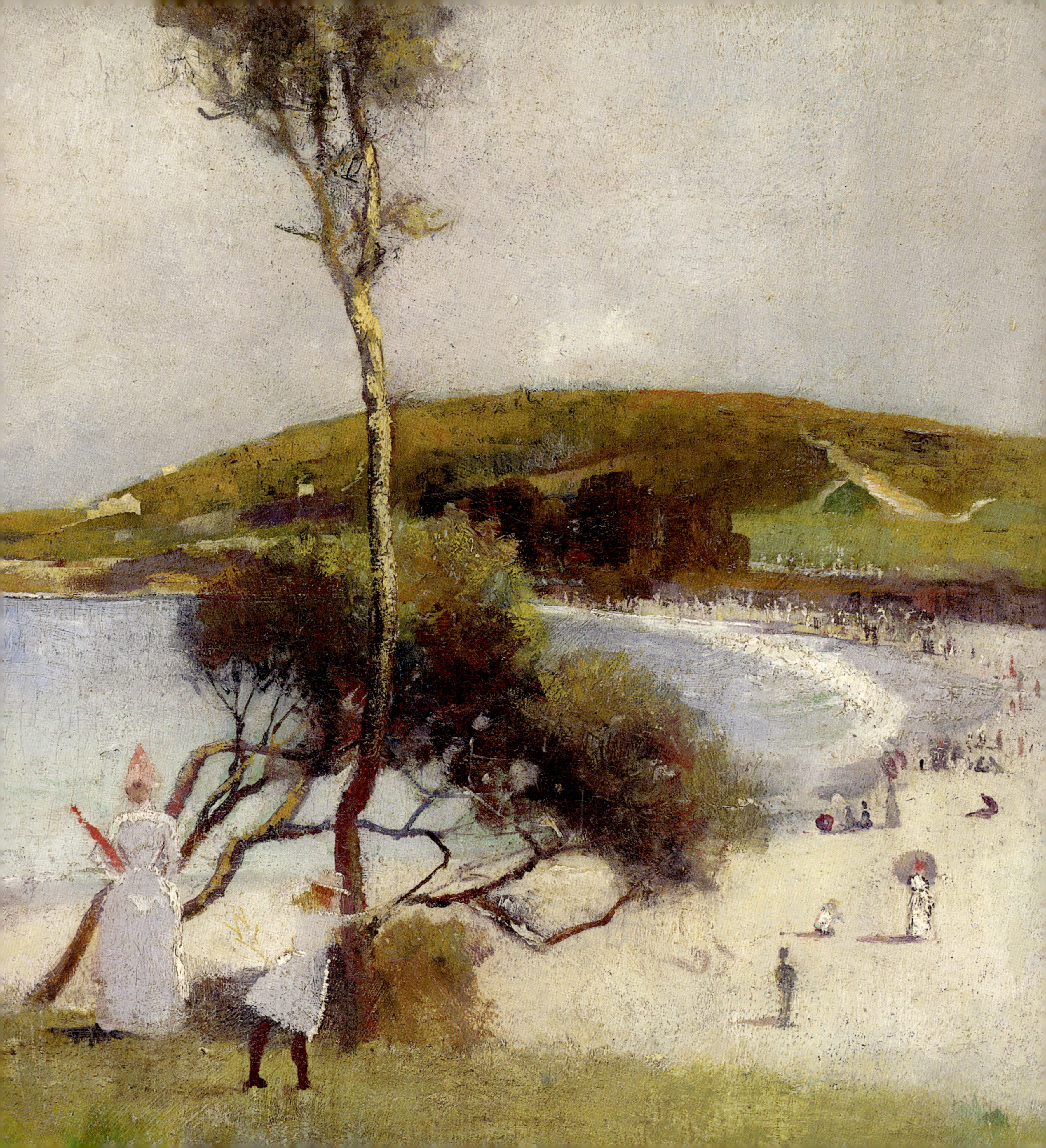

# Director's Foreword

In August 1889 an exhibition of contemporary art opened at Buxton's Rooms in central Melbourne called 'The 9 by 5 Impression Exhibition'. The curious title referred to the dimensions in inches of the cigar box lids that served as the supports for many of the pictures on display, but more significantly, it reflected the exhibiting artists' commitment to the aesthetic principles of Impressionism, to 'plein-air' landscape painting and the representation of the urban environment.

The leading painters were Tom Roberts (1856–1931) and Charles Conder (1868–1909), who had emigrated from England in their teens, and the Melburnian Arthur Streeton (1867–1943). Together with Sydney-born John Russell (1858–1930), who was already living in France where he became friends with Monet, Van Gogh and the young Matisse, they came to be known as Australia's Impressionists. Over the course of the 1880s and 1890s, as the sense of Australian nationhood became ever more keenly felt in the run up towards Federation in 1901, they forged a language of painting that celebrated the distinctive character of the Australian countryside and coastline and the bustling vibrancy of its fast-growing cities, particularly Sydney and Melbourne.

This is the first exhibition of Australian painting ever to be held at the National Gallery and it includes 41 works by these four artists. In his introductory essay in this catalogue, 'Australia's Impressionists in a World Context', Christopher Riopelle, co-curator of the exhibition together with Allison Goudie, refers to the Gallery's increased interest in recent times in less well-known aspects of nineteenth-century painting, both those which differ significantly from our own holdings and those that are related to them. Although this is the first exhibition of Australian painting held here, the Gallery has since the summer of 2015 displayed Arthur Streeton's *Blue Pacific* (cat. 27), a striking vertical-format landscape showing a coastal view at Coogee, Sydney, on loan from a private collection. The brilliant blue of the ocean and the dazzling glare of the Australian landscape – qualities that Streeton was particularly skilled in capturing – make it a spirited companion to the Gallery's landscapes by Monet and Seurat.

I want to express our gratitude to our partner museum in the organisation of the exhibition, the Art Gallery of New South Wales, Sydney, its Director, Michael Brand, and Wayne Tunnicliffe, Head Curator, Australian Art, with whom we have enjoyed an excellent working relationship. Our colleagues in Australia have been extraordinarily generous in making important loans available to us and I register our thanks to the Directors and curators at the National Gallery of Australia in Canberra, the Art Gallery of South Australia in Adelaide, the National Gallery of Victoria in Melbourne, and to the private collectors both in Australia and in Europe who have allowed us to show their paintings to the public in Trafalgar Square for a few months. I am sure that for our visitors Australia's Impressionists will be an engaging and memorable experience.

I would like to thank the Australian High Commissioner in London, His Excellency The Hon Alexander Downer AC, and his staff for their support. The exhibition has been made possible thanks to donations from The Packer Family Foundation and the Australia's Impressionists Exhibition Supporters' Circle. Finally, I am grateful to Mr Kerry Stokes AC and Mrs Christine Simpson Stokes who have funded this publication.

**Gabriele Finaldi**

Left
**Charles Conder** (1868–1909)
*Coogee Bay*, 1888
Detail of cat. 25, p. 89

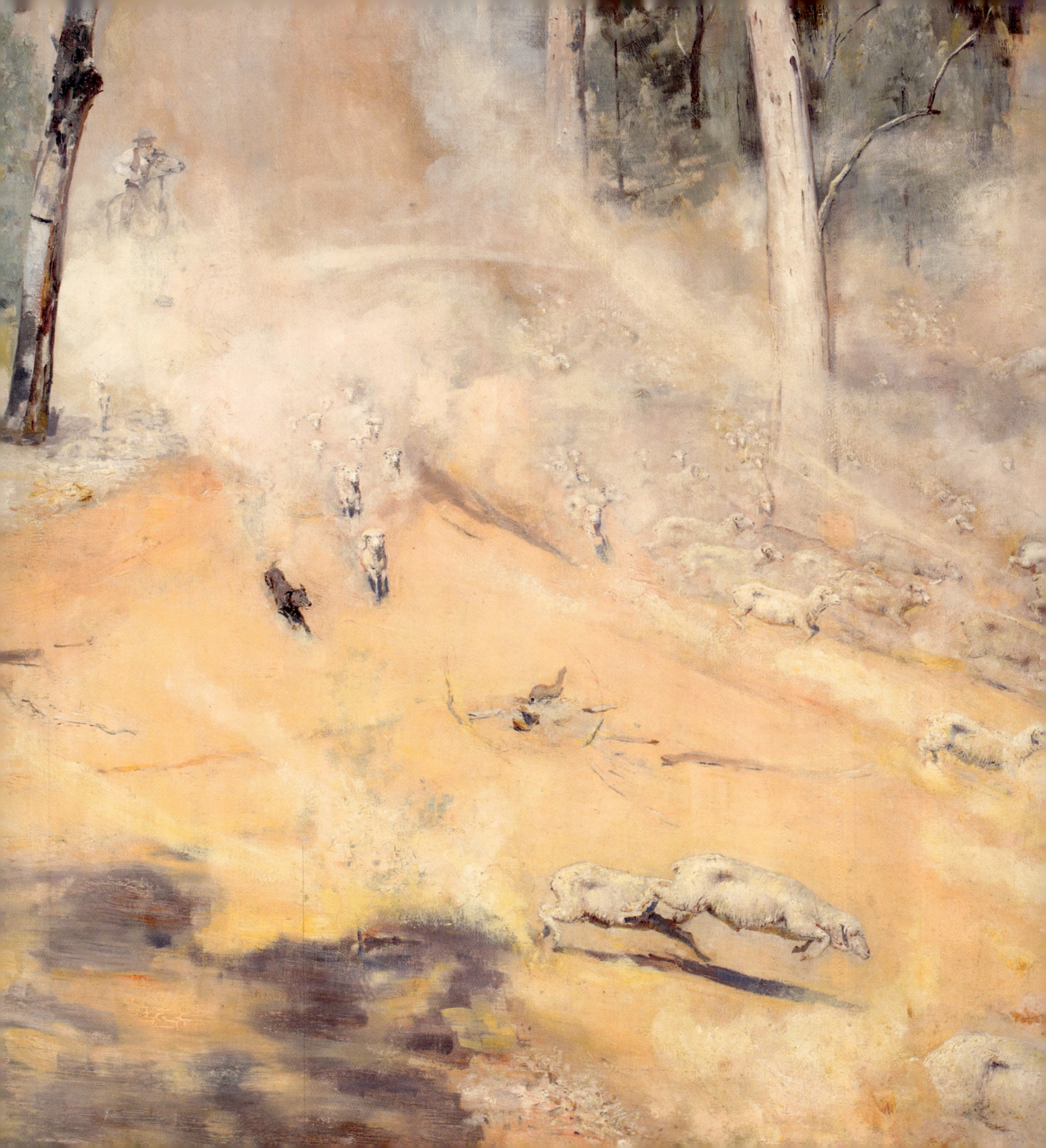

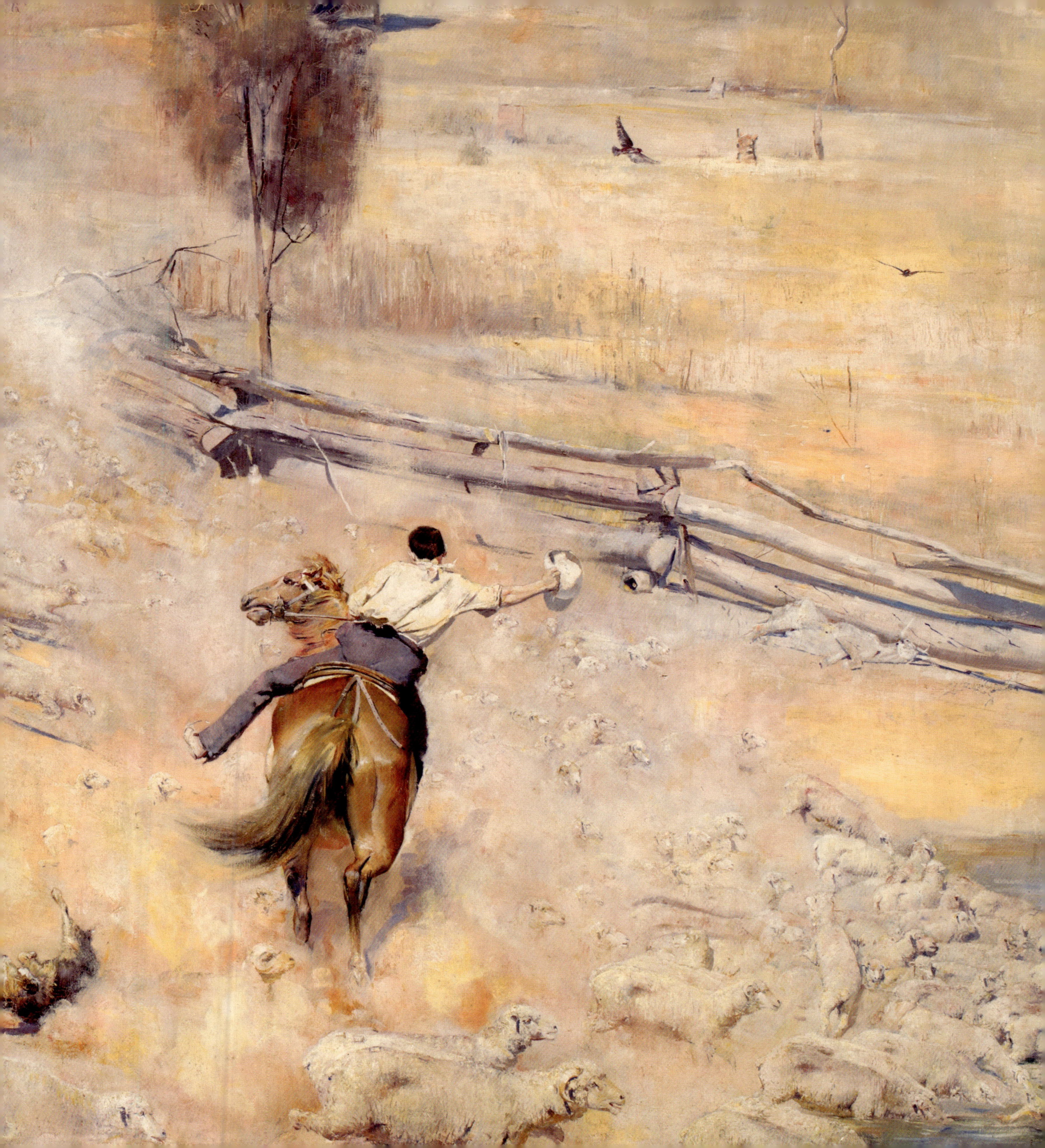

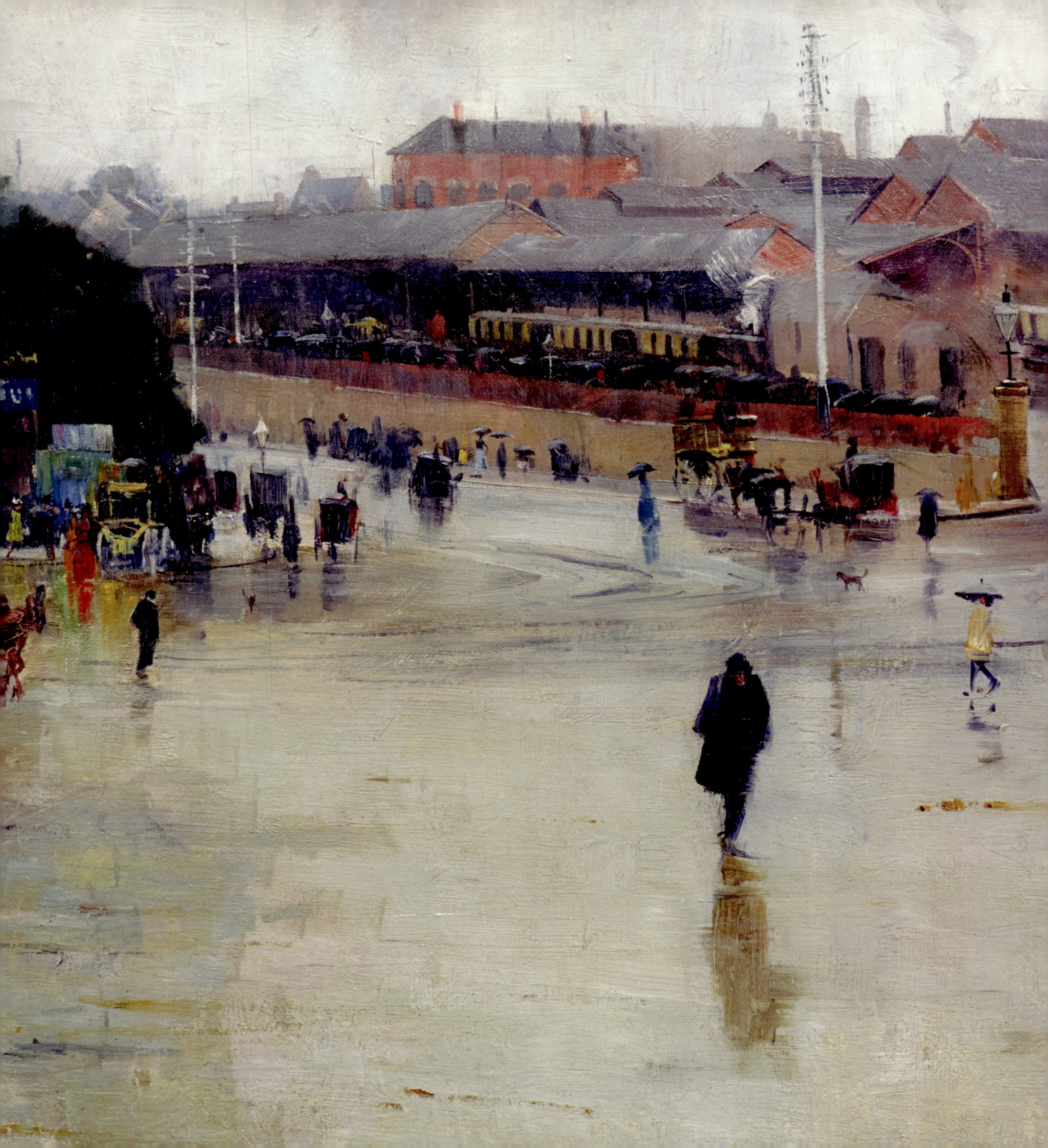

Australia was not alone in the late nineteenth and early twentieth centuries in its growing fascination with its own unique landscape, burgeoning cities, distinctive ways of life. Nor were its artists alone in adopting new, freer and more improvisatory modes of painting in order to capture these rapidly evolving realities. National self-consciousness was an international phenomenon of modern times. From Scandinavia to America to Japan, artists were exploring new modes of expression. Often, they kept a close eye on innovations made in the metropolitan art capitals, Paris and London in particular, seeing what they could profitably use to their own ends. We consider here how four Australian artists engineered their engagement with international avant-garde art and where it led Australian art in the run up to national Federation in 1901. It is an exciting story, unique, as all such stories are, but also representative of a worldwide trend. We look too at the National Gallery's growing interest in the phenomenon of national landscape painting and the broader context in which it mounts its first-ever exhibition of Australian painting.

Studying art in London, Tom Roberts (1856–1931) fell under the sway of James Abbott McNeill Whistler's silvery views of the Thames, exhibited there in May 1884. He was soon painting atmospheric oil sketches in a Whistlerian mode; *Fog, Thames Embankment* among them (cat. 2). Back in Melbourne from early 1885, he continued to execute sketches indebted to Whistler's moody tonal landscapes; *By the Treasury* could almost be a rain-swept London scene (cat. 3). He told younger contemporaries like Charles Conder (1868–1909) and Arthur Streeton (1867–1943) about Whistler's innovations and they too took up the style (cats 7 and 4). The 9 by 5 Impression Exhibition of 1889, spearheaded by Roberts and recognised even before it opened as a turning point in Australian art was, among much else, a testament to the role the distant Whistler and avant-garde London played in the collective imagination of ambitious young Australian painters.[1]

# AUSTRALIA'S IMPRESSIONISTS IN A WORLD CONTEXT

Christopher Riopelle

Fig. 1
**Arthur Streeton** (1867–1943)
*The Railway Station, Redfern*, 1893
Detail of cat. 13, p. 76

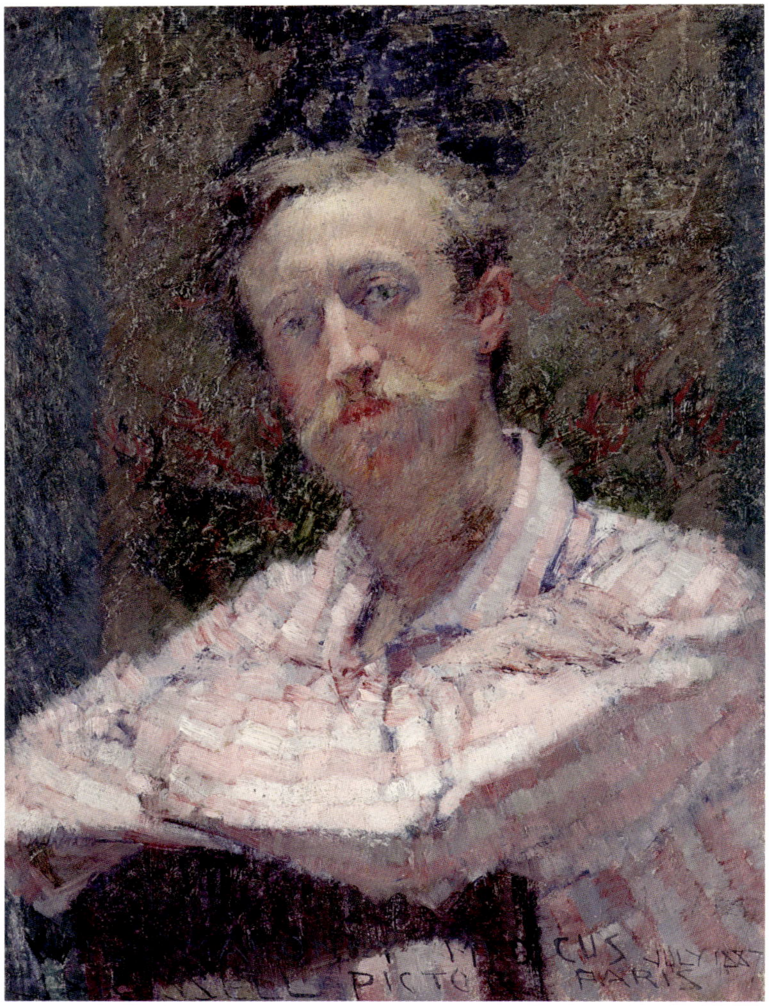

Fig. 2
**John Russell** (1858–1930)
*Dr Will Maloney*, 1887
Oil on canvas, 48.5 × 37 cm
National Gallery of Victoria, Melbourne
Purchased, 1943
(Accession no. 1242-4)

Years later Roberts recalled that he had always held on to *Fog, Thames Embankment* and other London sketches. They held up well to his later works, he said. They were for him 'a kind of touchstone', paintings he could go back to over and again for a renewal of artistic energy. Long after his art had moved on to distinctly Australian themes, and his obvious debt to Whistler and foreign models had faded, the heady lessons of 1880s London remained alive to Roberts. It was there, 'in my innocence' as he phrased it, that he confronted something entirely novel and, under its impact, made the breakthrough to a new kind of painting. Thus Roberts set the course his generation of Australian artists would follow.[2]

In Paris in 1887 John Russell (1858–1930) painted the portrait of a dashing young medical doctor, Will Maloney, inscribed it AMITIE, and gave it to the sitter as he prepared to return to Australia (fig. 2).[3] The portrait was more than a gift to a departing friend. Russell wanted it to be seen by fellow artists in Australia, particularly Roberts. It would show them the advances he had made in his art in the two years since Roberts himself had left Europe. Russell had thrown in his lot with the French avant-garde and it was taking him in the direction of bold Impressionist colour and broken brushstrokes as yet little seen in Australia. He followed up in December 1887 with a letter to Roberts describing the bright new palette he had now adopted and the struggle he faced 'chasing colour' by which, he confessed, he had been 'floored again and again.'[4]

The challenge never abated. Facing it and pushing ahead further and ever more fearlessly with his colour experiments lay at the heart of Russell's artistic project. He wrote to his friend Vincent van Gogh (1853–1890) in July 1888, commenting on the strengths he admired in Claude Monet (1840–1926), including the French artist's 'courage in attacking difficult problems.'[5] He would do the same. Even if Streeton later complained that Russell spent too much time fidgeting over the technical aspects of painting, 'ways and means' as he dismissed them, for Russell the problems were never merely technical but commensurate with the moral dimensions of his art and with the demands of his role as an artist. He would go on to pursue an artistic career in France at the forefront of fearless formal experiment and buoyed by friendships with modern masters from Monet and Van Gogh to Auguste Rodin

(1840–1917) and Henri Matisse (1869–1954) who themselves never ceased to push at barriers. It was the leitmotif of Modernism; henceforth, contemporary art would be characterised by an ever more rapid succession of styles and formal innovations, grouped under that inadequate heading, as artists sought new ways to confront a rapidly changing world. And Russell continued to send detailed reports on his work back to Roberts and the artistic community around him just so a vital connection with Australia would not be broken.

As these anecdotes suggest, early engagement with European avant-garde painting played a crucial role in the direction Australian art would take in the 1880s and 1890s. Having travelled vast distances to London and Paris, young Australians like Roberts and Russell found the training they had come for something of a disappointment; Europe's academies were hardly more exciting than the ones they had left behind. Conversely, independent-minded artists like Whistler and Monet pointed them in new directions. The Australians were far from alone in responding to such stimuli. Young artists from across Europe and North America were pouring into London and, increasingly as the century progressed, Paris.[6] There they confronted cosmopolitan art scenes, lively pockets of resistance to convention, sceptical attitudes to traditional art pedagogy, disdain for the status quo, both artistic and social, and boldly experimental new ways of making art, endlessly renewed. Students at the Parisian Atelier Cormon were as likely to encounter fellow foreigners as they were Frenchmen; it was there that Russell met Van Gogh and their lively exchange of ideas began. The artist to whom Roberts most powerfully responded in London, Whistler, was an American reared in Russia. The influence of Japanese art, especially prints with their bold flat patterning and abrupt shifts of scale, was sweeping avant-garde Europe. Internationalism was in the air, nowhere more so than in the cities that spanned the Seine and the Thames.

For searching spirits supposedly from the far side of wherever, the possibilities were electrifying. After their metropolitan sojourns most of them intended to, and did, return home, fired now by a mission to change art as it was practised where they came from. A brilliant-hued variant of French Impressionism, inspired particularly by the landscapes of Monet, soon swept American painting. Italians like Giuseppe de Nittis brought word south of innovations by Degas and Whistler and a generation, anxious to escape art training based on superannuated Renaissance principles, responded with alacrity. Edvard Munch, Auguste Strindberg, Helene Schjerfbeck and Akseli Gallen-Kallela brought the fresh air of Paris – and a disconcerting propensity for raw psychological confrontation – to Scandinavian art and began to forge the lineaments of a distinctive Nordic contribution to Modernism.

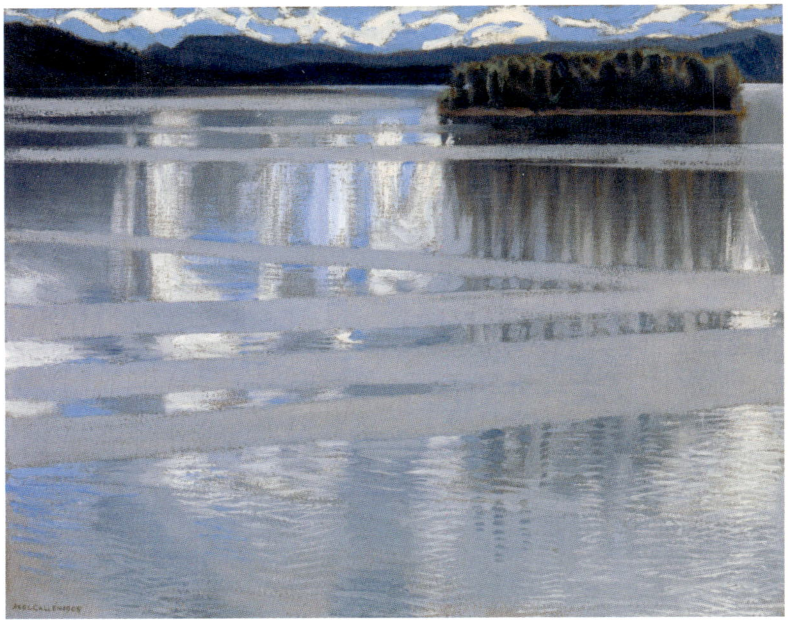

From Brussels to Berlin and Vienna, from St Petersburg to New York and Melbourne, artists responded to the new possibilities not slavishly but seeking to understand how the experimental styles and improvisatory techniques emerging in Paris and to a lesser extent London could be adapted to specific circumstances back home. Nowhere was this process of assimilation and adaptation livelier than in the field of landscape painting. An evolving sense of national identity was a global phenomenon in the later decades of the nineteenth century. In Australia it anticipated by decades the political union that came with Federation. Each nation looks different from its neighbours; it has its typical and distinctive landscape features; landscape imposes a way of life, as an Australian jackaroo or North Sea fisherman can attest. Each nation can recognise itself in landscape and so in the nineteenth century its representation on canvas became a privileged forum for collective self-reflection. This proved particularly so in places as yet without a strong visual tradition based on the European model. Here was where that tradition would be forged. Thus, what came to be called national landscape painting emerged as a highly varied international movement and an engine for the spread of Modernism.[7]

## WHY IS THE NATIONAL GALLERY SHOWING AUSTRALIA'S IMPRESSIONISTS?

Fig. 3
**Akseli Gallen-Kallela** (1865–1931)
*Lake Keitele*, 1905
Oil on canvas, 53 × 66 cm
The National Gallery, London (NG 6574)

Fig. 4
Installation view of exhibitions at the National Gallery, London. Russian Landscape in the Age of Tolstoy (2004), and Forests, Rocks, Torrents (2011).

In recent years the National Gallery in London has set out to trace the lineaments of this evolving engagement with landscape painting, the questions it poses about the relationship between art in the cosmopolitan centre and the rise of national art movements in the most distant reaches of its orbit. Further, what role did this process of assimilation and adaptation play in the spread of Modernism? That engagement has taken the form of acquisitions, loans to the permanent collection, and exhibitions. Acquired in 1999, Gallen-Kallela's *Lake Keitele* (fig. 3), to take one example, is formally indebted in its high horizon, simplified forms and broad swathes of colour to the landscapes of contemporary French artists like Pierre Puvis de Chavannes and

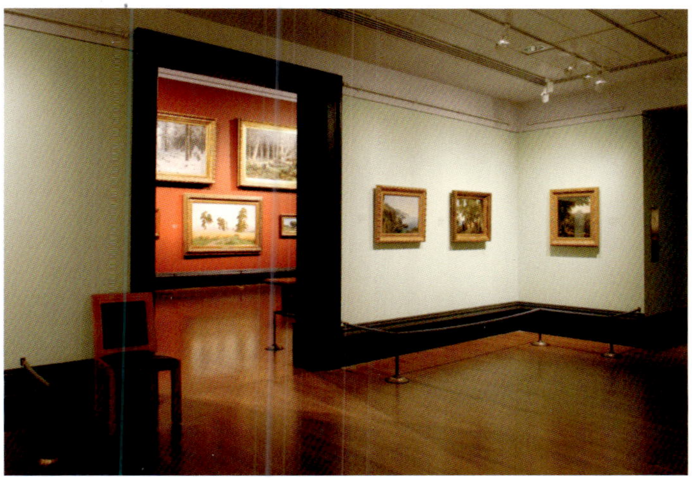

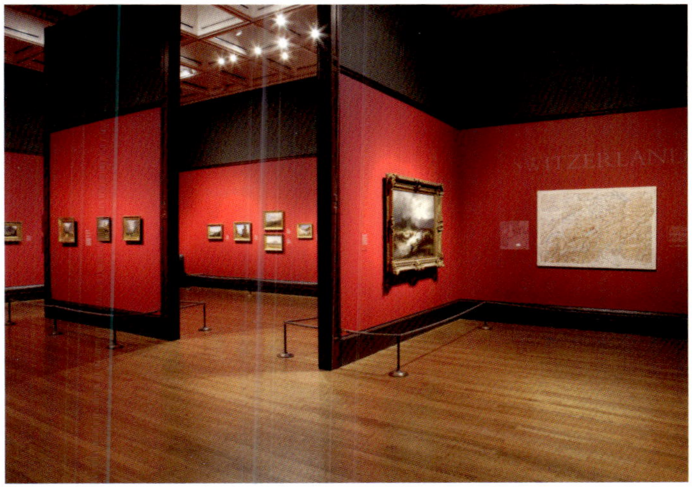

Paul Gauguin but at the same time is profoundly engaged with the artist's native Finland; an ancient hero of the Finnish national epic *Kalevala* has just rowed across the lake and it is his silvery wake we see.[8] The core group of predominantly French modern paintings assembled for the nation from the beginning of the First World War has been expanded by formally audacious paintings by Danish, Norwegian, German, Belgian and Italian artists.

Temporary exhibitions have provided even wider scope for investigation. The political dimension of landscape in circumstances of oppression was explicitly addressed in Russian Landscape in the Age of Tolstoy, an exhibition of 2004 in which concepts of Motherland (*rodina*) were seen to permeate Russian self-consciousness (fig. 4, top). Thus an austere landscape like Isaak Levitan's *The Vladimirka Road* of 1892, utterly devoid of human figures, could nonetheless function as an indictment of Siberian exile and a metaphor for Tsarist tyranny.[9] In 2008 the exhibition Radical Light: Italy's Divisionist Painters showed how Italian artists absorbed, largely sight-unseen, the coloristic lessons of French pointillist painting to evolve a uniquely Italian manner of depicting both sunlight and artificial illumination. It proved a strong tool for confronting modern themes and, as the exhibition demonstrated, led directly to Italy's greatest contribution to twentieth-century art, Futurism.[10] Forests, Rocks, Torrents, an exhibition of 2011, compared the oddly similar landscape traditions of nineteenth-century Switzerland and Norway, showing the special role landscape played in evolving national self-definitions (fig. 4, below).[11]

Such phenomena were not restricted to Europe. Recently the National Gallery has expanded its mandate from the commitment to collect, display and study European painting; it now addresses painting further afield, works that, broadly speaking, fall within the European representational tradition but which may have been created anywhere in the world. Thus, exhibitions have been, or are planned, devoted to such American landscape painters as Thomas Cole, Frederic Church and George Bellows and his contemporaries, and an impressive Bellows cityscape of 1912 has been acquired.[12] In 2015, Streeton's *Blue Pacific* of 1890 (cat. 27), a view of Coogee Bay in Sydney, came on long-term loan to the Gallery, the first Australian painting to hang here. In the future, visitors to Trafalgar Square will see an increasingly diverse display of international modern art.

This is the context in which the present exhibition has been mounted. Australia's Impressionists are seen here as constituents of a wider, indeed a worldwide dialectic in which nation after nation finds its way to self-expression and to Modernism. It is an introduction to the subject, directed at an audience that knows little about Australian art. It paints with a broad brush – only four key painters represent many more. It is profoundly indebted to the work of generations of Australian art historians who continue to assess the national tradition with impeccable precision, and not without scholarly disagreements robustly expressed. But it proposes an international perspective and asks, from afar, why we here should be concerned with understanding the motivations that led artists 130 years ago to decide they needed to find a way, their own way, to describe Australia. The answer is that it forms one chapter in an international story in which Britain and France and Europe and America, no less than Australia, are vitally implicated and that lies at the heart of Modernism.

Three of the four artists worked 'at home'. Two of them, Roberts and Conder, were actually British-born and the latter spent only seven years in Australia, never to return. Yet their engagement with Australia was complete. Born in the suburbs of Melbourne, Streeton had never been abroad, indeed he had never been much further than Melbourne itself, when he took up painting. Natural gifts, meeting ambitious friends like Roberts and Conder, and discovering plein-air painting soon allowed him to reveal his startling originality. The three artists led a revolution in Australian painting, first announced in the winter of 1889 with the 9 by 5 Impression Exhibition which they organised and which, as we have seen, was deeply informed by what they knew of Whistler and his art, and by word of something called Impressionism coming out of France which promised a new freedom and spontaneity in painting the modern world.

Soon, they grew increasingly ambitious in the scale and complexity of their image-making as they took on purely Australian themes like Roberts's proto-cinematic *A Break Away!* (cat. 22) and Streeton's monumental and tragic *Fire's On* (cat. 23). The emphasis on international developments gradually fell away as these artists found their distinctive, indeed unmistakeable Australian 'voices'. Perhaps because he had not yet been to Europe, Streeton felt that bit more free from foreign influence than his companions. By 1891 such paintings as *A Dusty Road, Templestowe* (fig. 5) engaged with an essentially monochromatic and largely featureless local landscape in ways that could not be mistaken for any other in Europe or America, one that Australian viewers could unfailingly recognise as their own. The exhibition traces this relatively rapid development so that by the time of Federation Australia could boast a fully-fledged and proudly self-aware national school.

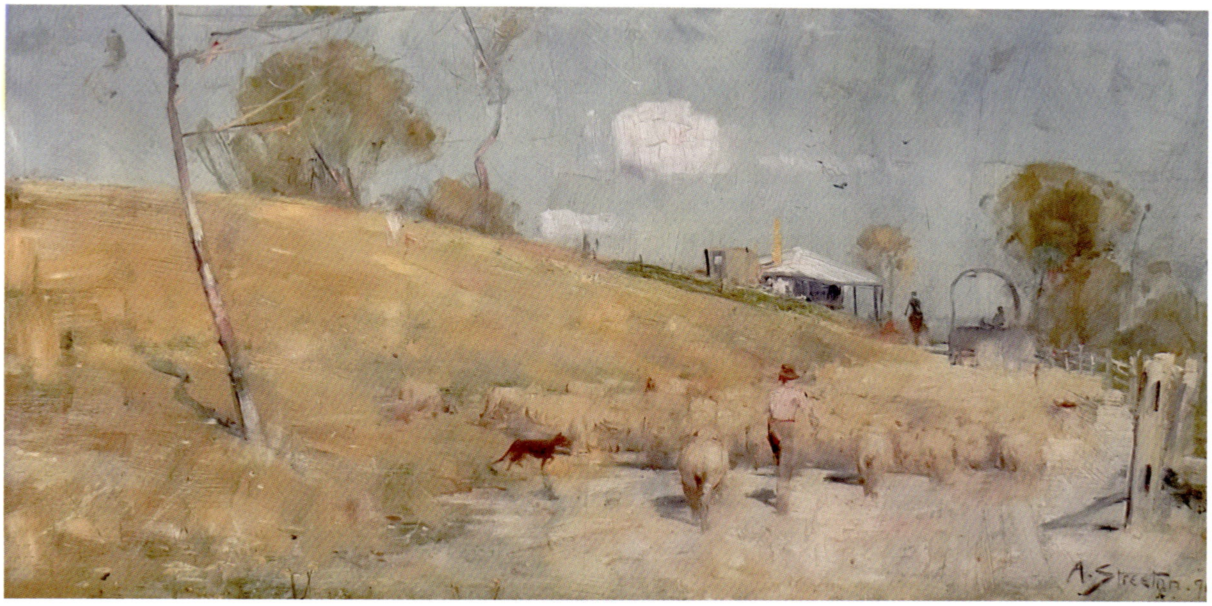

Fig. 5
**Arthur Streeton** (1867–1943)
*A Dusty Road, Templestowe*, 1891
Oil on canvas, 29.5 × 60 cm
Private collection, London

Russell is the odd man out. He chose to work abroad among the French avant-garde and by the time he returned to Australia in 1921 had for all intents and purposes given up art-making. Until relatively recent times and the pioneering investigations of Ann Galbally,[13] he is conspicuously absent in Australian art history, as if his decision to remain too long in France and to paint in a 'foreign' style disqualified him from consideration in the context of 'real' Australian art. He might be a lively foreign footnote in the history of French Modernism, like the Irishman Roderic O'Conor or the Canadian James Wilson Morrice, but seemingly was of little import back home.[14] As recently as 2013 he was simply omitted from the otherwise-close-to-exhaustive survey Australia mounted at London's Royal Academy of Arts. It is as if Americans were to omit Mary Cassatt from accounts of their art for her temerity in choosing Paris over Philadelphia.

We do know, from his letters to Roberts in particular, that Russell was determined to keep in contact with his native land. He wanted Australian artists to know about his paintings and his engagement with the most advanced artists in the world. What we propose here is that the Australian connection was more profound than geographical proximity, that the boldness with which Russell prosecuted his painterly vision, his conviction that Australia should confront Modernity on an equal footing with his French friends – and with one odd and rebarbative Dutchman who had been his confidante and, amazingly, turned out before long to be the most famous and influential artist in the world – was an Australian trait. By giving Russell 'equal billing' here with those masters of the Australian theme, Roberts, Streeton and Conder, we propose a slightly different reading of the dynamics of Australian art at the birth of Modernism than has previously been seen in London.

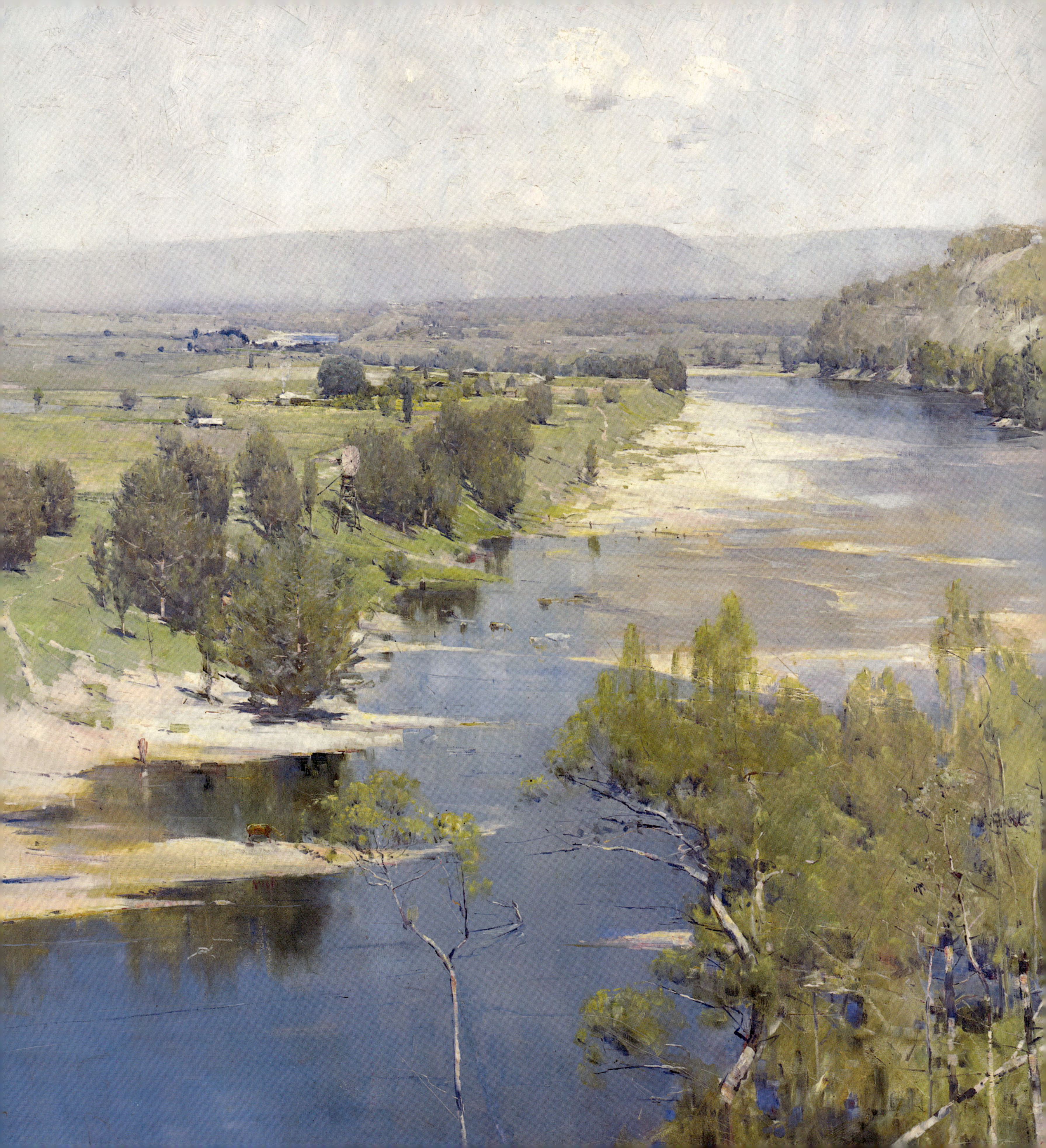

A photograph, as much as any painting, illuminates Australia's Impressionism. Arthur Streeton (1867–1943) is on the edge of Sydney Harbour at Little Sirius Cove, sitting cross-legged on the sand just a few yards from the water (fig. 7). With back turned to the camera, brush in hand, at work on a small board propped up creatively by a long branch, Streeton appears immersed in the act of painting, oblivious to the photographer, though another photograph reveals that he knew the camera was there. Apart from a hat worn because of the midday sun, and a necktie, he is topless. No settler artist in Australia had been pictured like that – so much part of Australian nature, working under what Streeton described as the 'palpitating sky of the Sunny South'.[1]

Many other artists from diverse European backgrounds had depicted the harbour since the eleven ships of the First Fleet, sent by Great Britain to establish a penal colony in Australia, reached Sydney Cove in 1788 with a multitude of draughtsmen among its officers and convicts. Through the mid-nineteenth century, Conrad Martens, a one-time shipmate of Charles Darwin on the *Beagle*, was the artist who made most of the harbour in watercolour. The photographer Charles Bayliss, working with one of the tycoons of Australian gold, Bernard Holtermann, approached the harbour with particular ambition in the 1870s, using glass negatives, 3 by 5 feet or 91 by 152 cm, then the largest wet-plates in the world. Streeton also offered something new.

A typically evocative letter, almost a prose poem, describes Streeton's first experience of Sydney on arriving from Melbourne by steamer with his fellow artist Tom Roberts (1856–1931) in June 1890:

> *We enter the heads, slowing wind up the harbour, past men-of-war who salute and dip their flags... Then Circular Quay with many steamers busy and bright... puffing hard & skipping over the blue water clouds of smoke... Roberts & I go to Mossman's Bay* [sic] *& pull through the lazy green water, & then lunch under the shade in the open air, eggs, meat, cheese, & 2 big bottles of claret... In the afternoon down to Coogee – where the great green rollers tumble in like huge heavy cylinders of liquid glass, spreading glory everywhere.*[2]

Fig. 6
**Arthur Streeton** (1867–1943)
*'The purple noon's transparent might'*, 1896
Detail of cat. 20, p. 83

# THE SUNNY SOUTH

Tim Bonyhady

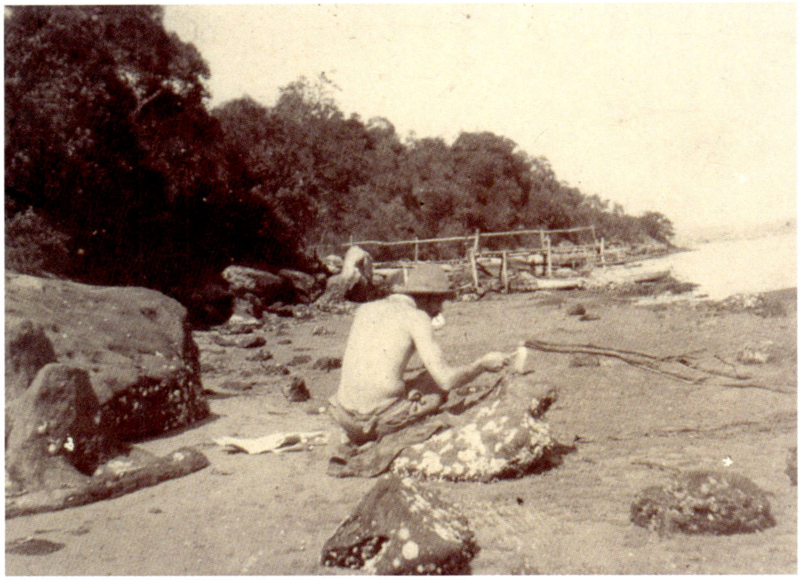

Fig. 7
Arthur Streeton painting 'a little rotter' (sketch-painting) at Sirius Cove, probably 1893.
Private collection

That first day was more than the usual sightseeing. It was a tour of three painting grounds: Circular Quay; Mosman, three miles north across the harbour; and Coogee, six miles to the south-east of the Quay by tram. Roberts, on his one previous visit in April 1888, had painted with Charles Conder (1868–1909) at Coogee, resulting in their pair of pictures, *Holiday Sketch at Coogee* and *Coogee Bay*, looking over the beach from its north headland (cats 24 and 25). *Departure of the Orient* (cat. 11), acquired immediately by the Art Gallery of New South Wales in September 1888 when the precocious Conder was not yet twenty, was of the Quay. A few years later, Roberts would paint *Mosman's Bay* with its 'lazy green water' (New England Regional Art Museum, Armidale).

In taking the 23-year-old Streeton across the harbour to Mosman, then to the ocean at Coogee in June 1890, the 34-year-old Roberts was showing his fellow artist what he too might paint. Streeton's summation was 'an artist's city – glorious'.[3] He was soon rendering the water of the harbour with unprecedented intensity of blue in his two versions of *From McMahon's Point – Fare One Penny* (National Gallery of Australia). He was also painting at Coogee, including one canvas which he called *The Sunny South* – a title already used by Roberts in Melbourne (fig. 8). A couple of years later, Streeton painted his first *Circular Quay* (cat. 30).

The Curlew Camp was just a short walk from Mosman at Little Sirius Cove, run much like a boarding house, but with the residents living in tents, it became Roberts's home from September 1891 and Streeton's from December 1892.[4] The photograph of Streeton on the water's edge probably dates from 1893, when Streeton described himself as 'sailing, getting sunburnt, painting a bit'.[5] Through these years, the harbour was central to Streeton's art. Where Roberts would hit on a great subject but often paint it only once, when Streeton found his, he pictured it again and again – large and more 'finished' canvases for major exhibitions with a view to public acquisition; smaller panels for private sales, including many narrow boards, usually horizontal, but sometimes vertical. In 1900, the Sydney *Bulletin* celebrated Streeton as 'the discoverer of Sydney Harbour'.[6]

Roberts was the immediate catalyst of this new mode of Australian painting, begun in Melbourne when the city was booming. The trigger was Roberts's return in 1885 from four years in Europe where he probably saw little French Impressionism, but was clearly influenced by the Anglo-American James Abbott McNeil Whistler, who was often

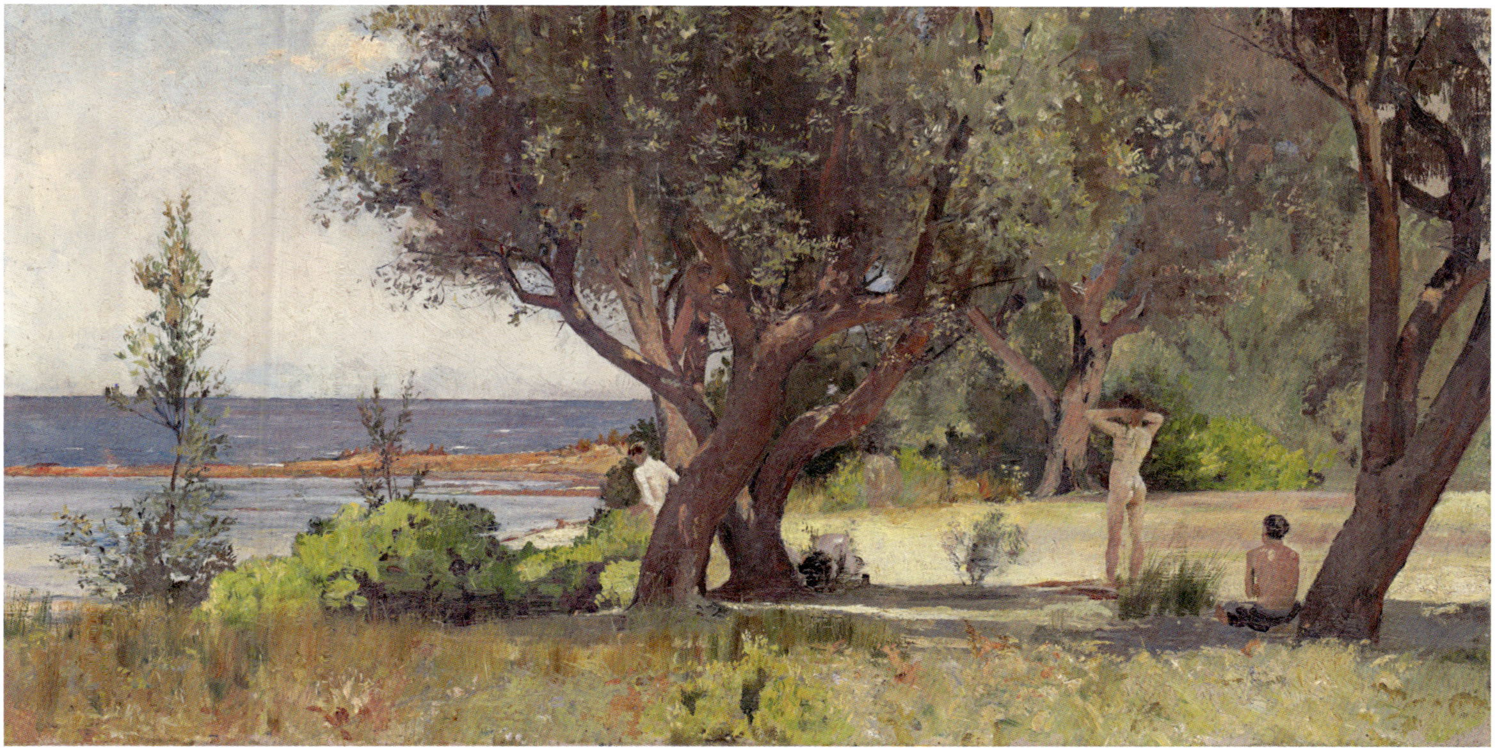

Fig. 8
**Tom Roberts** (1856–1931)
*The Sunny South*, about 1887
Oil on canvas, 30.8 × 61.4 cm
National Gallery of Victoria, Melbourne

Felton Bequest, 1940
(Accession No. 1078-4)

identified as an Impressionist in England, as he was occasionally also in Australia.[7] Roberts brought a new freedom and freshness of painting to Melbourne, taken up by a group of artists with shifting membership but with Roberts at its centre. His small oil *A Quiet Day on Darebin Creek* (cat. 15), exhibited in December 1885, is the first sign of this new school of artists. Painted primarily on site, an hour's journey from Melbourne's centre, it depicts two of Roberts's early painting companions, most likely John Llewellyn Jones with either Frederick McCubbin or Louis Abrahams (fig. 11, p. 28).[8]

That summer, Roberts painted with McCubbin and Abrahams at suburban Box Hill, a thirteen-mile train ride from the city centre, which would remain one of their painting grounds for three years. The following summer, this trio, eager for beach subjects, shifted to Beaumaris on Port Phillip Bay where they encountered Streeton who was also painting there. When Roberts first visited Sydney in April 1888, he met Conder who moved later that year to Melbourne, where he shared a studio with Roberts. Around the same time, Streeton found yet another outer-suburban painting ground, at Heidelberg on the Yarra Valley, again easily accessible by train, where Conder joined him, probably in January 1889, followed by Roberts, until Conder departed for England in April 1890. By then, the economy was in bust, which was one reason why Roberts and Streeton lived at Curlew Camp when they moved to Sydney.

Over the previous century, landscape painting had been the strongest artistic tradition of settler Australians. The British-born John Glover (fig. 27, p. 49) and the Austrian Eugene von Guérard had been the most accomplished. Contrary to much twentieth-century critique, these colonial artists were masters of the Australian landscape which they pictured variously as an Aboriginal arcadia, a pastoral arcadia and a wilderness intact.[9] Still, Roberts and Streeton and, to a lesser extent, Conder, transformed how Australia was visualised. They took up established subjects such as the city centre and Sydney Harbour in a new form. They introduced other subjects ranging from European men and boys, naked in the landscape, to fruit trees in bloom, to outback workers, often engaged in 'strong, masculine labour'. They pictured twilights and moonrises as well as intense light and heat.

'Glare' was a keyword. The Melbourne critic, Fred Broomfield, who believed that an 'Australian School of Art' was imminent in 1889, wanted pictures of 'the torrid glare of a fierce and unrelenting noonday sun'.[10] A review in 1890 observed that Streeton and Conder had 'evidently set before themselves the task of reproducing ... the impression of the glare and heat and dust which is such a common feature of our summer landscape'.[11] Another review of Streeton's Sydney Sunshine exhibition of 1896 identified the great majority of paintings – including *'The purple noon's transparent might'* (fig. 6, p. 18) – as 'vivid transcripts of Australian landscape seen beneath the fierce glare of noonday summer sun'.[12] A retrospective of Streeton's art in 1919 lauded his 'extraordinary fidelity' in capturing 'the dazzling, shimmering glare of the Australian landscape'.[13] While 'glare aesthetic' was coined in the 1970s by American art historians for a mode of American painting which was primarily academic,[14] in Australia a 'glare aesthetic' is integral to the Impressionist mode.

The greatest Australian expression of the 'glare aesthetic' is Streeton's *Fire's On* from 1891 (fig. 9), showing the construction of the Lapstone Tunnel through the Blue Mountains west of Sydney. Streeton always intended this picture as a painting of labour – that favourite nineteenth-century subject, so often heroicised or sentimentalised. Streeton was aware from the outset of the hazards for navvies of blasting new track, their deadliest job.[15] 'Awful work', Streeton observed. His initial plan was to show navvies filling wheelbarrows and wagons with blasted rock.[16] That changed when a young navvy, Edward Brown,[17] was killed. 'Blown to death 20 yards from me', Streeton wrote, deeply affected, having spoken to Brown only the day before. While Baudelaire's dictum – 'modernity is the random, the fugitive, the accidental' – has been applied by Virginia Spate to Tom Roberts's *Allegro con Brio, Bourke Street West* (cat. 14),[18] it is at least as applicable to *Fire's On*. Having witnessed the accident, Streeton showed Brown's body being carried out on a stretcher.

Had Streeton called his big canvas *The Fatal Cutting* – as he described it in a letter to Roberts – anyone who looked at the painting with title in mind would have peered into it to see why. Instead, Streeton called it *Fire's On*, the warning shout used when a blast was about to occur, which regularly set Streeton himself retreating from his painting perch. In keeping with this title, Streeton showed dust and smoke rising from the blast. Yet when viewed from some distance, it is easy to overlook what is happening, as the most obvious relation of man and nature is one of scale: the immensity of the land and sky and the smallness of the figures. There is an area of intense yellow near the centre of the picture which catches the eye and then there is the shimmering sky, a masterpiece of Streeton's square brushwork.

In one of his letters to Roberts, Streeton wrote of a 'mirage, sizzling and jiggering'; in another letter to McCubbin he wrote of 'the deep blue azure heaven'. While Roberts achieved great intensity and comparable glare in his contemporary *A Break Away!* (cat. 22) which he worked on largely in a woolshed, Streeton painted *Fire's On* primarily on the spot over six weeks. The tragedy of the man's death is overwhelmed as the painting 'rejoices', as Streeton also wrote to Roberts, 'at the prosperous warmth all glowing before me'. Streeton's goal before he witnessed Brown's death was to 'paint a 6 foot [183 cm] Colory gem' and that was what he did, despite his picture's calamitous content.[19]

The appetite for an Australian school of painting was palpable, amidst heightened nationalism, as the six self-governing British colonies in Australia looked

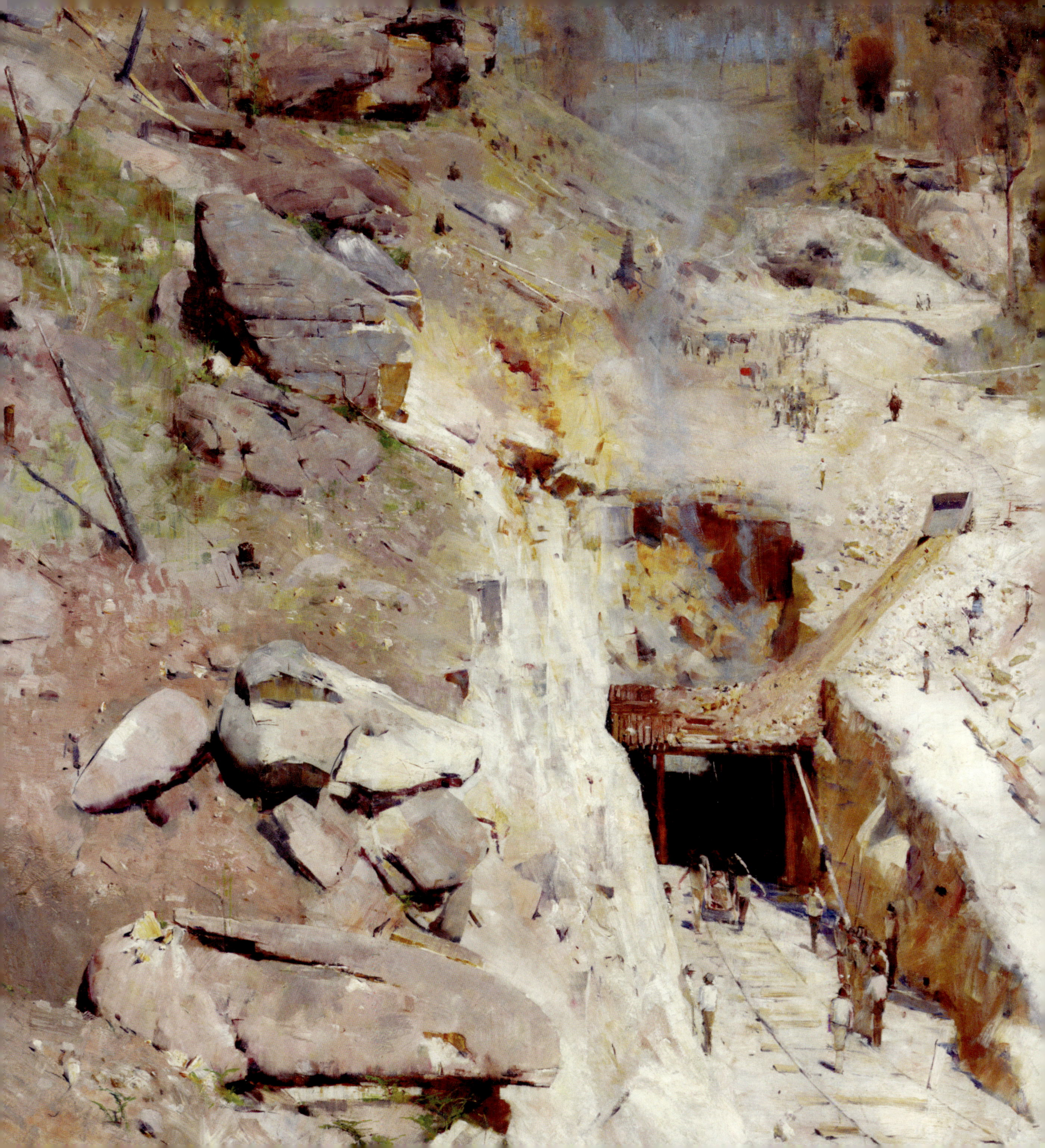

to become a nation, achieved through Federation in 1901. Oscar Comettant, a French member of the International Jury for the art gallery at Melbourne's Centennial Exhibition of 1888, thought the prospects of a distinctively Australian school bleak.[20] The Melbourne critic, Fred Broomfield, disagreed, declaring: 'the penumbra of a genuinely Australian School of Art... veritably visible'.[21] Roberts, Streeton and Conder invoked this debate in September 1889, casting their joint 9 by 5 Impression Exhibition as a step 'towards the development of what we believe will be a great school of painting in Australia'.[22] Conder, aboard a ship bound for England in May 1890, went further. In a farewell letter to Roberts, he remarked: 'If there is *any distinct school* in Melbourne – I won't say Sydney – it's entirely due to you'.[23]

This view became orthodoxy in the twentieth century, embraced by Streeton who dedicated an exhibition of his paintings in Melbourne in 1915 'To Tom Roberts, from whose quick perception and expression of the principles of Impressionism in the year 1886, sprang the first national school of painting in Australia'.[24] In 1929 the critic J.S. MacDonald identified Roberts as the 'father' of Australian landscape painting. The one matter of debate was whether Streeton was as important, or perhaps more so. In his *Story of Australian Art*, William Moore argued in 1934 that, while Streeton had 'generously given all the credit to Roberts', it 'was the influence of Streeton... which led to the creation of an Australian School of landscape painting'.[25]

The 'Australian School of landscape painting' or the 'national school' were the usual characterisations of this group through these years, but as other styles flourished, there was a need for a more specific name. 'Heidelberg School', named after the Melbourne suburb on the Yarra River, was a coinage in 1891 of the art critic, Dickinson, occasionally used in the first decades of the twentieth century. The Melbourne *Age* wrote in 1926 of the painter David Davies being 'associated with Arthur Streeton, Tom Roberts and Charles Conder in the famous Heidelberg School of landscape painters'. A decade later, Streeton identified Roberts, Conder and himself as the 'chief workers' of the 'Heidelberg School'.[26] But 'Heidelberg School' was not generally accepted as their collective identity until Bernard Smith, Australia's foundational art historian, embraced it in his *Place, Taste and Tradition* of 1945, triggering its widespread adoption.[27]

It was – and remains – a useful label, but was flawed if taken as implying that Heidelberg was the artists' principal painting ground. In 1973 the pre-eminent curator of Australian art, Daniel Thomas, declared it 'unsatisfactory', named with 'insufficient justification'. Thomas argued that Box Hill was 'more important' in Melbourne,[28] and Sydney was at least as significant – a point made most sharply by the cultural historian Humphrey McQueen. In his *Tom Roberts*, the greatest biography of an Australian artist, McQueen identified what took place as 'A Tale of Two Cities'.[29]

Fig. 9
**Arthur Streeton** (1867–1943)
*Fire's On*, 1891
Detail of cat. 23, p. 87

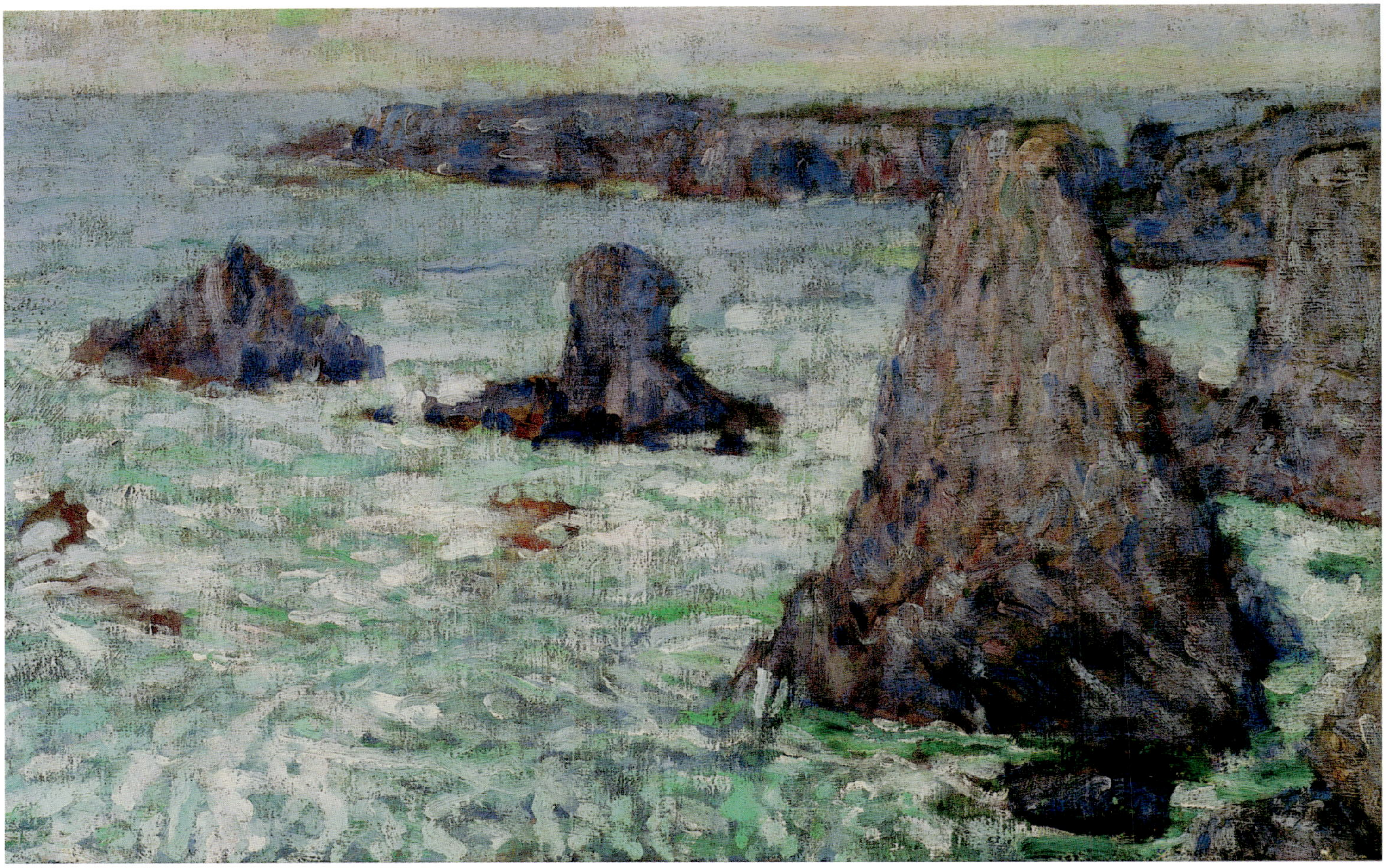

Fig. 10
**John Russell** (1858–1930)
*Les Aiguilles, Belle-Île*, about 1890
Oil on canvas, 40.4 × 64.7 cm
Queensland Art Gallery, Brisbane

Gift of Lady Trout 1985
(Accession No 1985.027.006)

In the catalogue of the Australia show at the Royal Academy in 2013, and the Tom Roberts exhibition at the National Gallery of Australia in 2015–16, 'Heidelberg School' does not get a mention, excised from the art historical lexicon. Instead, the dominant term has become 'Australian Impressionists', supported by substantial contemporary usage involving, significantly, the artists themselves. Conder titled one of his oil sketches at Heidelberg *Impressionists' Camp*; he inscribed a sketch portrait of Roberts, *An Impressionist* (fig. 16); and Roberts, Streeton and Conder titled their one joint show an exhibition of 'impressions'. The group was also often identified with 'Impressionism' by the contemporary Australian press and 'Impressionists' and 'Australian Impressionists' were recurrent, almost ubiquitous characterisations of these artists for much of the twentieth century, exemplified by the 1963 exhibition at the Tate Gallery, Australian Painting: Colonial, Impressionist, Contemporary, where the middle, Impressionist section, focused on the art that followed Roberts's return to Australia.

The catalogue of one of the key exhibitions of this art, the National Gallery of Victoria's *Golden Summers* of 1986, challenged this view, arguing that the Australian artists were plein-air painters, not proper Impressionists, which made Bernard Smith apoplectic. While lauding the Golden Summers exhibition, Smith lambasted its catalogue for adopting a Europeanist, unilinear approach, concerned only with style and technique. Adamant that the 'Heidelberg School' had created 'their own kind of Impressionism', Smith declared: 'The degree to which they were not imitators of Monet but creative artists deploying an Impressionist style when they had need of it, for their own purposes in their own ways and in another world with its own challenges and problems, is admirably revealed in the magnificent exhibition at the National Gallery of Victoria.'[30]

Twenty years later, with a different director and a different curator, the Gallery's next exhibition of this group involved a *volte-face*. The show's title, Australian Impressionism, revealed all. Rather than seeing Impressionism as a movement defined by how some French artists painted some of the time, the exhibition identified 'Australian Impressionism' as one of many forms of 'International Impressionism', defined in 1994 by the American art historian Norma Broude as 'the impulse to paint contemporary life and experience directly from nature, to study the effects of light, and to use a lighter palette and looser brushwork'.[31] Yet the characterisation of the Australian artists remained contested, even within the *Australian Impressionism* catalogue. In its final essay, David Hansen argued that Roberts, Streeton, McCubbin and Conder were best identified as exponents of Naturalism, which he identified as 'a synthesis of traditional academic drawing and modelling, plein-air tonal-realist atmosphere, and something of the brightness, brevity and contemporary subject matter of Impressionism and Aestheticism'.[32]

The Sydney-born John Russell (1858–1930) has always been identified as an Impressionist. A student at London's Slade School from 1881, resident in Paris from 1884, he accompanied Roberts on a walking tour of Spain in 1883, exchanged works with Van Gogh and was with Monet on the French island of Belle-Île in 1886 (fig. 10). A year later, as Russell informed Roberts in their regular correspondence, he was aiming for: 'Simple colour but strong... keep pure as long as possible'.[33] When Roberts forwarded one of these letters to Streeton in the first half of 1891, Streeton displayed no interest in Russell's account of technical matters. His much-quoted response was:

*Many thanks for Russell's letter. 'Tis very interesting. He seems to love the open air very much & therefore must be a fine chap... but he does seem to me to bother too much about the ways and means – really there's not enough time to do that. I should think twould take a man off his inspiration or idea.*[34]

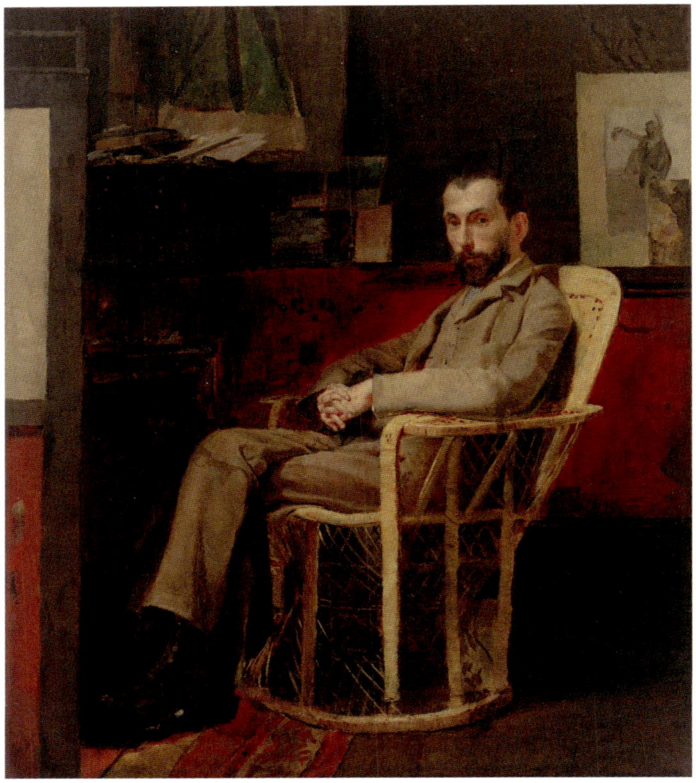

While Ann Galbally has assumed that Roberts shared Streeton's disdain for Russell's ideas,[35] it is at least as likely that Roberts considered them of interest – prompting him to give Streeton the opportunity to read them. This circulation of letters was a defining element of this close-knit fraternity which saw the artists share studios and camps, paint each other and paint the same subjects often from similar vantage points, travel together, exhibit together and engage in close, personal correspondence. While British officer-artists at Sydney Cove in the late eighteenth century had worked in much the same style, often copying each other's work, and Melbourne boasted a remarkable community of Germanic artist-scientists in the mid-nineteenth century,[36] Roberts, Streeton and Conder were at the core of the first school of settler Australian artists.

They depended on many others. Louis Abrahams and his extended family provide one example. Briefly a painter, who had an adjoining studio to Roberts in Melbourne's Collins Street, Abrahams is best known as the provider of the cigar box lids which were the boards used by the artists for their 9 by 5 Impression Exhibition. But Abrahams was much more, intimately involved with the new movement. In 1886 Roberts painted Abrahams's portrait out of friendship (fig. 11). When Abrahams married Golda Brasch in Sydney in 1888, with Roberts best man at the wedding, Roberts painted a companion portrait of her, the same size as the portrait of Abrahams, as a wedding gift (fig. 12). In between Roberts depicted Abrahams along with Frederick McCubbin in his Box Hill picture, *The Artists' Camp*, and, it has been conjectured, also represented Abrahams in *A Quiet Day on Darebin Creek* and *The Sunny South* (fig. 8).[37]

Abrahams was also very close to McCubbin: they named their sons after each other. In 1889, Abrahams was the model for McCubbin's *Down on his Luck* and, perhaps, a year later, a model for his *A Bush Burial*.[38] In the early 1890s, Golda Brasch's brothers ran the Curlew Camp in Sydney and, like Abrahams in Melbourne, Reuben Brasch gave painting materials to the artists. A wholesale clothier with a store on Sydney's Oxford Street, Brasch provided them with draper's boards – long, thin panels with bevelled edges, used for winding cloth around – which Streeton found ideal when painting Sydney Harbour.[39] The youngest of the Brasch siblings, Lena, also posed for a number of Roberts's paintings around this time when he possibly had a romantic interest in her.[40] When Reuben sailed for England in 1896, members of the camp staged a farewell dinner for him chaired by Roberts, presenting him with an illuminated address before adjourning to the camp's music tent.[41]

Fig. 11
**Tom Roberts** (1856–1931)
*Louis Abrahams*, 1886
Oil on canvas, 40.6 × 35.6 cm
National Gallery of Australia, Canberra

Acquired with the assistance of Alan Cowen and Mavourneen Cowen, Kerry Stokes AC and Christine Simpson-Stokes, and Krystyna Campbell-Pretty in memory of Harold Campbell-Pretty 2015 (Accession No. NGA 2015.1122)

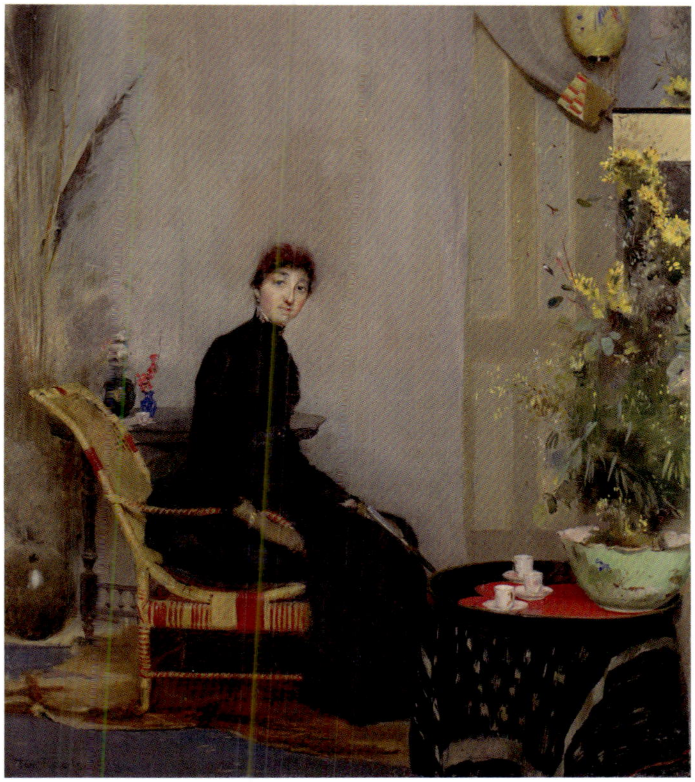

Fig. 12
**Tom Roberts** (1856–1931)
*Mrs L.A. Abrahams*, 1888
Oil on canvas, 41 × 36 cm
National Gallery of Victoria, Melbourne
Purchased, 1946
(Accession No. 1650-4)

'Organised by kind brothers (Jews)', Streeton would write much later of this camp, as if surprised by this conjunction.[42] But as was commonplace with modern art movements in the late nineteenth century, Jews were much more than that for Roberts, Streeton, Conder and McCubbin. One of Melbourne's most prominent Jews, the lawyer, politician and newspaper tycoon Theodore Fink, was not only a major patron but also promoted the artists in his weekly *Table Talk*.[43] The extended Abrahams family was at least as significant. Louis built a significant collection by a mix, most likely, of gift and purchase.[44] His brother Laurence was another collector, as was his in-law and business partner Barnett Snider, confirming, as Gerard Vaughan of the National Gallery of Australia has recognised, the importance of Australia's Jewish community to its most innovative art.[45]

The work of Roberts, Streeton and Conder has proved so popular within Australia because of their accomplishment as painters, distinctive form of Impressionism and rendering of light. It has also had great appeal because of the group's treatment of key subjects for the Australian mythos – the harbour, the beach, the ocean, the city centre, the suburban frontier, the pioneer, the outback worker. Yet the artists' 'Tale of Two Cities' has also been pivotal. Roberts, Streeton and Conder were – and to a large extent remain – exceptional among Australian artists in having lived in and painted in both Sydney and Melbourne when they were in their artistic prime. Unmarried and relatively mobile in those years, their shifts between the cities were primarily in search of patronage, not always happily. But because Roberts, Streeton and Conder were Melbourne and Sydney painters, their work speaks to Australia's two pre-eminent cities – their environs and experience – in rare fashion.

While the artists' subtle, tonal pictures infused with greys and pinks are beautiful, their paintings of 'glare' have had greatest resonance. 'The Sunny South' was an international phrase with many usages in the second half of the nineteenth century – applied by Britons to Mediterranean countries; by Americans to their Southern States, where it was the title for a literary magazine in Atlanta, Georgia; and used again as a title by the Australian playwright George Darrell for one of the most popular plays of Australia's colonial era. But it was also an idea embraced and pursued by Roberts and Streeton in many of their pictures from Roberts's *Allegro con Brio, Bourke Street West* (cat. 14) to Streeton's *Fire's On* (cat. 23) and beyond. As the photograph of Streeton painting on the sand at Little Sirius Cove suggests, they gloried in being part of *The Sunny South* while creating an Australian Impressionism.

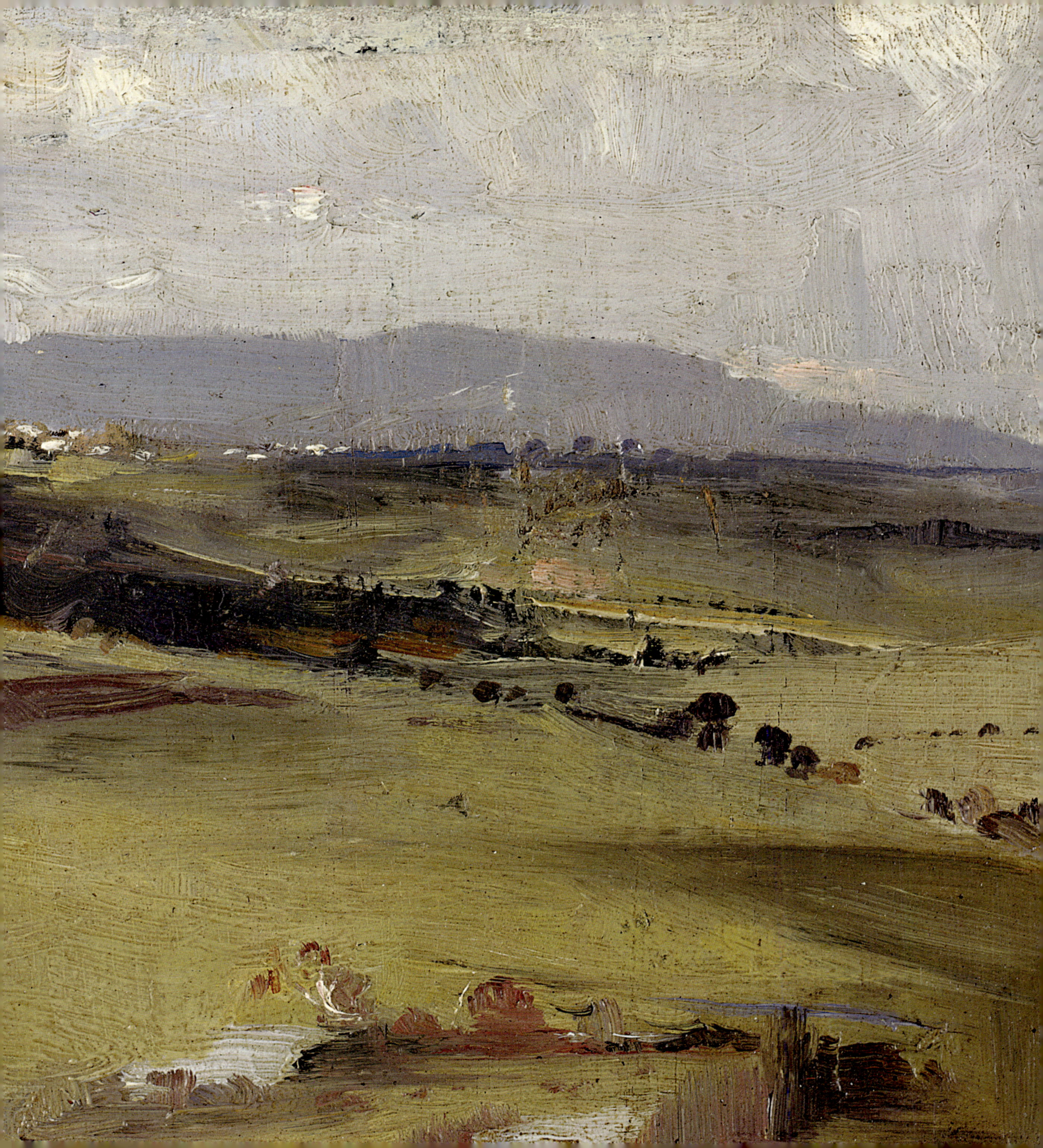

*Mr Tom Roberts, the well-known, popular, esteemed and representative Australian artist, meets you on the threshold of his… studio… with the cheeriness and heartiness all who know him know so well. He is without his coat – which looks like work – and whistling merrily, which betokens happiness. Work and happiness! What more can man require – except health? And as you emerge from the darker anti-chamber into the studio proper you are pleased to see he has that too, and abundantly.*

Thus opened a feature in *Melbourne Punch* in May 1889 titled 'An Australian Artist: A Little Talk with Mr Tom Roberts'.[1] The 33-year-old protagonist had spent the first half of the 1880s in Europe, training at the Royal Academy in London, briefly at the Académie Julian in Paris and, perhaps most instructively, travelling through Spain with John Russell (1858–1930) where, encouraged by Spanish students Ramón Casas and Laureà Barrau, he started painting en plein air.

# THE 9 BY 5 IMPRESSION EXHIBITION

## 'It seems to be believed that a little coterie of painters, in one corner of Australia, is about to revolutionise landscape art.'

Allison Goudie

Fig. 13
**Tom Roberts** (1856–1931)
*Across the Dandenongs*, 1889
Detail of cat. 9, p. 71

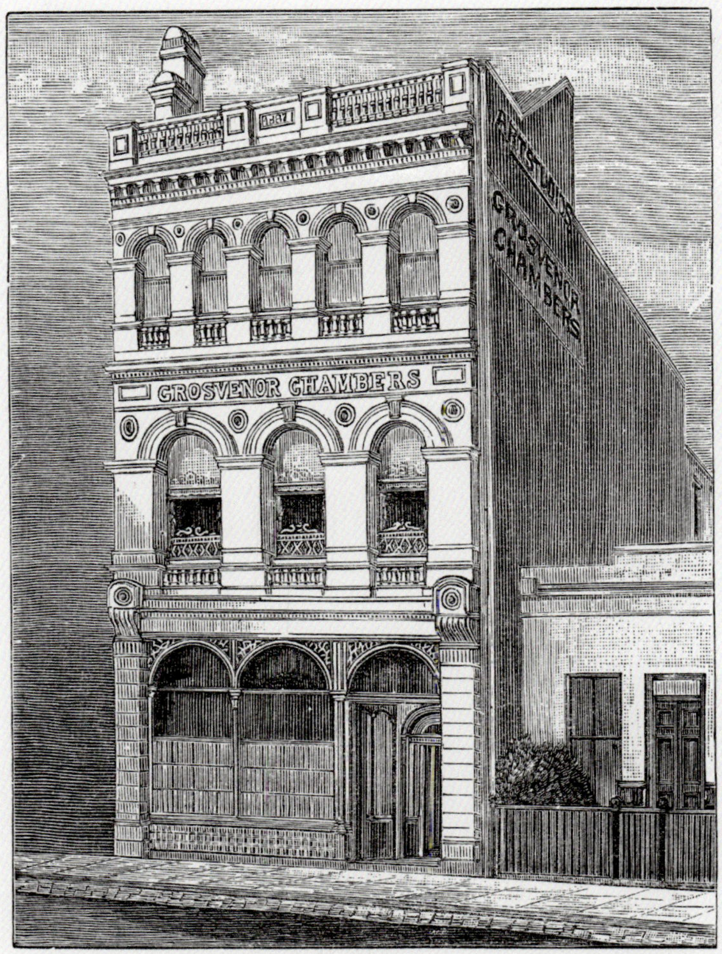

GROSVENOR CHAMBERS, COLLINS STREET EAST.

Fig. 14
Engraving of Grosvenor Chambers, Collins Street East, 1888.

The interview's setting was the newly erected Grosvenor Chambers artists' complex at 9 Collins Street (fig. 14), on which Tom Roberts (1856–1931), now an active figure in the local art scene and one of its first studio tenants, had acted as a consultant.[2] We catch a glimpse of Roberts's studio from a photograph of him intently inspecting a picture, with a young Arthur Streeton (1867–1943) looking over his shoulder (fig. 15). The wicker chairs are the same as the ones that feature in Roberts's portraits of his friend Louis Abrahams and Abrahams's wife Golda (see figs 11–12, pp. 28–9). The former was painted before Roberts moved to Grosvenor Chambers, whereas the latter is a velvety evocation of the new studio, described in *Punch* as 'distinctly quiet… in its appointments… mostly in neutral tints… with quiet hangings, Japanese screens… and much else in keeping.'[3]

In decking out his studio in this manner, right down to the 'quiet' muslin-draped walls, Roberts was aligning himself with the international vogue for Aesthetic interiors, and specifically an artistic setting espoused by the cosmopolitan James Abbott McNeill Whistler.[4] Even the name of this new artists' residence invoked that most favoured exhibiting venue of Whistler's circle, London's Grosvenor Galleries, which in 1887 had sent a loan exhibition of contemporary British art, the Grosvenor Gallery Intercolonial Exhibition, to Melbourne.[5] Yet the inclusion, in the bold flower arrangement in Golda's portrait, of wattle and eucalyptus, pinpoints the portrait geographically, infusing it with a specifically Australian sensibility.[6]

Though muted in tone, the portrait is bathed in light from the large south-facing windows[7] (the European principle of painters' studios being illuminated from the north adapted for the southern hemisphere), which buffered this Aesthetic oasis from the urban maelstrom outside.

*The trams may clatter, and their bells jingle and clang – you hear them not; the rushing trains may roar and rattle, you need not heed them… the city's hum is silenced at the window-sill, and breaks upon you only once and again in apologetic whispers.*[8]

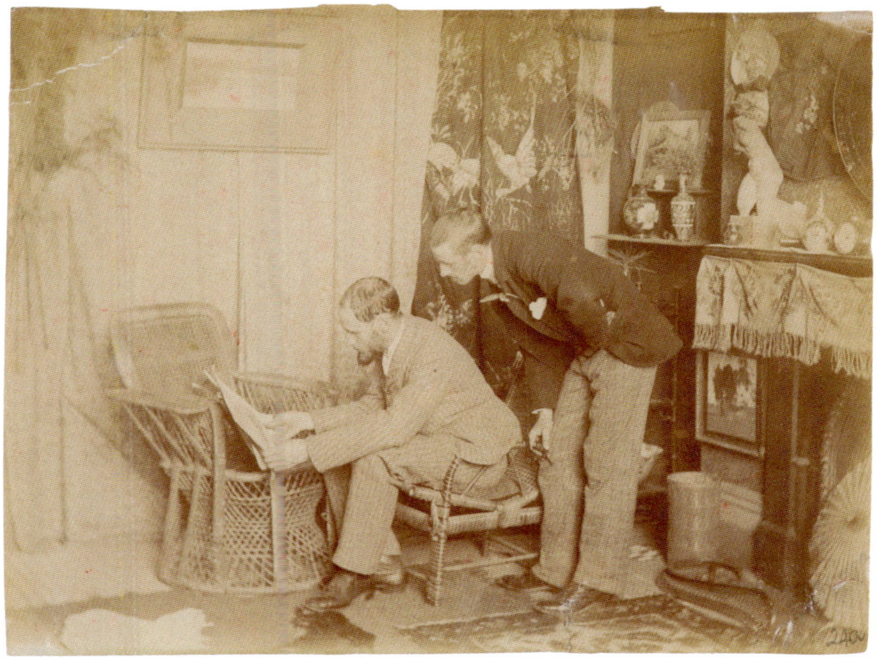

What lay beyond was 'Marvellous Melbourne', so-named by British journalist George Augustus Sala, who described it as 'teem[ing] with wealth, even as it does with humanity'.[9] Sala belonged to a steady stream of 'old-world impressionist[s]' – in the sense of a writer recording his impressions – of which Australians 'silently bore the trespass'.[10] A letter to the editor of the Bathurst *National Advocate* headed 'It's English You Know', complained:

*[The old-world Impressionist...] sees us only through English eyes... unable to appreciate Australia's native characteristics. Where we have departed from the fixed ideas of old-world proprieties there do we incur his condemnation.*[11]

The letter would not have been lost on Roberts. The interview in *Punch* was less a 'little talk' than an outpouring of indignation from Roberts at comments made by the composer F.H. Cowen regarding 'the difficulty [of] writing an Australian symphony owing to the absence of local colour'. Roberts protested that 'local colour' was in fact 'remarkably characteristic of Australia' and that painters 'travel to England and France to find much less'.[12]

Moreover, the Australian landscape, by virtue of its difference to Europe, was inherently liberating, demanding a new sort of artistic vision: 'there is so much character in the scenery [that] its reproduction [has the potential] to demolish conventionality in the ordinary picture-liking mind'. Roberts offered an example to illustrate his point, recounting an exchange with a fellow visitor at the latest exhibition of the Victorian Artists' Society:

*I was speaking to some one the other day... in front of an excellent Australian study, and was praising it, when my companion said, 'but I don't see anything in it; it's not my idea of a landscape.' 'What kind of a landscape do you like?' I asked. 'A reedy brook with a few trees overhanging it, and a strong sky, and all that sort of thing, perhaps?' 'Exactly,' was the reply. Well it's just that reedy brook kind of picture you don't get here – and we are the better for the change.*[13]

Fig. 15
Tom Roberts and Arthur Streeton at Grosvenor Chambers, about 1889.

State Library of New South Wales, Sydney (Accession no. PX*D 310, no. 24)

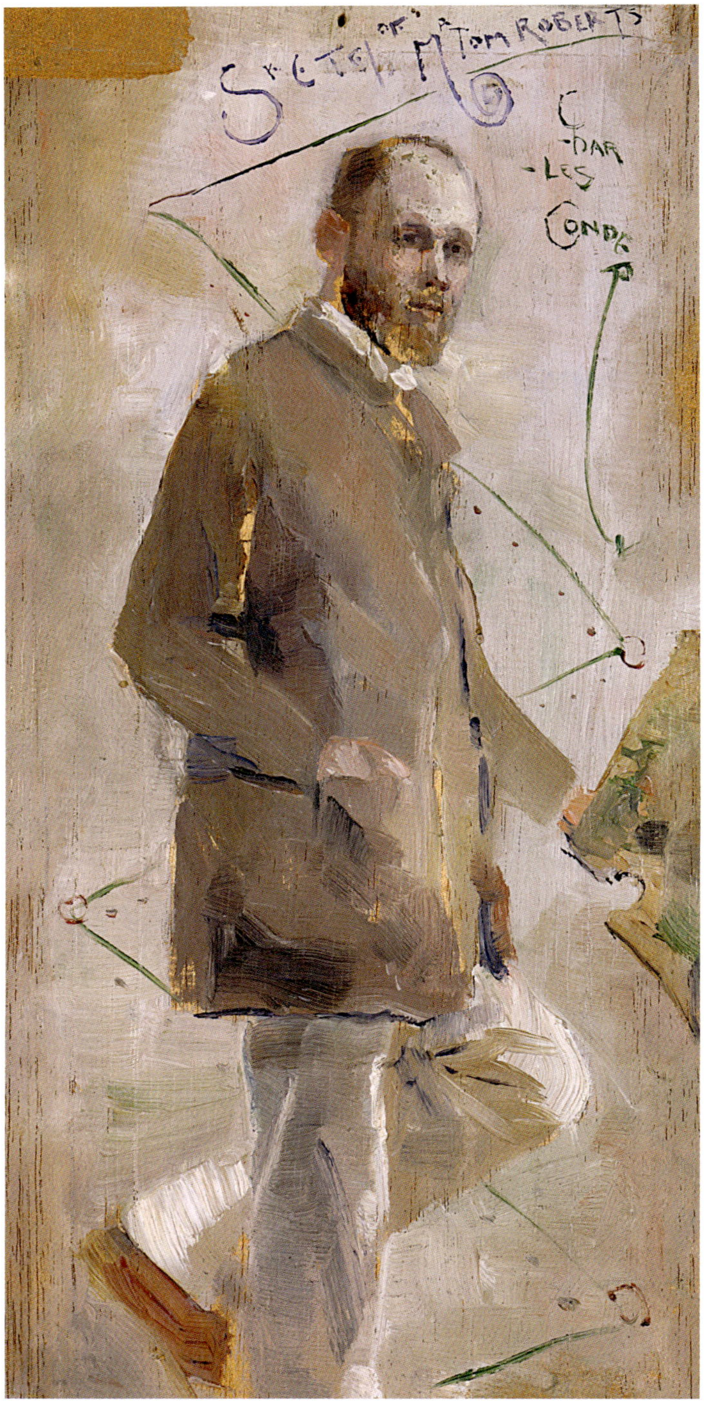


Roberts did not pass up the opportunity presented by the *Punch* interview to tie in the work of the nascent Australian Impressionist painters – quite a different phenomenon, to be sure, to the 'old-world impressionist' commentators like Sala – with his defence of the unconventionality of the Australian landscape. The new movement had been the subject of lively discussion in the Australian press, and Roberts became its father figure, the sitter for Charles Conder's (1868–1909) spirited portrait *An Impressionist* (fig. 16). Little wonder, then, that Roberts should tell *Punch*: 'such painters are on the right path – they are honestly… doing their best to represent the truth.'[14]

Shortly after returning from Europe, Roberts embarked on what is now one of his most famous compositions, *Allegro con Brio, Bourke Street West* (cat. 14). The urban subject was popular with artists around the world; but with its rendering of the midday glare, clouded only by the dust kicked up from the road and the belching chimney smoke, Roberts's picture is unmistakeably Australian. An altogether less urbane corner of Melbourne than the area around Grosvenor Chambers, Roberts has nonetheless endowed the scene with an Aesthetic elegance, using the dust and pollution to harmonise the composition, elevating it to the status of a rhythmic arrangement of creams, ochres and grimy blues punctuated by lyrical accents of red and black. The *Sydney Morning Herald*'s attempted explanation of 'Impressionism' reveals something of its amorphous character as understood in the nineteenth century, and of the reality of its transnational nature: 'started by the French painter, Manet: its most successful exponent at the present time is the American painter John Singer Sargent'.[15] The musical title Roberts gave his painting of Bourke Street is a tribute to that other American abroad, Whistler, whose 1884 exhibition of small works, Notes – Harmonies – Nocturnes, (fig. 17 and see fig. 24, p. 45) Roberts must surely have seen while in London and whose *Note in Blue and Green* (now lost) was exhibited in Melbourne in 1885.[16] The subject and composition find parallels in Monet's views of the *Boulevard des Capucines* (see fig. 39, p. 112), while the handling has something of the smudginess of Degas's work that similarly recalls the blur of a photograph

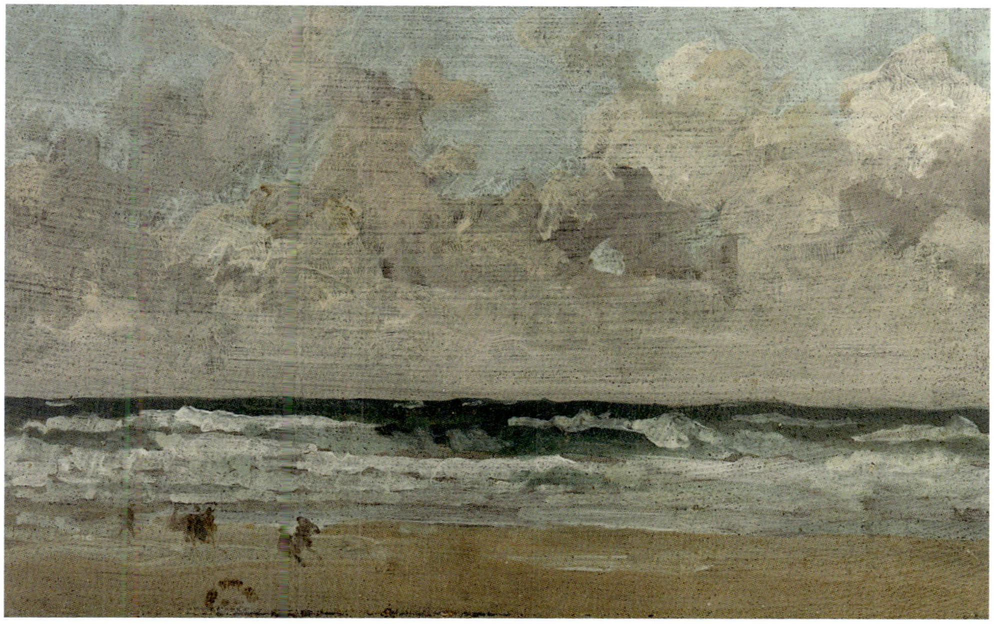

Fig. 16
**Charles Conder** (1868–1909)
*An Impressionist (Tom Roberts)*, about 1889
Oil on cedar panel, 28.5 × 23.4 cm
Art Gallery of New South Wales, Sydney
Purchased with funds provided by the Art Gallery Society of New South Wales 1997 (Accession no. 63.199)

Fig. 17
**James Abbott McNeill Whistler** (1834–1903)
*Violet and Silver: The Great Sea*, about 1884
Oil on wood panel, 13.8 × 23.5 cm
Freer Gallery of Art, Smithsonian Institution, Washington DC
Gift of Charles Lang Freer (Accession no. F1902.148a-b)

as its exposure seeks in vain to fix the transient bustle of city life. Roberts would have had opportunities to see works by Monet (including one version of his *Boulevard des Capucines*[17]), Degas and Pissarro in London at exhibitions organised by the dealer Paul Durand-Ruel in the early 1880s, and possibly also during his short stay in France; though whether or not he actually did remains unclear.[18]

Conder's reflections upon his arrival in Paris in 1890, published by the Melbourne newspaper *Table Talk,* help situate the Australian take on 'Impressionism' in its international context:

*Most of the best painters here are what would be called impressionists in Melbourne, but they are not regarded in at all the same light as they are here… I fear I am rather a Goth, but I cannot at present admire much of what is called the impressionist school – they are 'ultra extremists'.*

Conder was instead 'tremendously struck' by the work of Jules Bastien-Lepage (1848–1884) ('he is perfect'). He further observed that Streeton, whose ambitious *Between the Lights – Princes Bridge* (cat. 10) shares something with Bastien-Lepage's characteristic colouring and had been described by an Australian critic as 'of the school of French Impressionists', 'would be thought infinitely more of [in Paris] than he is in Australia'.[19] Another Australian artist in Paris, Emanuel Phillips Fox (1865–1915), was similarly apprehensive upon encountering the French Impressionists (and by this point, Post-Impressionists) first-hand:

*I went some time back to an exhibit of impressionists… I like their ideas, but I think a great many of them carry them to excess, and reduce painting to an absurdity. The particular ones I refer to are by an artist who paints everything in spots and pure colour. It looks awfully funny at first sight; however, if you close your eyes till they are almost shut and get a very broad view of the picture one finds out what the artist has been aiming at, some of them being very sunny and true.*[20]

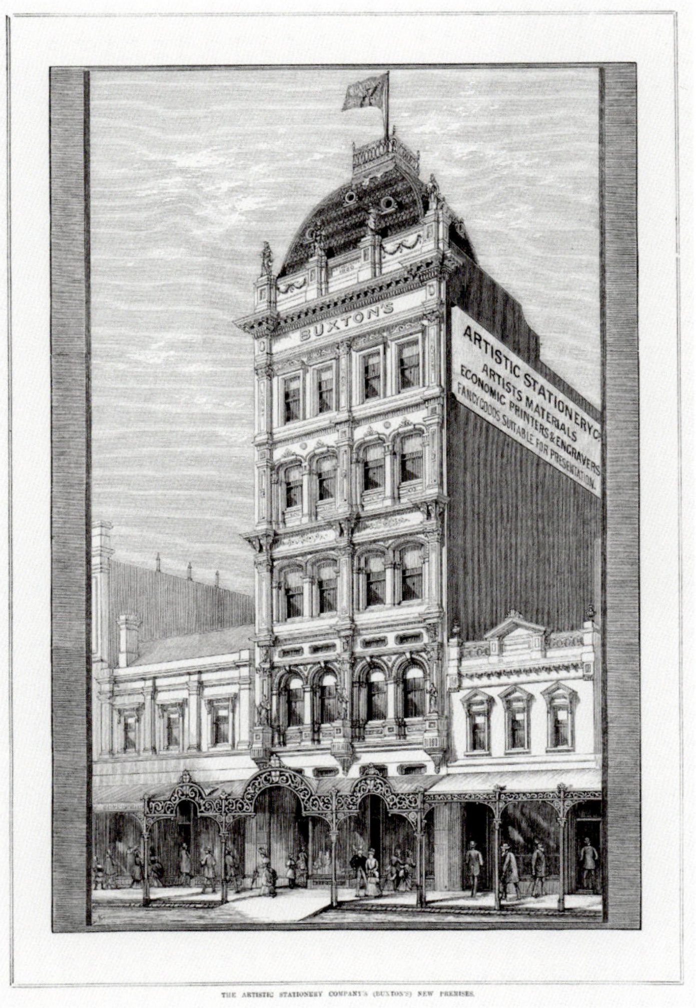


Fig. 18
**Albert Charles Cook**, engraver (1836–1902)
'The Artistic Stationery Company's (Buxton's) New Premises', Alfred Martin Ebsworth, Publisher, Melbourne, 21 October 1885
Wood engraving
State Library of Victoria, Melbourne
(Accession no. A/S21/10/85/173)

With so many notions of 'Impressionism' circulating, yet no reproductions (at least of the more analytical style of the French Impressionists), it is hardly surprising that confusion reigned among the Australian public as to its nature.[21] The *Sydney Morning Herald* reported that 'the term "Impression" is little understood, being often applied to pictures which impress one only by their bad workmanship'.[22] According to *Table Talk:*

*So much has been said and written about impressionism in art… it is scarcely to be wondered at that the frequenters of the picture galleries are much exercised in their minds as to the proper understanding of the subject.*[23]

Roberts's mention of the Impressionists in May 1889 in his interview with *Punch* was carefully calculated, for he was planning, together with Streeton and Conder, an exhibition of 'Impressions' for the forthcoming winter. 'Now', announced *Table Talk,* 'the public will have an opportunity of judging for itself what Impressionism really is'.[24]

Opening on 17 August 1889 at Buxton's Rooms (a multi-storey art supplies and gallery establishment housing studios, a gallery and a stationery emporium opposite Melbourne Town Hall, (fig. 18), the exhibition offered no shortage of examples of 'Impressionism'. Under the title the 9 by 5 Impression Exhibition, it consisted of 183 'impressions': primarily oils – landscapes and figurative works – contributed by Roberts, Streeton and Conder, as well as a number of sculptural works including 'sketch[es] in wax' by Charles Douglas Richardson (fig. 19). Many of the works had cigar box lids for supports, many of roughly nine by five inches, obtained inexpensively via Abrahams, whose family were tobacconists. The catalogue bore a statement 'To the Public', which functioned as a sort of manifesto:

*An effect is only momentary: so an impressionist tries to find his place. Two half-hours are never alike, and he who tries to paint a sunset on two successive evenings, must be more or less painting from memory. So, in these works, it has been the object of the artists to render faithfully, and thus obtain first records of effects widely differing, and often of very fleeting character.*[25]

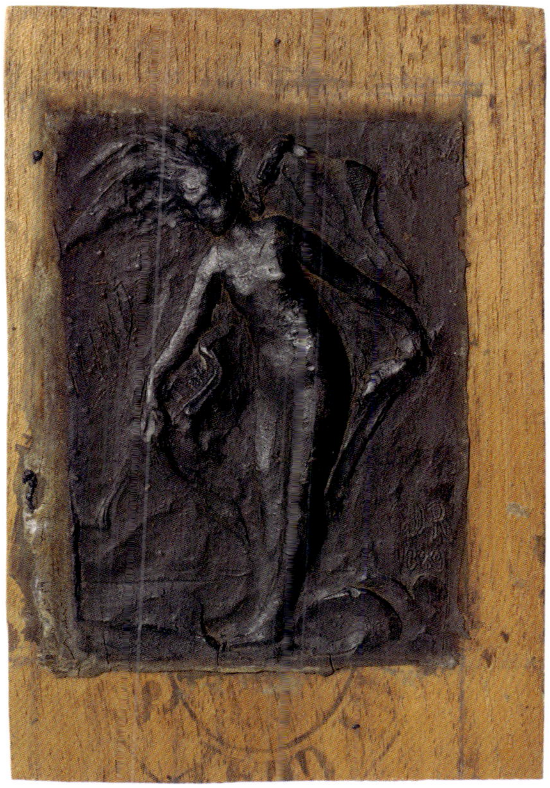

Fig. 19
**Charles Douglas Richardson** (1853–1932)
*Wind*, 1889
Wax, carved and modelled on
cedar panel, 11.7 × 8.9 cm
National Gallery of Australia, Canberra

Rudy Komon Fund, 1981
(Accession no. NGA 81.1650)

True to the ideals of plein-air painting, this statement recalled a paraphrasing of Corot from the June 1889 issue of the American *Century Magazine*,[26] one of the international journals that were pooled together and discussed at the 'conversaziones' Roberts regularly hosted.[27] The statement 'To The Public' was accompanied by a quote given to the French master Jean-Léon Gérôme, likewise probably harvested from the *Century Magazine*,[28] declaring that: 'in painting the first thing to look for is the general impression of colour' (emphasis as given in the 9 by 5 catalogue). This was a telling choice, given that Gérôme vociferously opposed the French Impressionists.

The idea of independent, artist-led exhibitions had been initiated by the French Impressionists in the 1870s, but Roberts, Streeton and Conder took their cue more immediately from Whistler's 1884 Nocturnes exhibition, presenting their works as part of an all-encompassing Aesthetic scheme.[29] This was achieved in part through the furnishing lent by the decorating firm Cullis Hill & Co., including 'soft scarves and draperies of Liberty silk of the reds that Millais has popularised, and the greens and yellows beloved of the aesthete' which 'were hung and knotted and looped among the sketches in such a way as to harmonise with the colouring of the frames and the pictures'. These were complemented by 'Japanese screens and parasols, quaintly carved *jardinieres* and cabinets, and great Japanese vases of japonica and daphne'[30] which made the air 'sweet with... perfume'.[31] The works were given wide timber frames, chosen for reasons of economy but conveniently 'avant-garde' in appearance, many stained in dark tints or embellished with metallic paint.[32] The decorative scheme extended to the catalogue, printed in olive green ink on handmade paper and charged at sixpence in addition to the sixpence entry fee (fig. 20).

This veneer of elegance was not without a certain calculated irreverence. A 'surreptitious peep' at the exhibition by *Table Talk* during installation revealed 'a state of confusion', surely publicised to promote an image of the artists as *enfants terribles* of the Victorian art world:

*A handsome ebony and gold easel stands gawkily in the middle of the room... compelled for the nonce to fraternize with a broom, which leans against the more aristocratic article with truly democratic freedom. Beside the broom, two or three pictures have just fallen over in sheer inability to support themselves under the existing conditions, and in their fall also knock over a tin of nails and a can of water [which] runs off in a stream towards the mass of 'whistler'* [sic] *draperies... Conder, perched on a very high ricketty* [sic] *stool sweeps whole splashes of bronze fluid on to the frame of his 'impression', occasionally splashing himself.*[33]

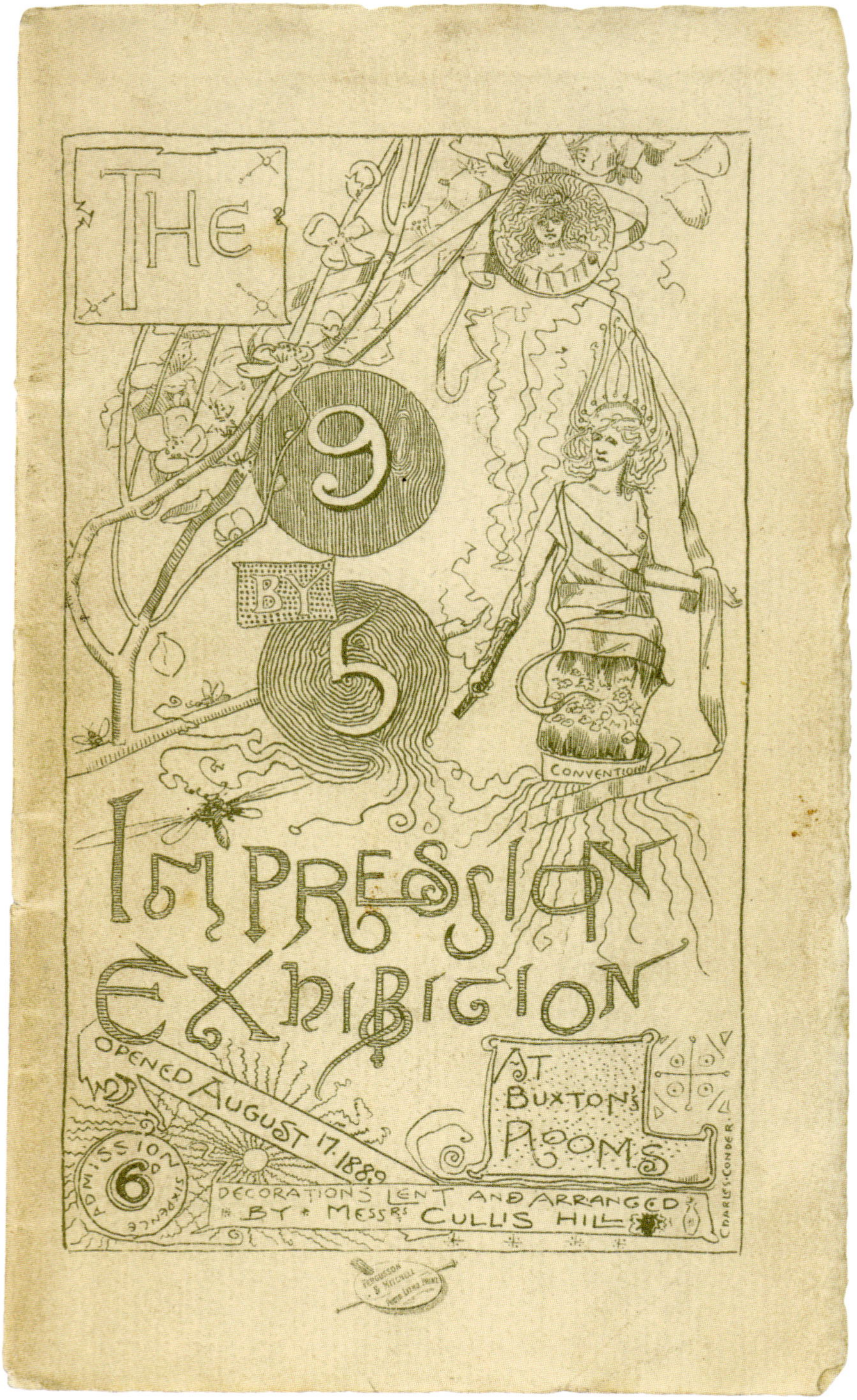


Coverage such as this leading up to the exhibition, courted by Roberts and his fellow exhibitors, gave the exhibition the status of a hotly anticipated event, itself a very Whistlerian characteristic.[34] For all the 'chaos' accompanying the installation, it possessed many of the features and amenities of a modern-day exhibition or museum, from the 'private view' ('a study of human nature itself'[35]) to the recitals held in the exhibition, the daily afternoon tea and the Friday evening 'lates'. The arrangement with Cullis Hill & Co. was a form of sponsorship, providing a pleasing backdrop against which the 9 by 5s could be marketed as desirable ornaments for the middle-class Aesthetic domestic interior.[36] Even the wife of the acting Governor of Victoria attended; as Virginia Spate has noted, 'this was as much a social event directed at Melbourne's tiny cultural and social elite as a challenge to an established system'.[37] The paintings were cheap and many sold quickly to prominent members of fashionable society (albeit often friends of the artists), with newspapers duly reporting who had bought what.[38] More were left unsold though, and Conder later complained that the undertaking had left him out of pocket.[39]

The PR campaign did pay off, however; the exhibition excited press interest 'of the liveliest kind'.[40] The critical reception was mixed, 'by no means unanimous either in praise or blame'.[41] *Table Talk* conceded however that regarding the more vitriolic reviews, the artists would 'have need of all their philosophy to bear the abuse that has been showered upon them for their bold undertaking'.[42] David Christie Murray (1847–1907), another of the 'old-world impressionists', gave a damning assessment, describing the exhibition as 'the sublimest effort of human impudence I ever beheld'.[43] Whistler's influence, he concluded, had been 'especially injurious' in this corner of the Empire.[44]

Just as Roberts, Streeton and Conder took their cue from Whistler in their art, so critics such as Murray took theirs from John Ruskin, who had famously lambasted the 'impudence' of Whistler's work, which amounted, he complained, to 'flinging a pot of paint in the public's face'.[45] The leading local exponent of the latter was James Smith, Trustee of the National Gallery of Victoria and critic for the *Argus*, who *Table Talk* cast as having said nothing at the press view 'beyond his opening saluation [*sic*] of "More eccentricities?"'[46] Recalling Ruskin's accusation, Smith condemned the pictures in the exhibition as 'suggest[ing] that a paint-pot has been accidentally upset over a panel nine inches by five'.[47] The artists pasted the review to the door of the exhibition, the result, Streeton recounted, being that 'people thronged... to see the dreadful paintings'.[48]

Smith identified a handful of oils, along with Richardson's 'plastic sketches', that were among the one fifth of works on display he deemed not 'a pain to the eye'. His primary complaint was that most of the work on display did not merit even the label of a 'sketch', not to mention that of a finished work of art worthy of public exhibition.[49] More positive newspaper reviews were given on the mistaken basis that the works exhibited were preparatory for larger compositions, 'shadows of coming events'.[50] Even the ever-faithful *Table Talk* missed the point:

*The sketches are really so slight that they cannot stand the full blast of windy criticism... to single out individual sketches for lengthy scrutiny or description is ascribing to them an importance they do not, and are not meant to, deserve.*[51]

In a letter to the editor of the *Argus* in response to Smith's review, Roberts, Streeton and Conder made clear that their works were actually finished paintings in their own right.[52] What was at issue in the stand-off between Smith and the Impressionists was no less than the future of painting in Australia. For Smith, 'the exhibition... [would] cause one to despond with respect to the future of art in this colony, did we not believe, with Mr W.P. Frith, RA, that "Impressionism is a craze of such ephemeral character as to be unworthy of serious attention".'[53] The Impressionists, in their letter of response, argued that it was precisely the sort of rupturing of convention offered by their painting that would be vital to the artistic future of Australia:

*We believe that it is better to give our own idea than to get a merely superficial effect, which is apt to be a repetition of what others have done before us, and may shelter us in a safe mediocrity, which, while it will not attract condemnation, could never help towards the development of what we believe will be a great school of painting in Australia.*[54]

Fig. 20
**Charles Conder** (1868–1909)
Catalogue cover of 'The 9 by 5 Impressionist Exhibition', 1889. Photo-lithograph printed by Fergusson and Mitchell, using a letterpress on hand-made paper 17.7 x 10.6 cm
National Gallery of Victoria, Melbourne

Purchased 2006
(Accession no. 2006.2[illegible]7)

The condescending retort read: 'it seems to be believed that a little coterie of painters, in one corner of Australia, is about to revolutionise the entire theory and practice of landscape art'.[55] And yet Roberts, Conder and Streeton no doubt felt themselves representing in Australia what Russell later described to Roberts as 'a mighty revolution in art', no matter how amorphous, united by an effort 'to render what they see and not what they know to exist' and 'throwing out most old time conventions',[56] just as the allegorical figure in Conder's *art nouveau* design for the cover of the catalogue unravels herself from the mummifying bandages of 'Convention'. At the same time, a form of painting that embodied 'a revolt against conventionality'[57] must have seemed particularly apt for a 'young' country, whose landscape, as Roberts had proclaimed a couple of months before the 9 by 5 exhibition, refused to fit into a conventional European framework.[58] Convention belonged to the old world, as *Table Talk* delighted in implying via the image of a dog seen chancing upon the exhibition installation, an impoverished foil to the vigorous figure of Roberts that had greeted the *Punch* journalist at his studio door:

*A little dog, wet and muddy, limps in on three legs... nobody notices him, and he smells nothing but the mawkish odour of gold and silver enamel fluids. Hungry as he is, his inquiring and shivering glance round is not without a touch of contempt, as if he remembered something of high art in his good days – before painters took to setting up impressionist exhibitions; or, perhaps the dog was a Londoner, and inclined to regard the colonies slightingly.*[59]

Fig. 21
**Charles Conder** (1868–1909)
*Riddells Creek*, 1889

Detail of cat. 7, p. 69

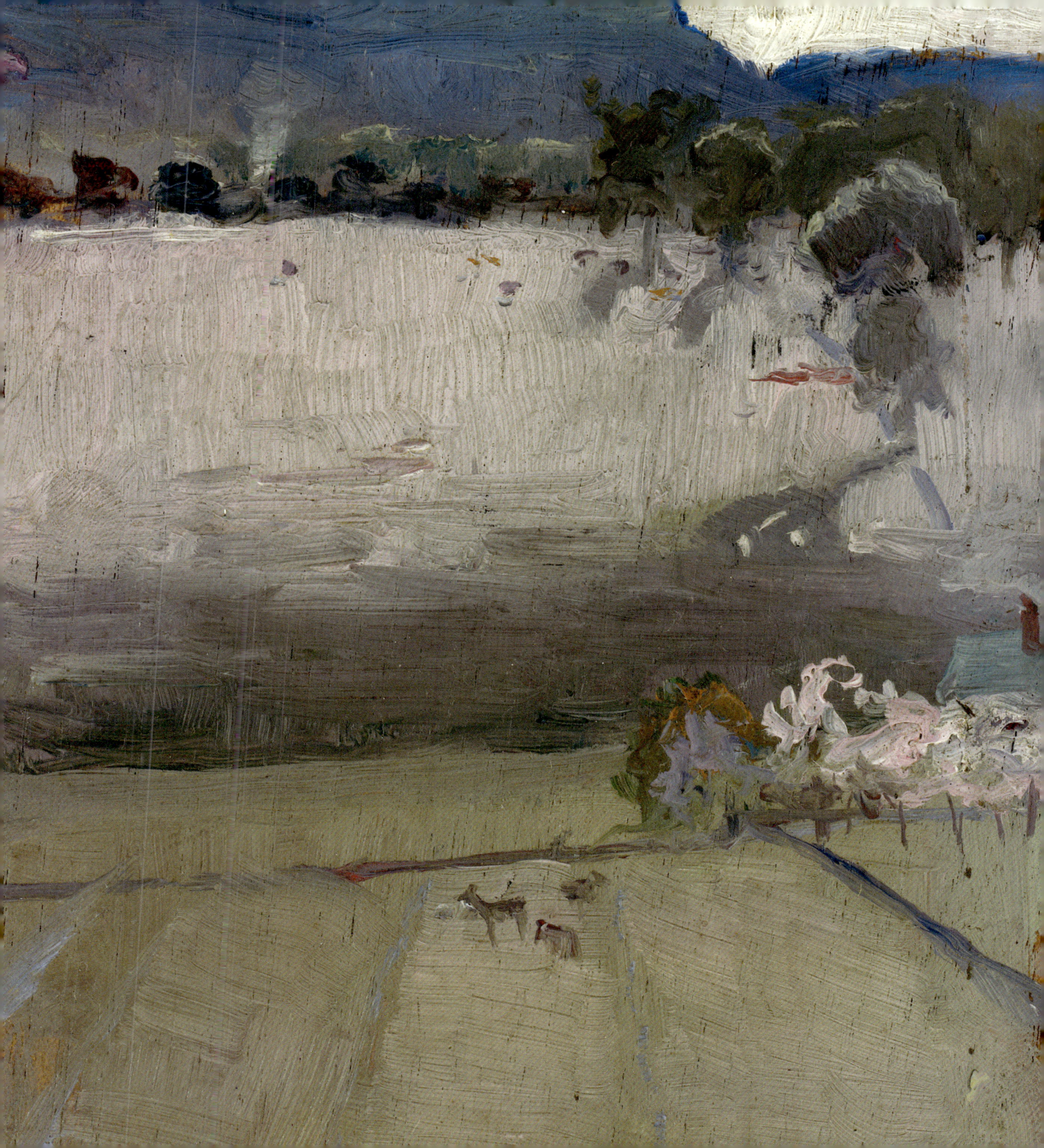

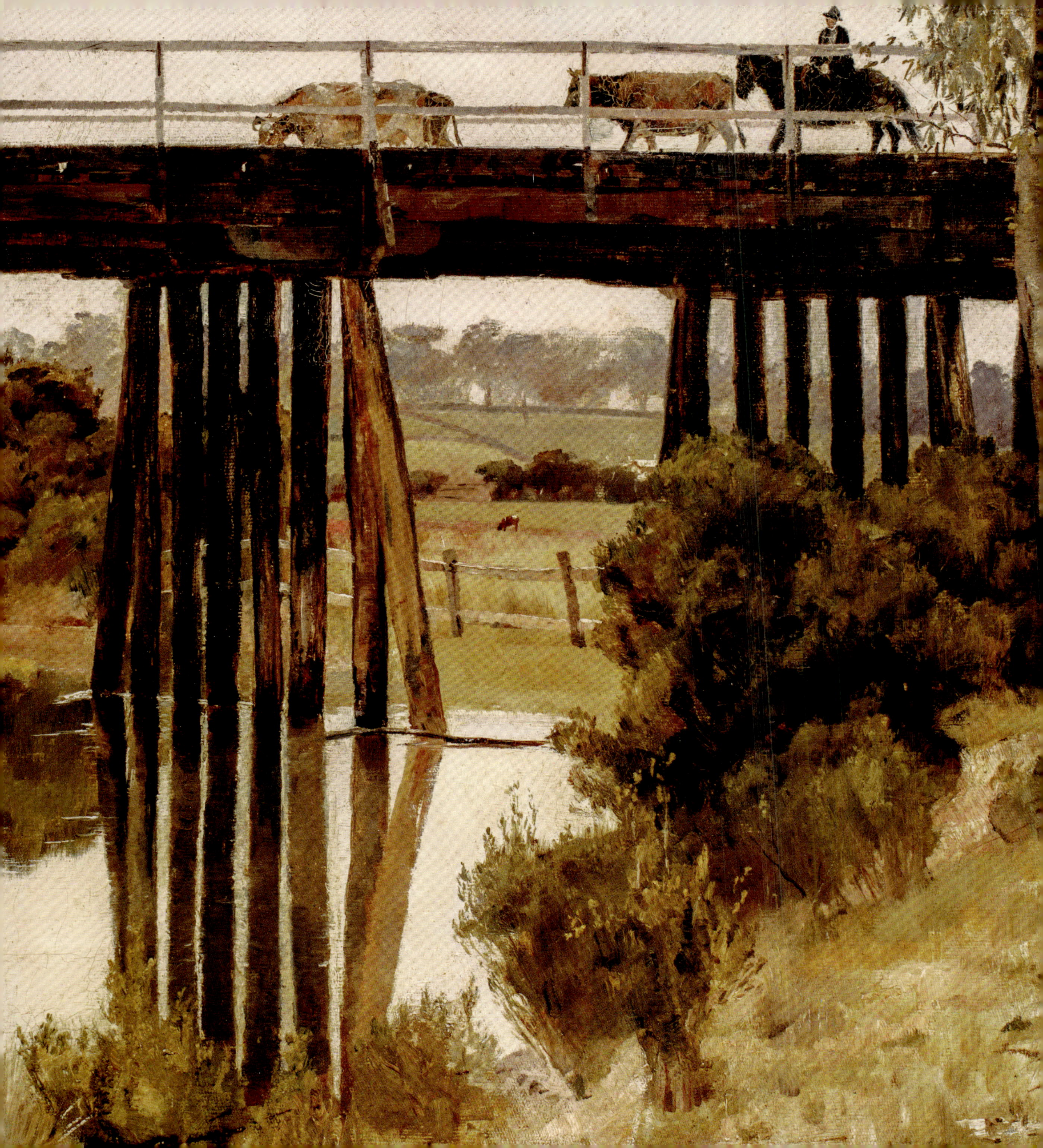

In the final decades of the nineteenth century Australia's Impressionist painters were at the vanguard of a nationalist movement that sought to create a distinctive local subject matter by adapting a style and approach that had, since its origins in 1860s Paris, spread across the world.[1] This was the age of empire, that witnessed the global circulation of people, ideas and goods on an unprecedented scale: improvements in steamship and navigational technologies allowed for greater movement of people across the globe than ever before. With the increased portability of oil paint in tubes and canvas supports by mid-century, as well as the rapid expansion of the railways, artists had ever greater freedom to roam. The Impressionist style, with its ethos of painting from nature ('en plein air') and concern for the transience of light, provided a radically modern tool kit for a new mobile generation of painters who had diverse reasons for wanting to break with the past. The style was embraced in Australia from the mid 1880s onwards, and was pivotal in forging a shared national identity, as six self-governing British colonies headed towards independent nationhood.

A new nation required new united values, symbols and institutions. As early as 1886 the painter Tom Roberts (once dubbed the 'father of Australian landscape painting'[2]) was a founding member of the Australian Artists Association. Yet the establishment of this new national body was not greeted with universal approval, particularly in Melbourne, where a 'National Gallery' had operated since 1861 (inaugurated on Queen Victoria's birthday). Purporting to speak on behalf of students from the National Gallery School, painter John Longstaff (1861–1941) wrote an incensed letter to a major local newspaper, the *Age,* complaining that 'The Australian Associated Artists [*sic*] are composed almost entirely of foreigners, and... many of [their works have]... not only been shown before, but have been painted in Europe.'[3]

# CREATING A NATIONAL IDENTITY

## Australia's Impressionist Landscapes

Sarah Thomas

Fig. 22
**Tom Roberts** (1856–1931)
*Winter Morning after Rain, Gardiner's Creek,* 1885
Detail of cat. 16, p. 79

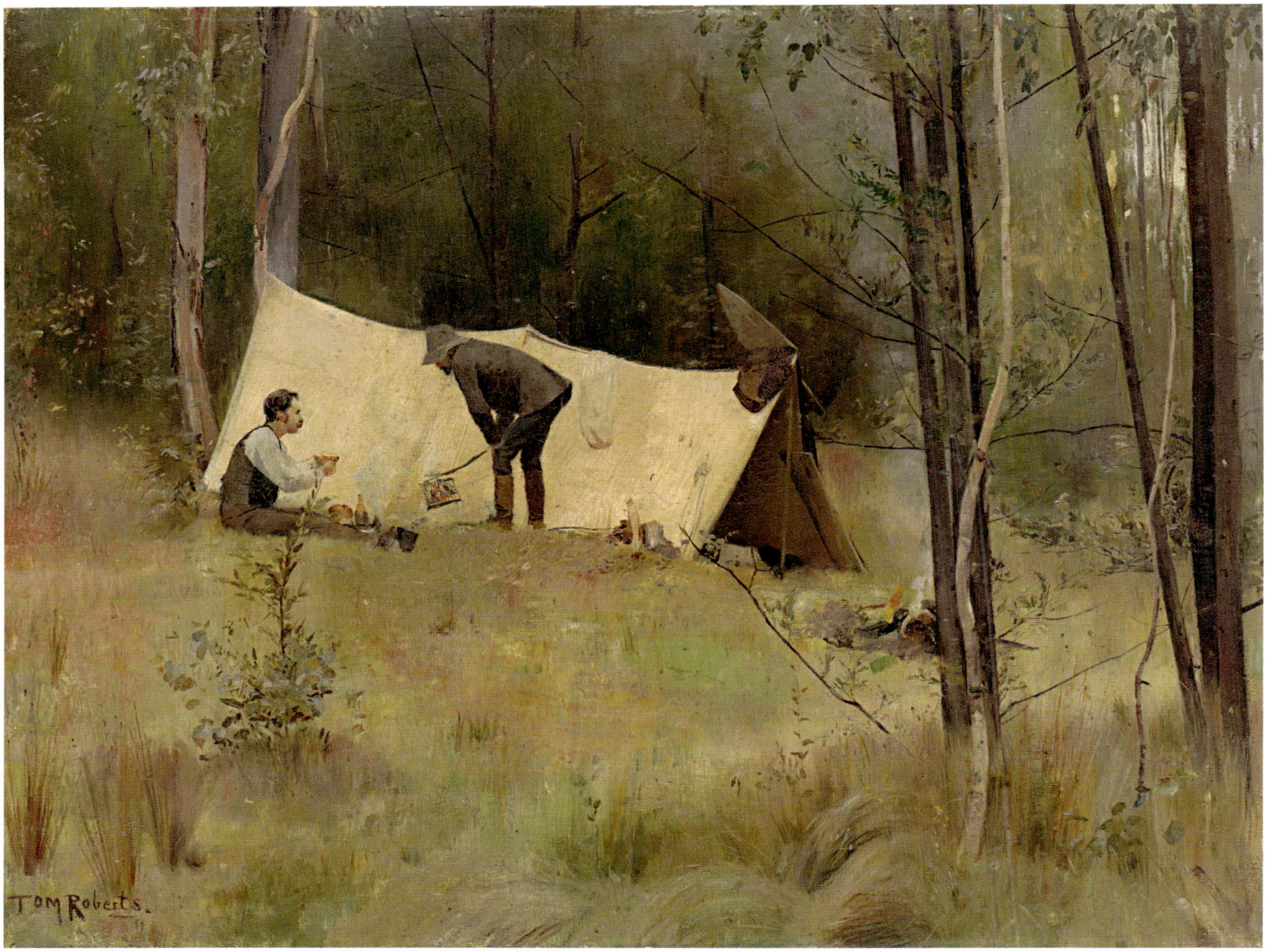


Fig. 23
**Tom Roberts** (1856–1931)
*The Artists' Camp*, 1886
Oil on canvas, 46 × 60.9 cm
National Gallery of Victoria, Melbourne
Felton Bequest, 1943
(Accession No. 1224-4)

Longstaff's missive was in large part aimed squarely at Roberts, who had been born in Dorchester, Dorset, and had trained at London's Royal Academy Schools (between 1881 and 1884). He had emigrated with his family to Melbourne as a 13-year-old boy, and would return there after his European training in 1885. He spent almost half of his life in Australia, where as an ambitious and talented plein-air painter he availed himself of great opportunities.

By the latter years of the 1880s, for the first time since colonisation, immigrants were starting to be outnumbered by those born locally: artists were encouraged to embrace local subject matter. 'We cannot... urge too strongly' wrote one commentator:

*... that we should as soon as possible fill our National Gallery with representative works of our artists and our nation, its early historical scenes, and pictures of the true rude life that must have and did exist in the early days of the colony.*[4]

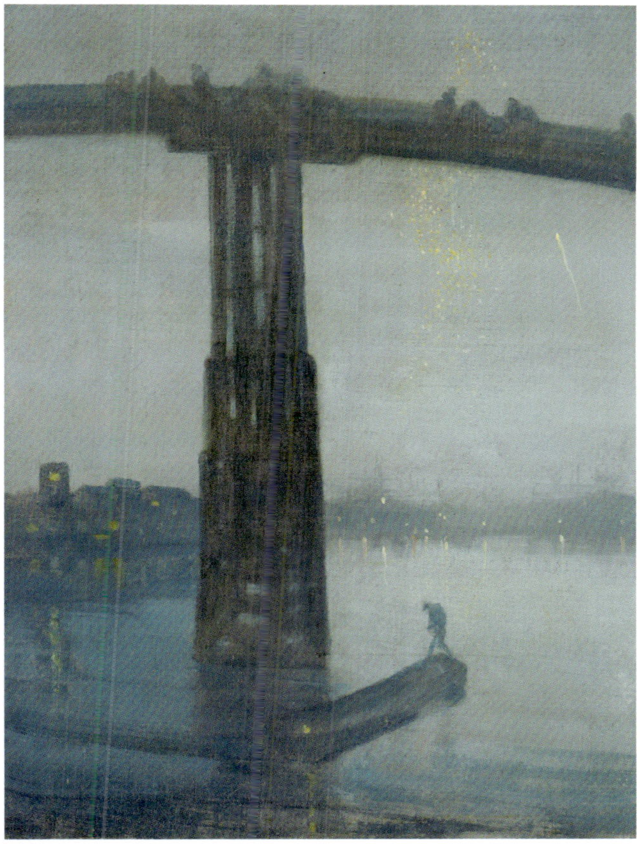

Fig. 24
**James Abbott McNeill Whistler** (1834–1903)
*Nocturne: Blue and Gold – Old Battersea Bridge*, about 1872–5
Oil on canvas, 68.3 × 51.2 cm
Tate, London

Presented by the Art Fund 1905
(Accession No. N01959)

Roberts and his Impressionist friends turned to the continent's natural environment – its untamed 'bush' as well as its agricultural landscapes and the labourers who toiled in them. They followed the exaltation of American critic Sidney Dickinson to 'present on canvas the earnestness, rigour, pathos, and heroism of the life that is about them'.[5] While seeking unique subjects, they also sought a 'closeness to nature' that equated the countryside with a nostalgic simplicity of life. In this they shared the sentiments of their plein-air forebears, French painter Jules Bastien-Lepage (1848–1884) and his British followers at the Newlyn School in Cornwall such as Stanhope Forbes (1857–1947). Rural artists' colonies were proliferating across Europe in such regions as Brittany, Cornwall and Scotland, many of which had been facilitated by the expansion of the railways. In 1885, the year prior to the formation of the Australian Artists Association, Roberts had encouraged a small group of Melbourne artists to immerse themselves in an area of dense bushland on the city's outskirts. Travelling by train to the Victorian town of Box Hill, only recently connected to the city by the railway and already in the process of being subdivided for urban development, Roberts and his city friends set up a bush camp less than a mile from the station.[6] In *The Artists' Camp*, (fig. 23) he captures the simple pleasures of their situation in his intimate portrayal of his artist friends Frederick McCubbin and Louis Abrahams, inspecting the lamb chops 'perfect from a fire of gum-twigs', the gentle scene of conviviality unfolding within a eucalyptus forest clearing.[7]

Close to the Box Hill camp Roberts also found the setting for *Winter Morning after Rain, Gardiner's Creek*, (fig. 22) infusing it with the same damp, cool light, and demonstrating a keen awareness of modern art in its compositional homage to James Abbott McNeill Whistler (1834–1903). Roberts had been living in London in the wake of the notorious 1878 trial, in which Whistler had sued the critic John Ruskin (1819–1900) for accusing him of 'flinging a pot of paint in the public's face'.[8] Roberts was familiar with some of Whistler's Thames *Nocturnes*, and works such as the controversial *Nocturne: Blue and Gold – Old Battersea Bridge*, (fig. 24) may well have been etched in his mind as he painted this wintry scene, his first work after returning to Melbourne in 1885.

A trip to Sydney in the early months of 1888 led Roberts to deploy an increasingly vibrant palette. Replacing the moody tonality of the Box Hill paintings, Roberts's joyful sun-drenched vista of Coogee Beach on a warm autumn day responds both to the dazzling intensity of the city's light, but also to his encounter with a young artist newly arrived from London, Charles Conder (1868–1909). The two artists set up their easels on the northern headland together to paint the bay, and both scenes – Roberts's *Holiday Sketch at Coogee* and Conder's *Coogee Bay*, (see cats 24 and 25) – remind us of the 'truth to nature' doctrine that plein-air painters abided by (especially in the repetition of physical features), but also of the infinite variability of perception (suggested, for example, by the distinct palettes and moods of each work). A third painter, Australian-born Arthur Streeton, having seen the two Coogee paintings, would be drawn there two years later, producing a different view along the cliff-tops, *Blue Pacific* (cat. 27).[9] These were not classical landscapes inhabited by a cast of mythical figures (although Conder's art in particular would soon move towards Symbolist allegory), but rather a joyful homage to the everyday life of the bourgeois Sydney-sider.

Conder's opalescent palette in his Sydney beach painting would burst into dazzling saturated colour later that year in *A Holiday at Mentone* (cat. 31). The artist had been lured to 'Marvellous Melbourne' by the temptations of wealth and fortune, and had admired the Whistler-inspired composition of Roberts's *Winter Morning after Rain, Gardiner's Creek* (fig. 22), which he saw in his friend's Melbourne studio.[10] Like *Coogee Bay*, *A Holiday at Mentone* also shows the modern life of the leisured – a dashing flâneur to the right, a fashionable woman settled on a wooden chair and a stiffly horizontal figure lying on the sand in the painting's centre (asleep after reading the radical Sydney journal, *The Bulletin*). This Baudelairean cast of metropolitan characters (and those scattered behind them), fashionable day-trippers, are comfortable in their occupation of this sun-drenched leisure zone, symbols of a growing national confidence painted in the centenary year of British settlement.

Yet Conder was never as interested in capturing the national mood as his fellow painters were: it would not be these urban sophisticates that would come to assume mythic proportions in the creation of federated Australia's national identity. Rather, it was the resilient and hard-working pioneer men (usually) of the bush – stockmen, drovers, shearers, wool-carters, gold-miners and other rural labourers – who came to occupy the increasingly large and ambitious canvases produced in the period. Frederick McCubbin's *Down on his Luck* (fig. 25) was one of the first works to portray the man of the bush as a heroic national figure. By this point the Australian Impressionist artists had developed enough confidence, in Virginia Spate's words, 'to believe they had something distinctive to say to the centre of Empire', and sent works with 'a leaning towards nationality' both to Britain and the Paris Salon.[11]

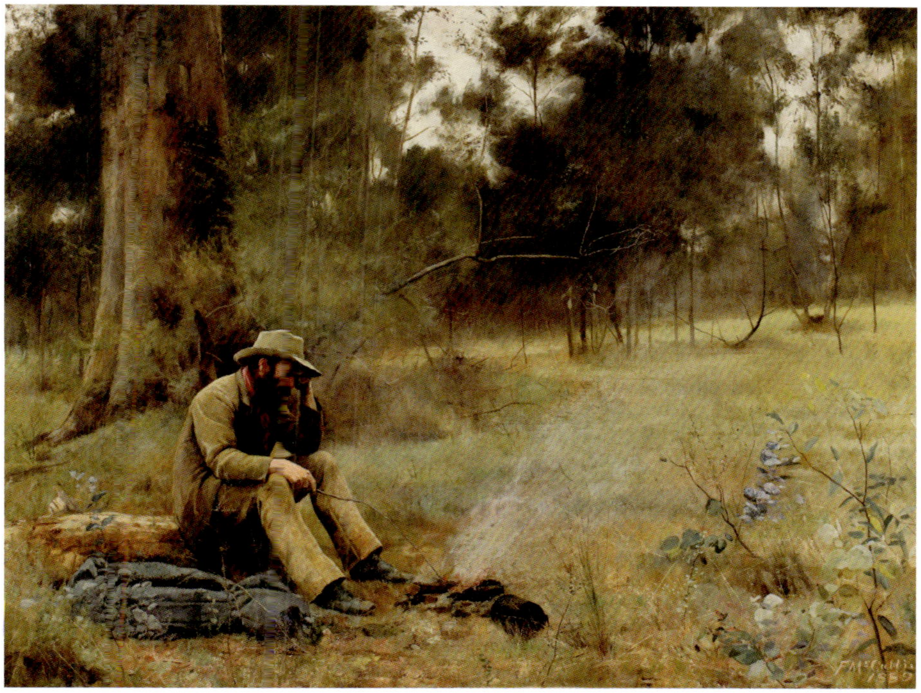

Fig. 25
**Frederick McCubbin** (1855–1917)
*Down on his Luck*, 1889
Oil on canvas, 114.5 × 152.5 cm
State Art Collection, Art Gallery of Western Australia, Perth

Purchased 1896
(Accession No. 1896/00P7)

Two years later Roberts travelled to a drought-stricken pastoral region of south-western New South Wales, specifically to paint a droving picture.[12] *A Break Away!* (cat. 22) portrays a drover on horseback striving to control the stampede of desperate sheep hurtling towards a muddy waterhole. He is undoubtedly the hero of the canvas (note the detailed realism of his muscular form looming out from the choking cloud of dust), but so too are the majestic gum trees that reach to the deep blue sky: these would soon become well-worn clichés in Federation-era Australian art, but in 1891 in the hands of the ambitious Roberts they seemed to embody the spirit and aspirations of a nation in the process of becoming. The production of wool – Australia's major contribution to Britain's imperial economy – would preoccupy Roberts in two of his other major national narratives, *Shearing the Rams*, 1891, and *The Golden Fleece*, 1894 (fig. 26).

A less muscular vision of the Australian pastoral landscape had been painted a couple of years earlier by Roberts's younger contemporary, Arthur Streeton (1867–1943). *Golden Summer, Eaglemont* (cat. 21) shows a distant view of the weatherboard homestead at Heidelberg (now a suburb of Melbourne) that Streeton shared with Roberts and Conder over two idyllic summers in 1888/9 and 1889/90. Like *A Break Away!* the vista here is bathed in warm sunlight. Yet Streeton's painting lacks the other's element of masculine endurance in the face of hardship: its genealogy links it less with history painting, like Roberts's monumental narrative, than with the works of an earlier plein-air painter, John Constable (1776–1837), with its careful attention to the transience of cloud formations and the timeless pleasures of rural life. Streeton's gentle vision of what he later called 'our hill of gold'[13] would become the leitmotif for a renewed swell of national patriotism that swept through (and divided) Australia in the years leading to the bicentenary of colonisation in 1988.[14]

The Australian landscape was not a new subject in colonial art: it had been painted from the very beginning of British colonisation by such immigrant

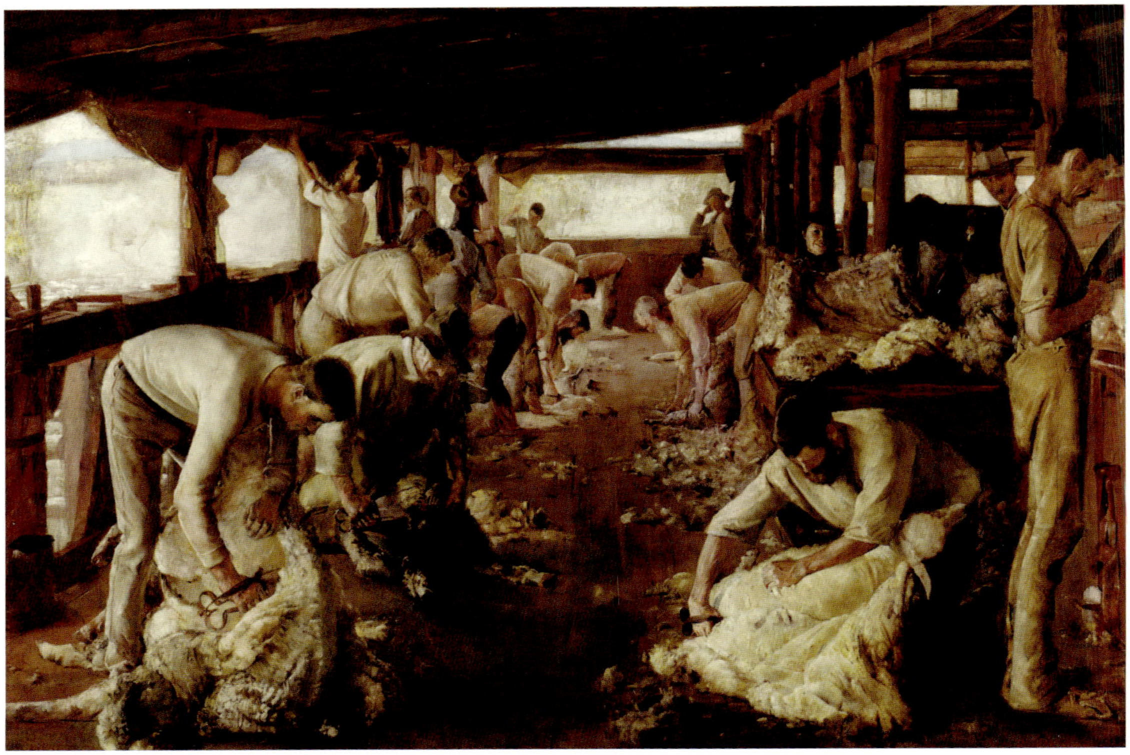

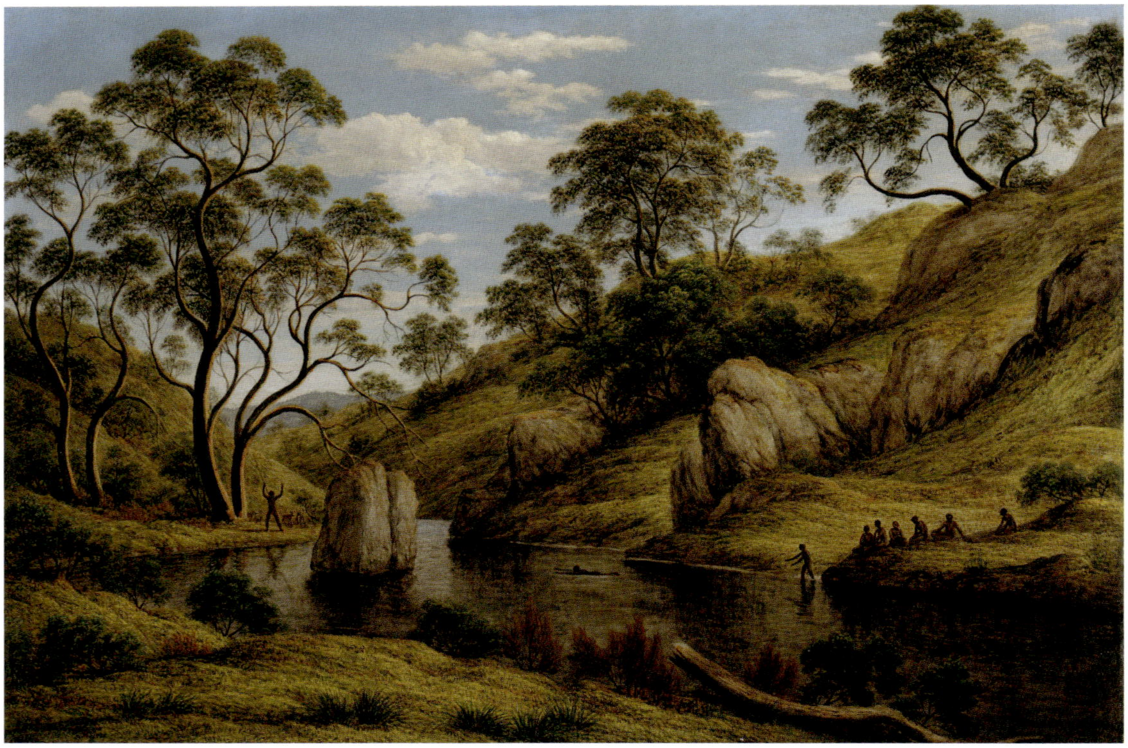

artists as John Glover, Eugene von Guérard and Louis Buvelot, who was championed as a great mentor by the Impressionists. These three artists all painted areas of colonial 'wilderness', but also regularly portrayed encroaching European settlement. When Glover landed in Van Diemen's Land (later Tasmania) in 1831, he set about creating an idealised classical vision of the Antipodean landscape, a pre-lapsarian world graced by distinctive undulating gum trees, and, significantly, Aborigines (fig. 27). However by the end of the century the Impressionists' golden landscapes, with their bush pioneers heroically forging the nation's future (while in fact clinging nostalgically to the past), had largely excluded their original occupants. By the time Streeton came to paint one of his most majestic vistas, *'The purple noon's transparent might'* (cat. 20), the editor of Melbourne's *Argus* would proclaim 'there can be no doubt that an Australian School of painting is in process of birth'.[15] In the Impressionists' national pictures Aborigines were largely excluded, as indeed they were in the Australian Constitution of 1 January 1901.[16]

Streeton, Roberts, Conder and their contemporaries deployed the radical new tools of Impressionism to produce an art that they understood as characteristically 'Australian'. Yet we should heed the late Benedict Anderson's assertion that nations are only ever 'imagined communities': the mythology of the white pioneer – resilient, determined, hard-working – is one that many Australians continue to identify with, despite its blindness to a more complex reality, both then and now.[17]

Fig. 26
**Tom Roberts** (1856–1931)
*The Golden Fleece*, 1894
Oil on canvas, 104 × 158.7 cm
Art Gallery of New South Wales, Sydney

Purchased 1894
(Accession No. 648)

Fig. 27
**John Glover** (1767–1849)
*The Bath of Diana, Van Diemen's Land*, 1837
Oil on canvas, 76 × 114 cm
National Gallery of Australia, Canberra

Purchased with the assistance of the
National Gallery of Australia Foundation 1993
(Accession No. NGA 93.1777)

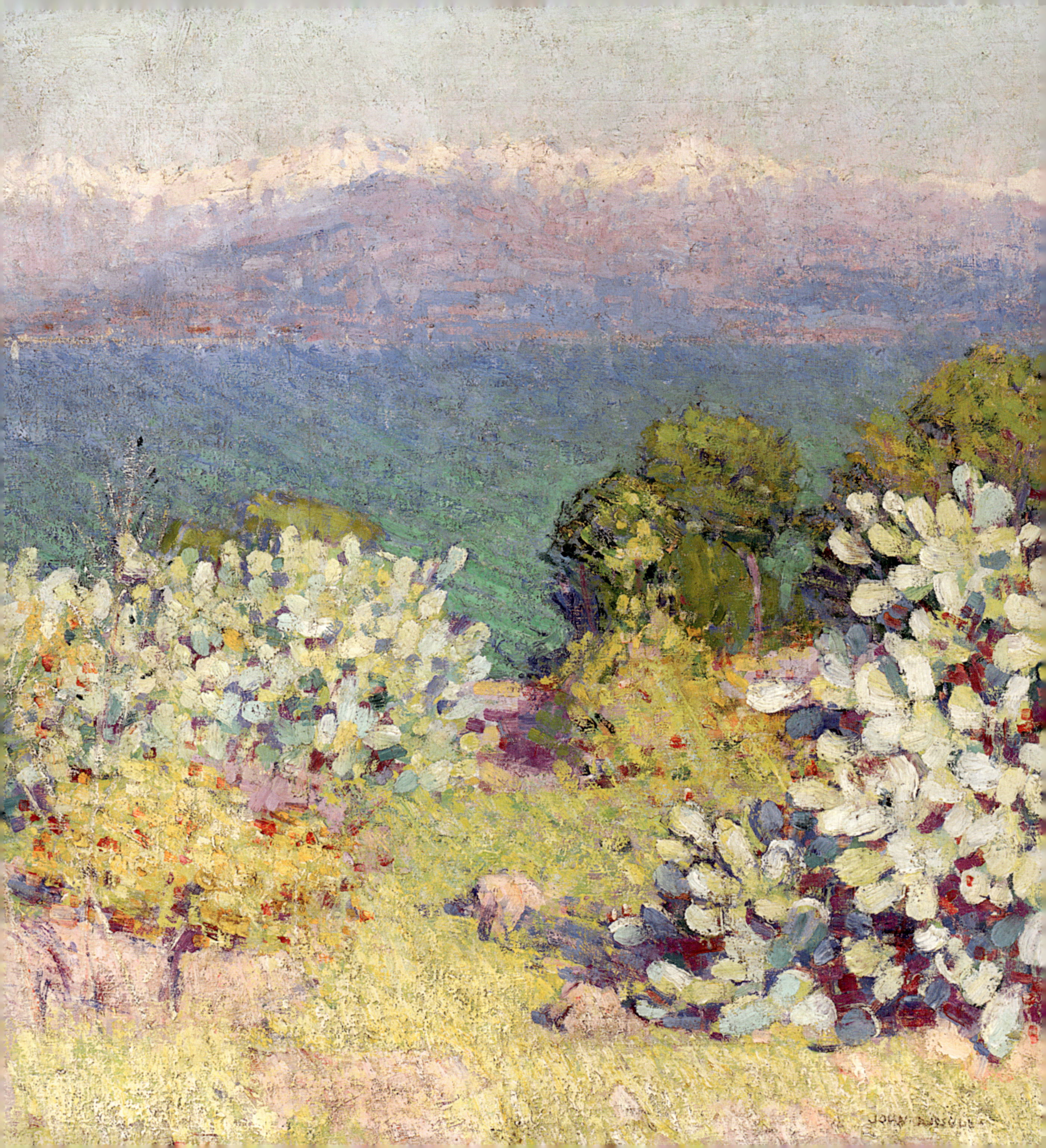
JOHN

*We are in the throes of a mighty revolution in art. The gropers after truth. Men who are searching things for themselves, seeking to render what they* <u>*see*</u> *& not what they know to exist are throwing out most old time conventions, as to the* <u>*rules*</u> *of composition, sentiment, colour & they are drifting towards what is best in Impressionism.*[1]

It is debatable whether the most Impressionist of Australia's Impressionists, John Russell (fig. 29), is an Australian Impressionist at all. Russell's development as a painter with a remarkable facility for colour was chiefly accomplished during twenty years spent painting one particular place, not his native Australia but the then remote island of Belle-Île-en-Mer off the coast of Brittany, France. Russell (1858–1930) was not the only Australian artist to live and work in France in the late nineteenth century, though while most others sought success and patronage through the accepted path of the salon exhibitions, Russell was unusual in his engagement with the avant-garde during a time of rapid change and charged debates about the nature of art.

Russell knew the Impressionist artists who had challenged the academic establishment in the 1870s and who were becoming increasingly recognised in the 1880s and 1890s, as well as the young mavericks who became known as Post-Impressionists and Neo-Impressionists. While Russell's practice gravitates towards Impressionism, it can be located within these three interrelated movements as he progresses through periods of intense engagement and relative isolation from the network of artist friends and peers who sustained his creative development.[2]

Sydney-born, athletic, adventurous and destined to work in the family engineering enterprises, Russell seems an unlikely participant in the fiercely

# JOHN RUSSELL

## A Landscape Apart

Wayne Tunnicliffe

Fig. 28
**John Russell** (1858–1930)
*In the Morning, Alpes Maritimes from Antibes*, 1890–1
Detail of cat. 33, p. 99

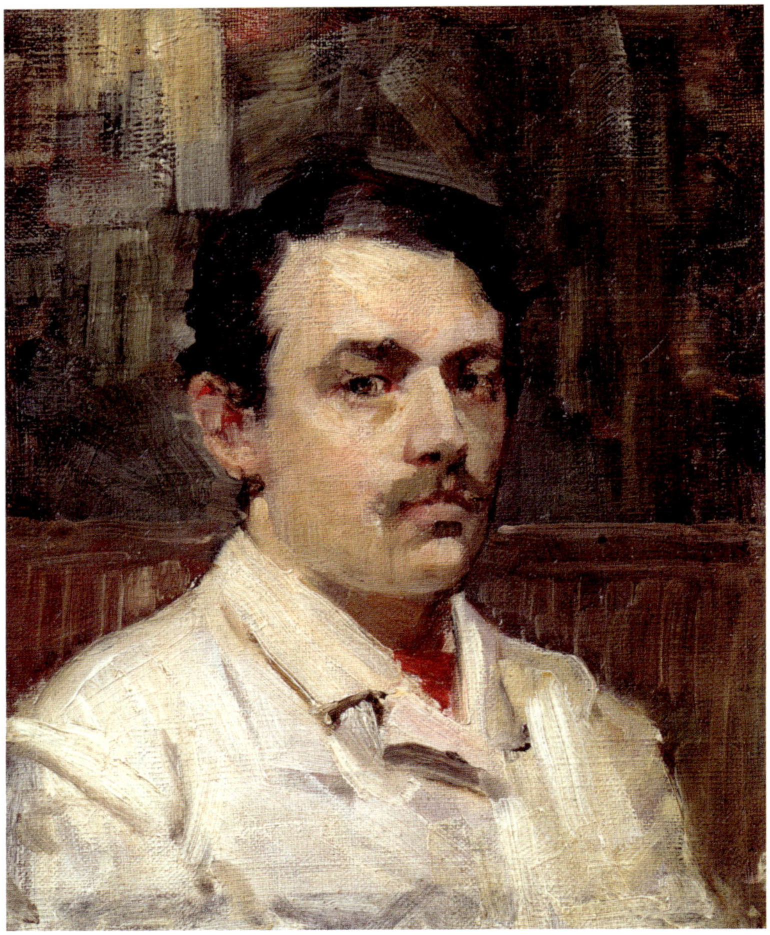

Fig. 29
**John Russell** (1858–1930)
*Self Portrait*, about 1886–7
Oil on canvas, 46 × 40.5 cm
Le Musée de Morlaix, Musée de France
(Accession No. D.997.1.1.1)

competing art movements unfolding in France in this period. The sudden death of his wealthy father in 1879, however, freed him from filial obligations and gave him the independent means to pursue his desire to train as an artist in Europe. Russell first enrolled at the Slade School of Fine Art in London in 1881, under the French artist and Professor, Alphonse Legros (1837–1911), who had been associated with the Impressionists in Paris in the 1870s.[3] During his time in London, Russell befriended Anglo-Australian art student Tom Roberts (1856–1931) who had left Melbourne to study at the Royal Academy Schools and after Roberts returned to Australia in 1885 they continued to correspond for several years. Russell's letters survive and trace his development as an artist through this period while he eventually embraced French Impressionism, which he communicated to Roberts just as Roberts became a driving force in developing what came to be known as Australian Impressionism.

Given his risk-taking and competitive nature it was probably inevitable that Russell would join the 1880s exodus of the more adventurous London art students to Paris, seeking to learn and test their artistic mettle in the European centre for both academic and advanced art.[4] Russell enrolled at the Atelier Cormon in 1884, led by salon artist Fernand Cormon (1845–1924) whose historicist paintings were conservative but who attracted a remarkable group of students to his small studio in the mid-1880s. During the three years that Russell remained at Cormon's his contemporaries included Louis Anquetin, Eugène Boch, Emile Bernard, Henri de Toulouse-Lautrec and in 1886 a newly arrived from Antwerp and awkwardly reserved fellow student, Vincent van Gogh (1853–1890). Van Gogh formed a friendship with Russell that was to last for the rest of his life and Russell both sketched and painted Van Gogh, giving his 1886 portrait to the artist 'in friendship' (fig. 30).[5] The tonal naturalist style and lively immediacy of this painting reflects Russell's earlier training under Legros who was known for his rapidly executed portraits which he demonstrated to his students.[6] Russell and Van Gogh's painting practices developed in tandem in 1886–7 and in a number of portraits, still lifes and small townscapes painted near Paris, there are considerable affinities between the artists' works both stylistically and in subject matter.

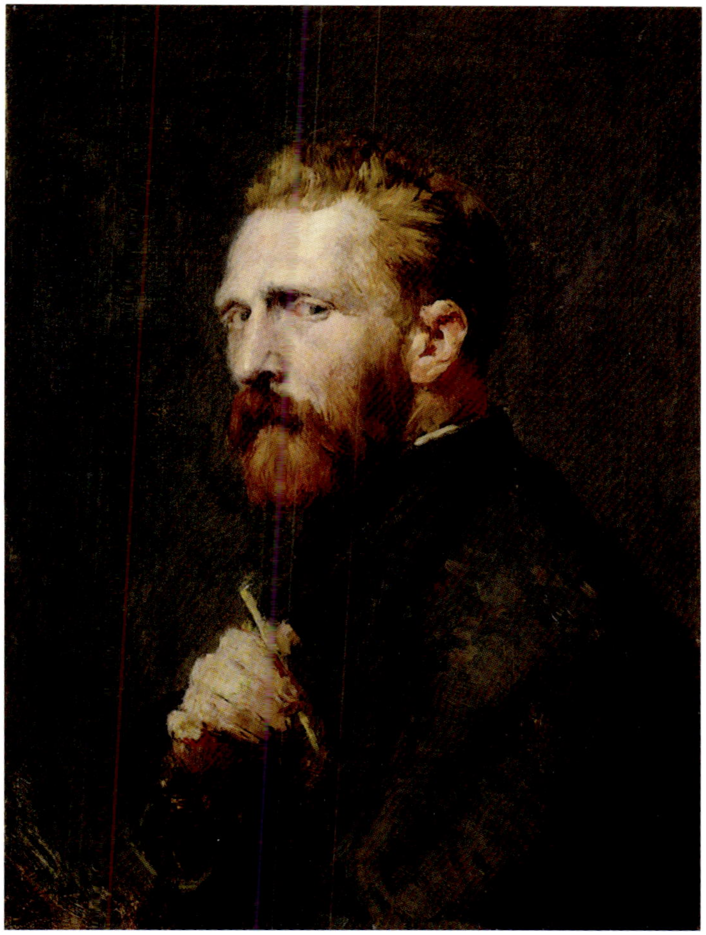

Fig. 30
**John Russell** (1858–1930)
*Vincent van Gogh*, 1886
Oil on canvas, 60.1 cm × 45.6 cm
Van Gogh Museum (Vincent Van Gogh Foundation), Amsterdam
(Accession No. s273V1962)

Van Gogh's and Russell's practices diverged later in 1887 as Van Gogh moved towards his own uniquely expressive Post-Impressionist style and Russell began to explore his developing interest in Impressionism in more depth. One catalyst for Russell's change in direction came from a chance encounter in 1886. Russell, accompanied by his mistress Marianna Mattiocco (1865–1908), escaped from Paris during the summer break to the savagely beautiful island of Belle-Île-en-Mer with its dramatic coastline and surging Atlantic seas. Like many of his urban contemporaries, Russell was looking for the authenticity of traditional beliefs and customs in rural agricultural or coastal fishing communities and Brittany was a particular magnet to artists with its distinctive language and culture unaltered by industrial modernity. The rise of plein-air painting during the nineteenth century and the dramatic redevelopment of Paris into an ultra-modern city led many artists to travel to remote areas on extended painting trips and to the establishment of artist's colonies which sustained anything from short visits to permanent residents. As well as local human subjects, landscapes – either wild or conveying age-old land management practices – were compelling to city-based plein-air painters as an antidote to the brittle sophistication of metropolitan living.[7]

Coincidentally Russell was visiting Belle-Île at the same time as Claude Monet (1840–1926) who he came across painting on the cliff tops near Port-Goulphar (fig. 31), addressing him as 'The prince of the impressionists' when he first met him. By the mid-1880s Monet was a well-known, if controversial, painter and he would seem to have allowed Russell to observe him at work during a time of great focus and productivity.[8] Monet immersed himself in the wild natural environment of the island, which defied picturesque conventions, as he sought to capture on canvas the often rapidly changing weather and light conditions during the course of the day, a process through which he moved closer toward working in series. While Russell was already an experienced plein-air painter, in response to this encounter and to the stimulus of his fellow students and the art he was seeing in Paris, he began experimenting with the stylistic and technical innovations associated with the Impressionists.[9] Russell began to abandon his careful tonal modelling and restricted use of colour in order to work more freely, applying broken higher-keyed colour with diverse and very apparent brushstrokes.

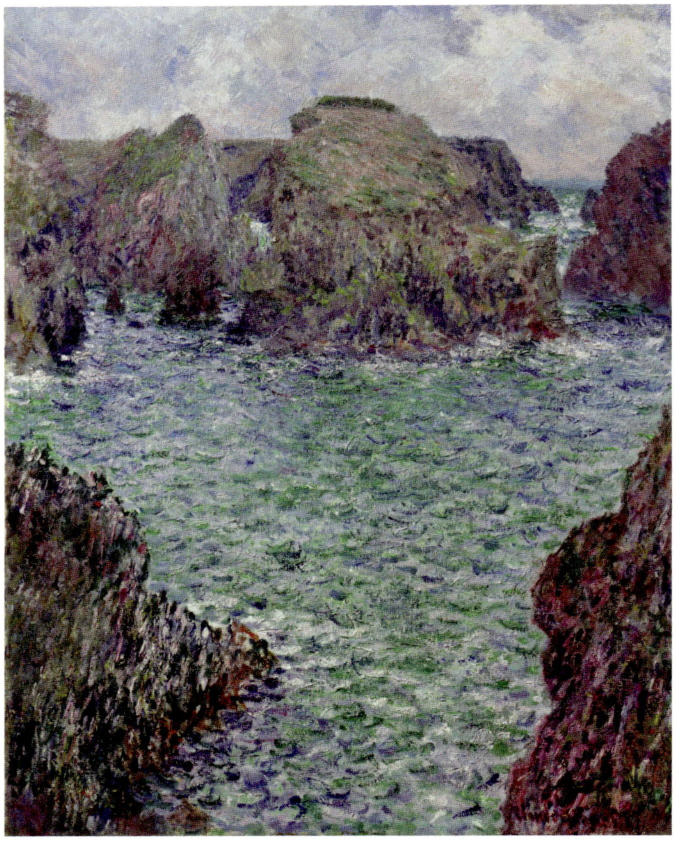

Fig. 31
**Claude Monet** (1840–1926)
*Port-Goulphar, Belle-Île*, 1887
Oil on canvas, 81 × 65 cm
Art Gallery of New South Wales, Sydney

Purchased 1949
(Accession No. 8356)

It was a gradual and at times conflicted process however and while Russell's surviving works from this period show Impressionist experimentation, a letter to Roberts in December 1887 suggests he still harboured salon ambitions (see fig. 35, p. 59) as it finishes with Russell describing his trials trying to complete a painting in his studio of Dante and Virgil crossing the River Styx: 'simple enough but I'm rapidly going through my hair'.[10]

In the same letter Russell writes that he is now using colour: 'pure or as nearly pure as possible', which is evident in a painting of Impressionist artist Alfred Sisley's partner Eugénie Lescouezec (1834–1898), undertaken in 1887 when Russell was staying at Moret-sur-Loing (cat. 32), a small village south of Paris where Sisley lived. The colours in this work are much more highly keyed than in Russell's earlier canvases, with extensive passages of white paint to represent the exposed limestone on the hills which includes bright blue reflections from the equally bright blue sky. Russell allows the pale primed canvas to show through as part of the overall tonality of the painting, particularly in the central tree trunk where it forms a sixth colour along with the green, brown, yellow, purple and blue dashes of paint. He has freely and energetically painted with diverse brushstrokes: the brief dabs to describe the central tree trunk, the short strokes used over much of the painting in varying directions, and the longer more fluid strokes that represent the shadows of the trees connecting the fore and mid grounds.

The unusual back view and cropping of Madame Sisley at the front edge of the canvas and the asymmetrical composition with strong verticals and horizontals reflects Russell's study of Japanese prints which greatly influenced many contemporary artists and which he and Van Gogh were collecting together at this time. Another influence is likely to have been photography, particularly as filtered through the unusual view points and cropping in Edgar Degas's paintings and drawings, an artist who Russell admired. Russell has not quite let go of his previous training, though, as recent conservation analysis has revealed fine underdrawing mapping out the composition and he does not quite trust his ability to convey form through colour modulation as he has added sketchy lines of red-brown paint over Madame Sisley's dress to emphasise its shape.

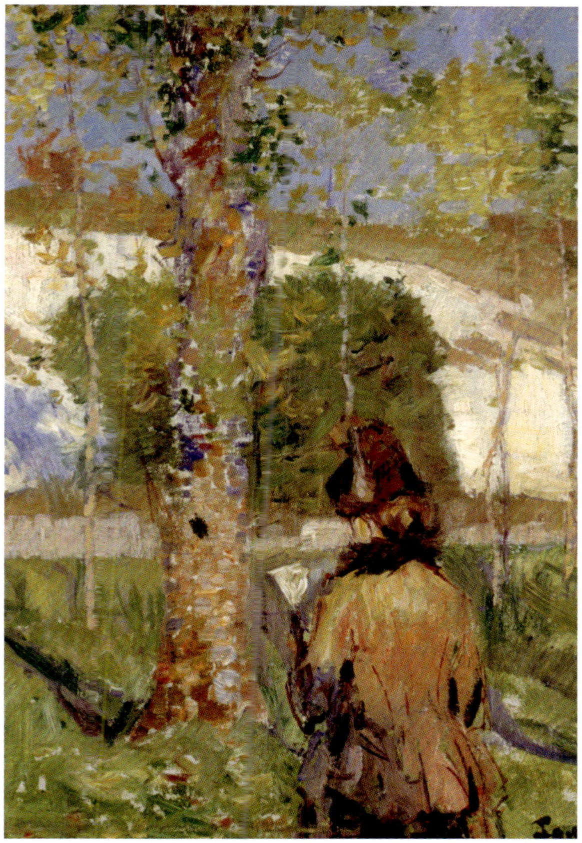

Fig. 32
**John Russell** (1858–1930)
*Madame Sisley on the Banks of the Loing at Moret*, 1887
Detail of cat. 32, p. 98

*But when we get to colour. The gorse and the heather. Yellow & purple, orange boat sails, blue sea, red rocks, green sea. All a matter of feeling. Tis in the man with brush & paint pot or it is not.*

*Here they were all time studying drawing & values, letting colour slide before the advent of Manet, Monet & the Impressionists.*[11]

Discontentment with city life and the constant café and studio arguments over which direction art should take contributed to Russell's decision to leave Paris permanently and in 1888 he, and his now wife Marianna, with their growing family, moved to a large house they had had built at Port-Goulphar on Belle-Île very near where Russell had first met Monet. Earlier in the year Van Gogh left Paris for Provence with the aim of eventually establishing a 'studio of the south' which failed after Gauguin's disastrous visit in 1888, while the Russell's house on Belle-Île practically became a 'studio of the north' as many visiting artists stayed with them over the subsequent two decades they lived on the island.[12] Russell pitted his athleticism against the elements on Belle-Île as he painted its inhabitants, land and seascapes in all types of weather and during all seasons.[13] Russell particularly focused on the sheltered bay in front of his studio and the nearby dramatic coastline within walking distance, developing a deep knowledge and sensory familiarity with this environment. Over the two decades he lived on Belle-Île, he repeatedly painted a dramatic local geographical feature, the spectacular rocky outcrops that rear out of the ocean known as the Needles, and they became something of a leitmotif for his time on the island and his development as an artist.

In early canvases painted soon after moving to the island such as *Aiguille de Coton, Belle-Île*, about 1890 (fig. 10, p. 26), Russell chose a very high horizon line with the sky barely present, bringing focus to the rocks and surging sea painted with obvious broken brushstrokes where he strives to capture the changing colour effects of moving water in the afternoon light. The canvas is a conventional horizontal format, however, with an encompassing view of the outcrops, headlines and ocean near the shore. By the early 1900s Russell often paints in a vertical or square format (as used by Monet) which brings much greater focus to the Needles themselves. In *Aiguille de Coton, Belle-Île* (fig. 33) there is no locating shoreline or broad view of the ocean, and sky and sea merge in the limited spatial recession barely suggested in the upper part of the canvas. This richly coloured work which makes use of intense blue-purples, greens and white is remarkable for the zig-zag brushstrokes which animate the painting. These brushstrokes vary from the tighter, smaller ones used to depict the rocks to the broad sweep of the intensely

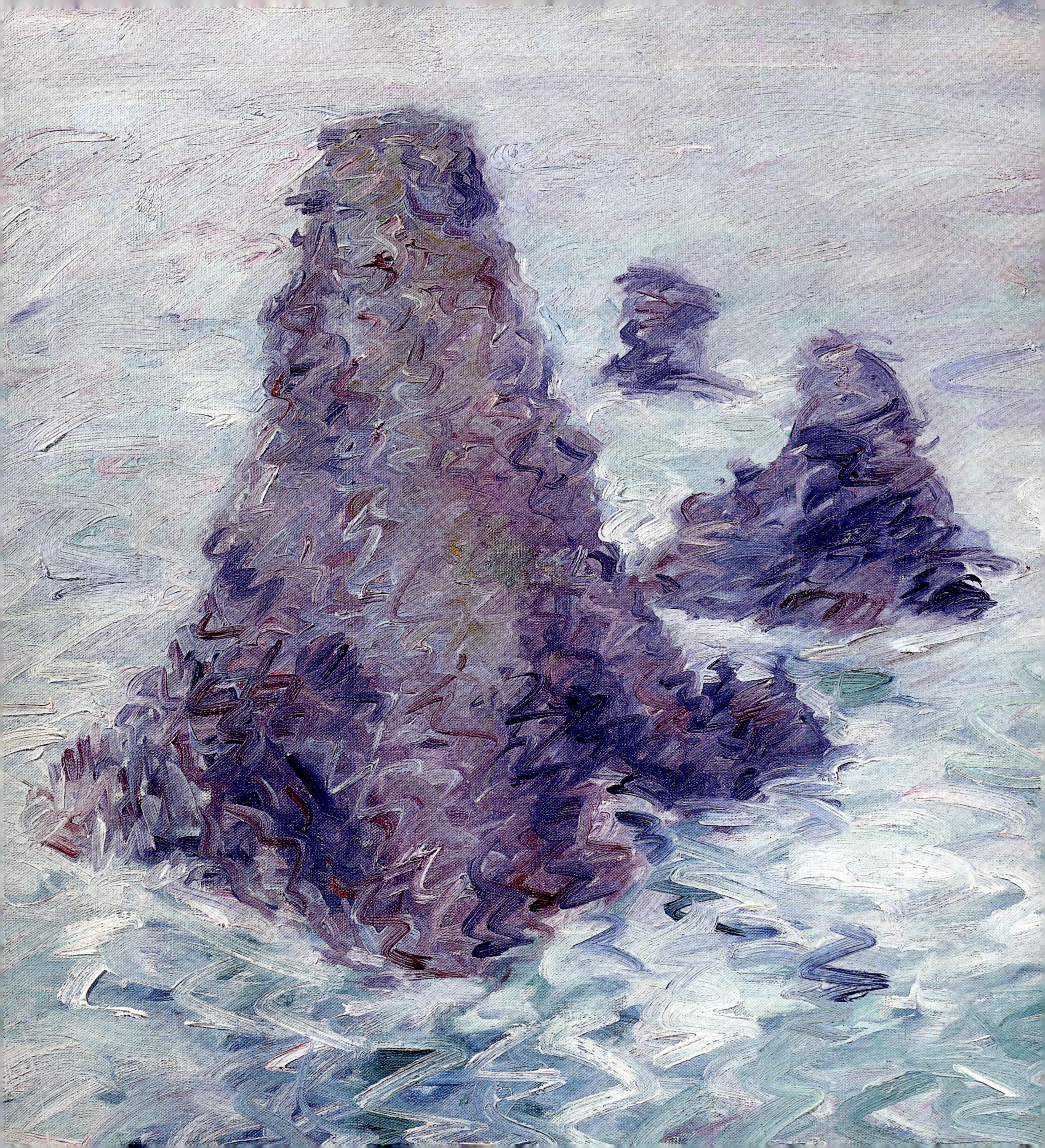

vigorous zig-zags that describe the ocean. Encapsulating the energy of the surging seas, the dense strokes loaded with paint in which the artist's physical gesture is highly evident seem to exist in their own right freed from representation. There is a remarkable raw expressiveness to this work that is essentially Post-Impressionist in nature.

In 1888 in Paris, Russell saw a group of recent light-saturated paintings by Monet of the Cap d'Antibes in the South of France:

*Before I left Paris I lunched with Mr Rodin (who has finished a fine head of my wife) and Mr Claude Monet. Saw ten of Mr Monet's pictures done at Antibes. Very fine in colour and light and a certain richness of envelop. But like nearly all the so-called Impressionist work the form is not enough studied... He is undoubtedly a remarkable colourist and full of courage in attacking difficult problems. We should all do the same.*[14]

Russell admired Monet's facility with colour while criticising what he saw as a lack of attention to form, and yet these paintings had a lasting effect, as when he later travelled to Antibes in the winter of 1890–1 he chose similar scenes to paint. Russell had a conflicted response to this popular resort area – after the isolation of Belle-Île, the Cote d'Azur seemed like well-trodden territory teeming with wealthy tourists from Paris and further afield – but he admired the 'Glorious views East. Bay of Nice with all the snow clad Alpes Maritimes in view. West. Bay of Cannes & the lovely high foothills of the Esterelles.'[15] Russell set to work on a series of highly resolved Impressionist canvases and small very experimental paintings. The former show a mature and remarkable facility with colours that he is now often mixing himself for greater vividness, applied in a complex and confident way as he has mastered Impressionist techniques. The latter have thickly applied paint in blunt brushstrokes where form is entirely subservient to bright pure colour that is almost proto-Fauve in its intensity. Russell communicates his new surety in a long letter to Roberts in which he shares technical information on his practice as well as declaring that Impressionism will win the revolution in art that is taking place.[16] The reception of this information in Australia seems to have been measured, though, and when Roberts shared this letter with Arthur Streeton, the latter wrote back to Roberts: 'Many thanks for Russell's letter Tis very interesting. He seems to love the open air very much & therefore must be a fine chap... but he does seem to bother too much about the ways and means.'[17]

Russell's 'ways and means' are central to his practice at this juncture and core to what he tries to communicate to Roberts in Australia about French Impressionism. In works such as *A Clearing in the Forest* (cat. 35) and *In the Morning, Alpes Maritimes from Antibes* (cat. 33), Russell layers paint in worked-up surfaces in which colour is also experienced as texture, achieving an overall chromatic and visual intensity.

Fig. 33
**John Russell** (1858–1930)
*Aiguille de Coton, Belle-Île*, about 1900
Detail of cat. 37, p. 103

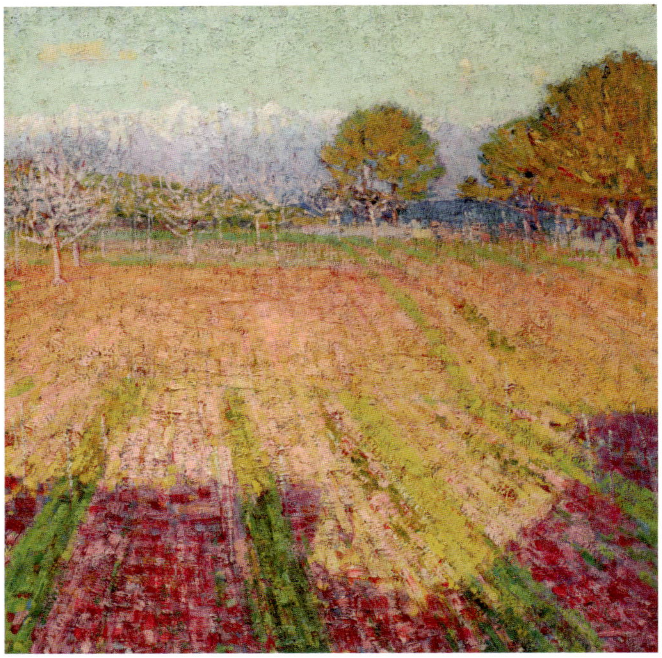

Fig. 34
**John Russell** (1858–1930)
*In the Afternoon*, 1891
Oil on canvas, 65.1 × 65.4 cm
Art Gallery of New South Wales, Sydney

Purchased with funds provided by the Art Gallery Society of New South Wales 2016 (Accession No. 324.2016)

In common with many other seemingly spontaneous Impressionist paintings, Russell's are considered compositions painted over a period of time, something he also observed about Impressionism in another letter to Roberts: 'As understood here it consists not of hasty sketches but in pushed work in which the purity of color & intention is kept. Monet for instance will put 10 or 12 sittings on a canvas.'[18] The layered interweaving of colours throughout these paintings shows an artist in full control of his technique to achieve a vision of the natural world based on both observation and subjective response. *In the Morning, Alpes Maritimes from Antibes* and its companion piece *In the Afternoon* (fig. 34) depict differing scenes but embody the Impressionist interest in changing light and colour effects at different times of the day. Russell exhibited this pair at the 1891 New English Art Club exhibition which showed the most advanced art in London at this time and, in addition to progressive artists working in England such as George Clausen, John Singer Sargent and Walter Sickert, the exhibition included work by French artists Edgar Degas and Monet. While reviews were mixed, Russell's paintings were seen as aligned with those of Monet amongst other painters with *The Times* critic noting: 'There is sunshine, real, genuine sunshine, in Mr J.T. [*sic*] Russell's *Morning* and *Afternoon*... [and] in Monsieur Claude Monet's *Orange and Lemon Trees*.'[19]

Russell's colour experimentation evolved further in the 1890s, becoming more non-naturalistic and expressive, and it was when Russell was at his boldest as a colourist that he encountered a young art student visiting the island, Henri Matisse. Painting in a conservative tonal style, Matisse first came to Belle-Île in 1895 and was disconcerted by the wild landscape and weather and promptly left, but he returned over the next two summers and met Russell in 1896. Matisse's art developed in response to what he learned from Russell in both colour theory and practice and his previously conventional approach changed as he awakened to a more expressive use of brushstrokes, a dissolution of modelled form and a much heightened colour palette. These changes alarmed his teacher Gustave Moreau and many of his fellow students when he returned to Paris, and yet Matisse did not resile from the new directions in which his art was developing, despite jeopardising his early career successes. Russell also introduced Matisse to Van Gogh's highly individual practice and he gave Matisse one of his twelve Van Gogh drawings, *Haystacks* (1888), surely as a mark of the respect in which he held the young student. While not the only influence on his transformation as an artist, Matisse's time on Belle-Île was undoubtedly a catalyst for change and by the late 1890s he embraced pure colour, explored both Monet's

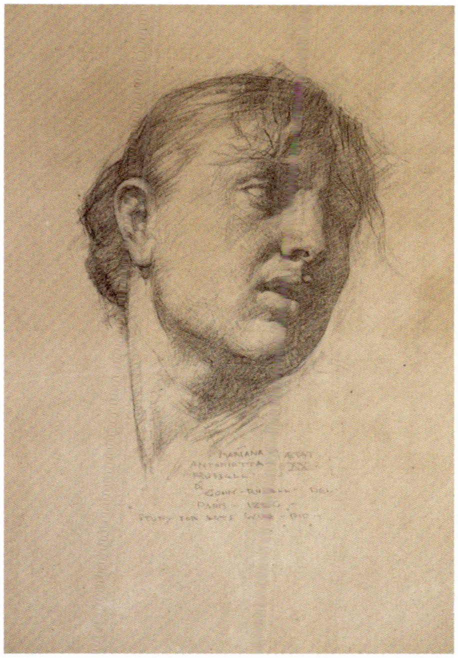

Fig. 35
**John Russell** (1858–1930)
*Study for 'Lot's Wife'*
(Marianna Mattiocco), 1886
Pencil, white chalk highlights on laid paper on thin card, 52.2 × 36.1 cm
Art Gallery of New South Wales, Sydney

Purchased with funds provided by the Gil and Shay Docking Drawing Fund 2007 (Accession No. 349.2007)

Impressionism and Van Gogh's Post-Impressionism, and experimented with Georges-Pierre Seurat's and Paul Signac's Neo-Impressionism as he worked towards the radical and violently coloured style that became known as Fauvism.[20]

*You are in your element – triple Triton – and you return to the grottoes of Amphitrite, or rather [those] of marine monsters. Enjoy yourself and don't forget that your painting is the precious thing for now and in the future.*[21]

At the fin-de-siècle, Russell began a remarkable group of paintings of tempestuous seas pounding the Belle-Île coastline. In some works, such as *Rough Sea, Morestil* (cat. 40), the ocean becomes a tumultuous pattern of waves crashing against rocky outcrops and cliffs with a repetition of highly animated forms that give great emphasis to the powerful natural forces he depicts. In others works, such as *Rough Sea, Belle-Île* (cat. 39), sea, sky and land dissolve into each other in swirling whorls of colour which approach complete abstraction. While sometimes suggesting Turner's late works, an artist admired by many of Russell's contemporaries, these paintings are a wildly energetic and individual response to the natural phenomenon that he had observed first hand for almost two decades.

Russell's masculine sporting pursuits and physical vigour finds expression in painting nature's raw forces, as tackling these plein-air subjects required considerable strength and stamina on the artist's part. Russell's increasingly expressive painting in the later 1890s is a distinctive development in his own practice, though his highly physical use of paint echoes Rodin's visceral use of materials from which forms emerge and submerge. While this may seem like a long artistic bow to draw, Russell and Rodin had been friends since 1888 when Russell commissioned Rodin to sculpt a portrait bust of Marianna (fig. 35) and Russell owned a small number of Rodin sculptures including a bust cast in silver.[22] The two artists were particularly close at this time and Rodin visited the Russell's in 1902, experiencing first-hand the adverse weather conditions that can quickly arise on this coastline.

Russell had been content for his work to be known amongst his friends and peers, but in the new century he sought a greater public engagement. A less agitated but nonetheless boldly coloured and painted seascape of sardine fishing boats on Port-Goulphar, *Cruach en Mahr, Matin, Belle-Île-en-Mer* (cat. 41), was accepted for the 1905 Salon d'Automne where the critic Louis Vauxcelles used the term 'Fauves' (wild beasts) to dismiss the work of Matisse and his confrères.[23] Russell also exhibited 21 paintings in the Salon de la Société des Indépendants over the years 1906 to 1909, his most sustained period of exhibiting, when it presented the most progressive painting in France. He may have been encouraged to participate in these exhibitions because of Matisse being on the selection jury for the Salon d'Automne, and Matisse and Signac on the

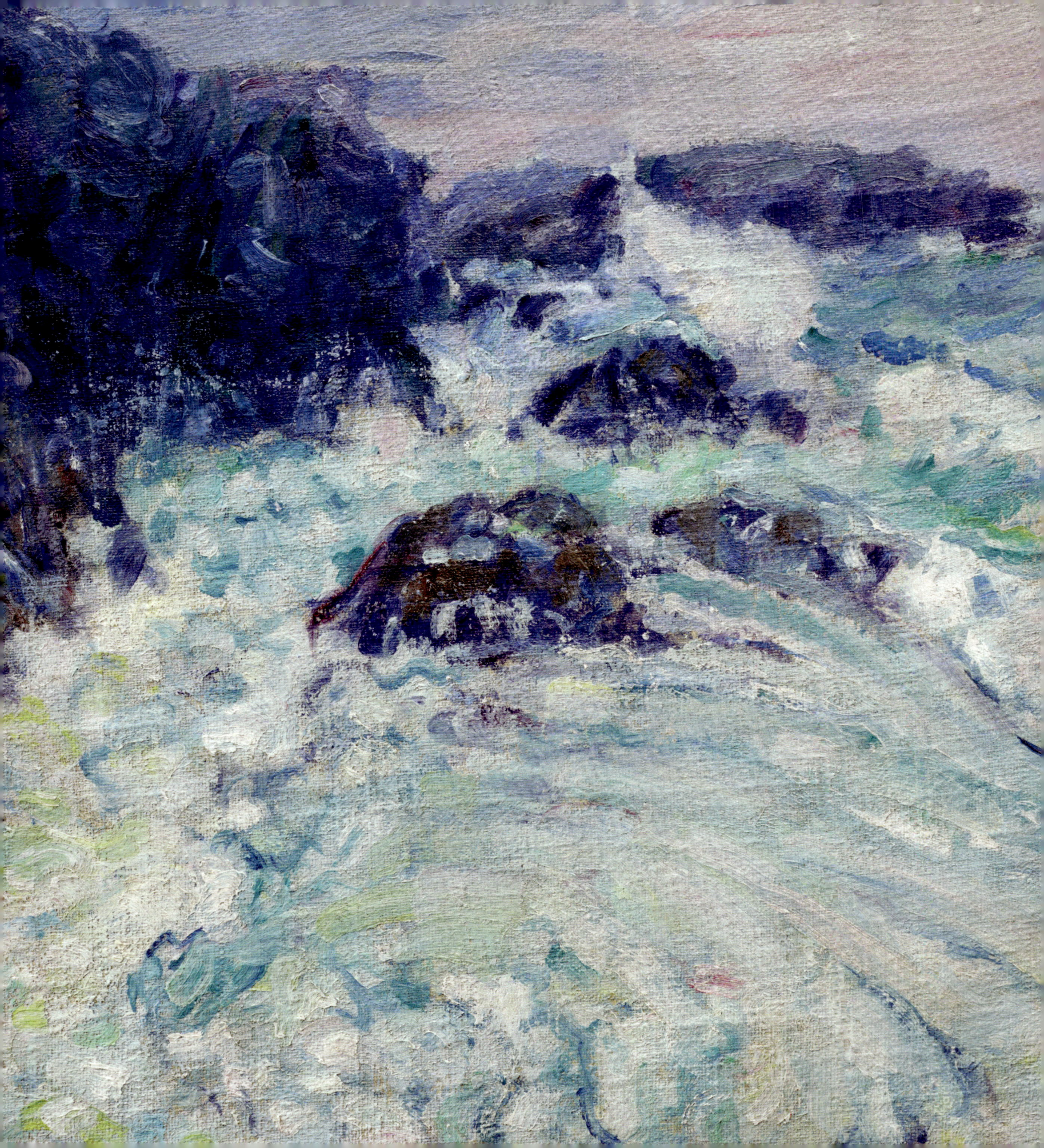

hanging committee for the Salon des Indépendants.[24] Significant critical notice eluded Russell, however, and when his beloved wife Marianna died after a short illness in 1908 he left Belle-Île and soon after France to live a peripatetic life in Europe before returning to the Antipodes in the early 1920s, eventually settling in Sydney in 1924 where he did not re-engage with the local art scene. Russell painted very few oil paintings after 1908 and his later production consists mainly of highly keyed luminous watercolours, a medium with which he had developed considerable facility and continued with until his death in 1930.

Was John Russell an Australian Impressionist? While he did not participate in the emergence of the local variant of international Impressionism in Australia, he was the only Australian-born artist to engage with the avant-garde in France in the 1880s and to embrace many of the qualities of French Impressionism at its height before moving towards his own version of Post-Impressionism. Russell tried to communicate what he was seeing and learning to Tom Roberts, one of the key protagonists of Australian Impressionism, though it is uncertain what, if any, effect Russell's letters had on Roberts's painting. Russell did not contribute to the painting of great landscape and figure subjects in Australia that helped a new national identity emerge in the 1890s and, while some artists knew he was painting in France, his work was virtually unknown in his birth country after 1883. It was not until the mid-twentieth century that his art and his life were rediscovered and became recognised at home, the two inextricably linked in the public's eye due to his close friendships with artists who came to define his cultural epoch. Russell's Australian-ness does not reside in such clichés as his adventurous spirit, athleticism and bold painting, but in his internationalism in the late nineteenth century when new world artists sought to test themselves against the old world art capitals. What Russell's surviving oeuvre reveals is an artist who developed exceptional abilities as a colourist through focusing on his subjective perception of the natural world that lay immediately around him. That he viewed this world through some of the most advanced ideas in French art of the time is remarkable for someone born so far away.

Fig. 36
**John Russell** (1858–1930)
*Rough Sea, Morestil*, about 1900

Detail of cat. 40, p. 106

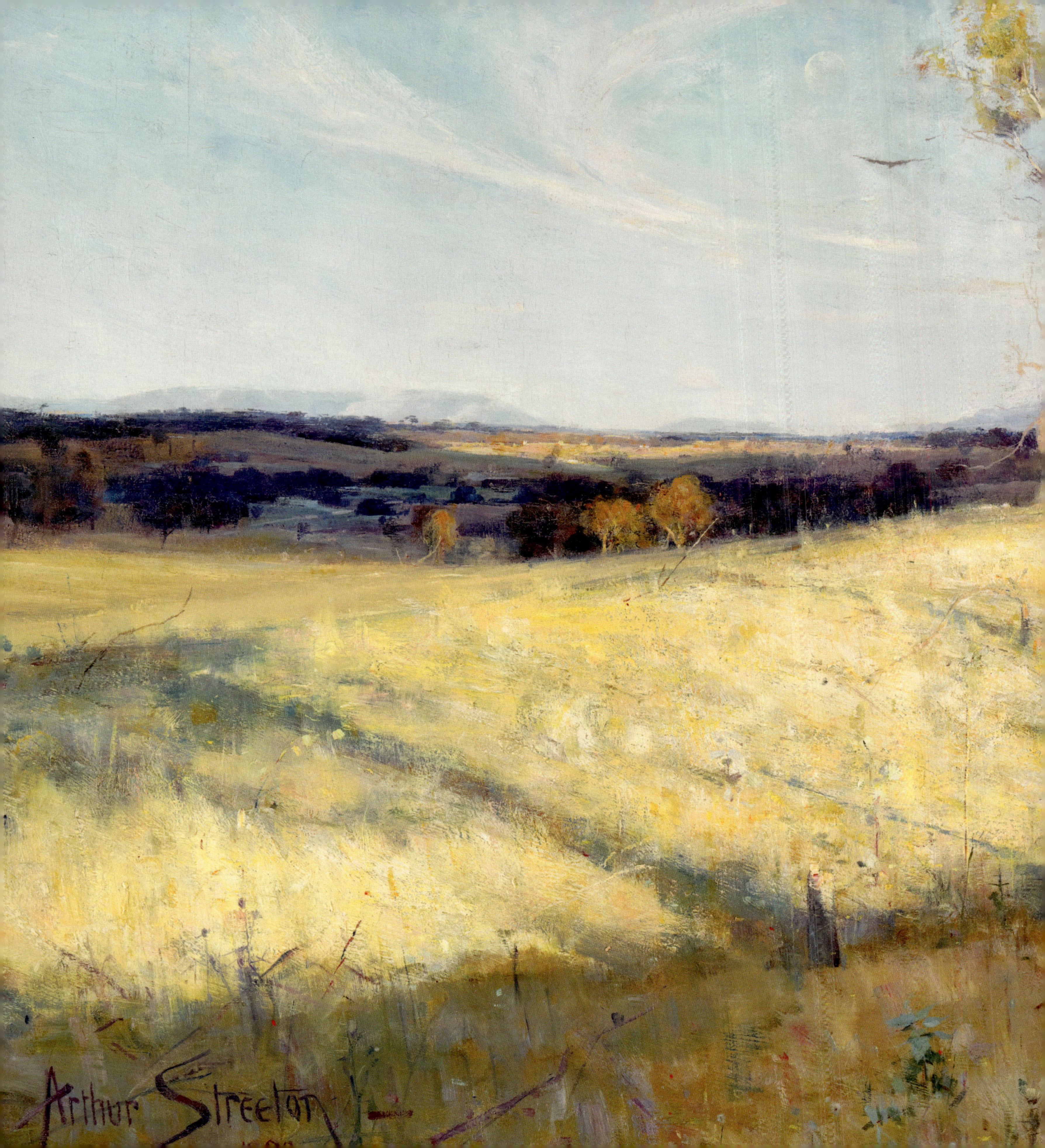
Arthur Streeton

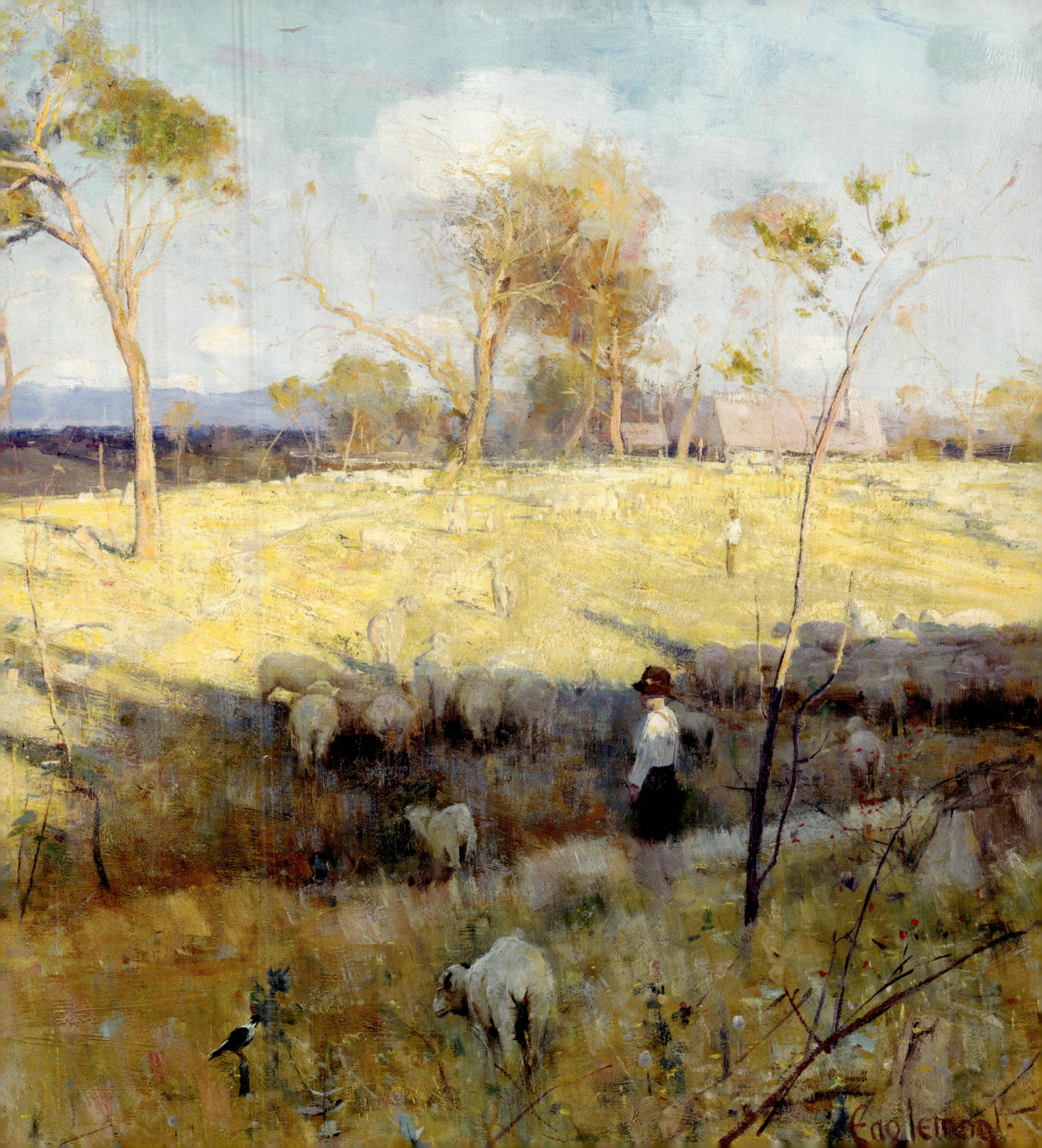
Eaglemont.

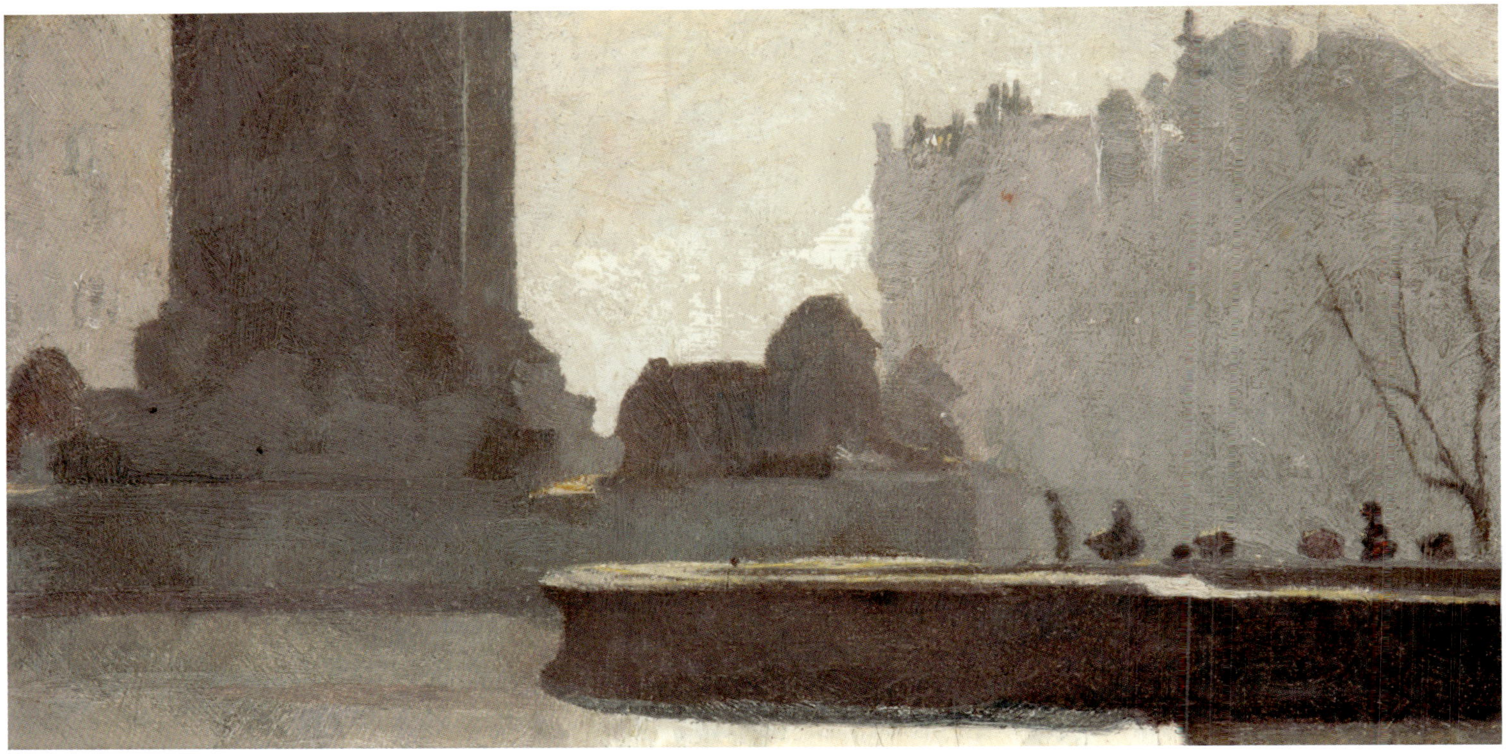

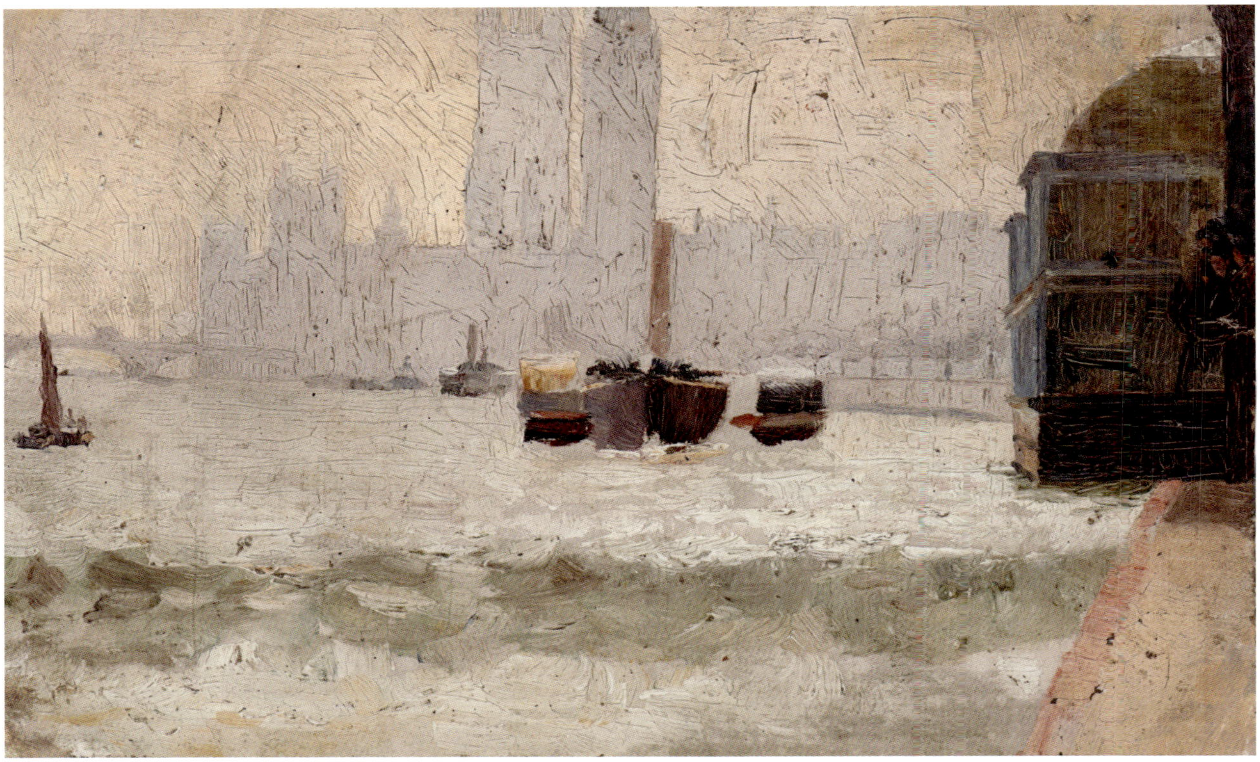

1
**Tom Roberts** (1856–1931)
*Trafalgar Square*, 1904
Oil on cardboard, 14 × 28 cm
Art Gallery of South Australia, Adelaide

South Australian Government Grant 1988
(Accession No. 8810P45)

2
**Tom Roberts** (1856–1931)
*Fog, Thames Embankment*, 1884
Oil on paperboard, 13.1 × 21.7 cm
Art Gallery of New South Wales, Sydney

Purchased with funds provided by the
Gleeson O'Keefe Foundation 2008
(Accession No. 1.2008)

3
**Tom Roberts** (1856–1931)
*By the Treasury*, 1889
Oil on wood panel, 23.6 × 14.2 cm
National Gallery of Victoria, Melbourne

Purchased through the NGV Foundation
by The Hugh D.T Williamson Foundation,
Founder Benefactor, 2002
(Accession No. 2002.304)

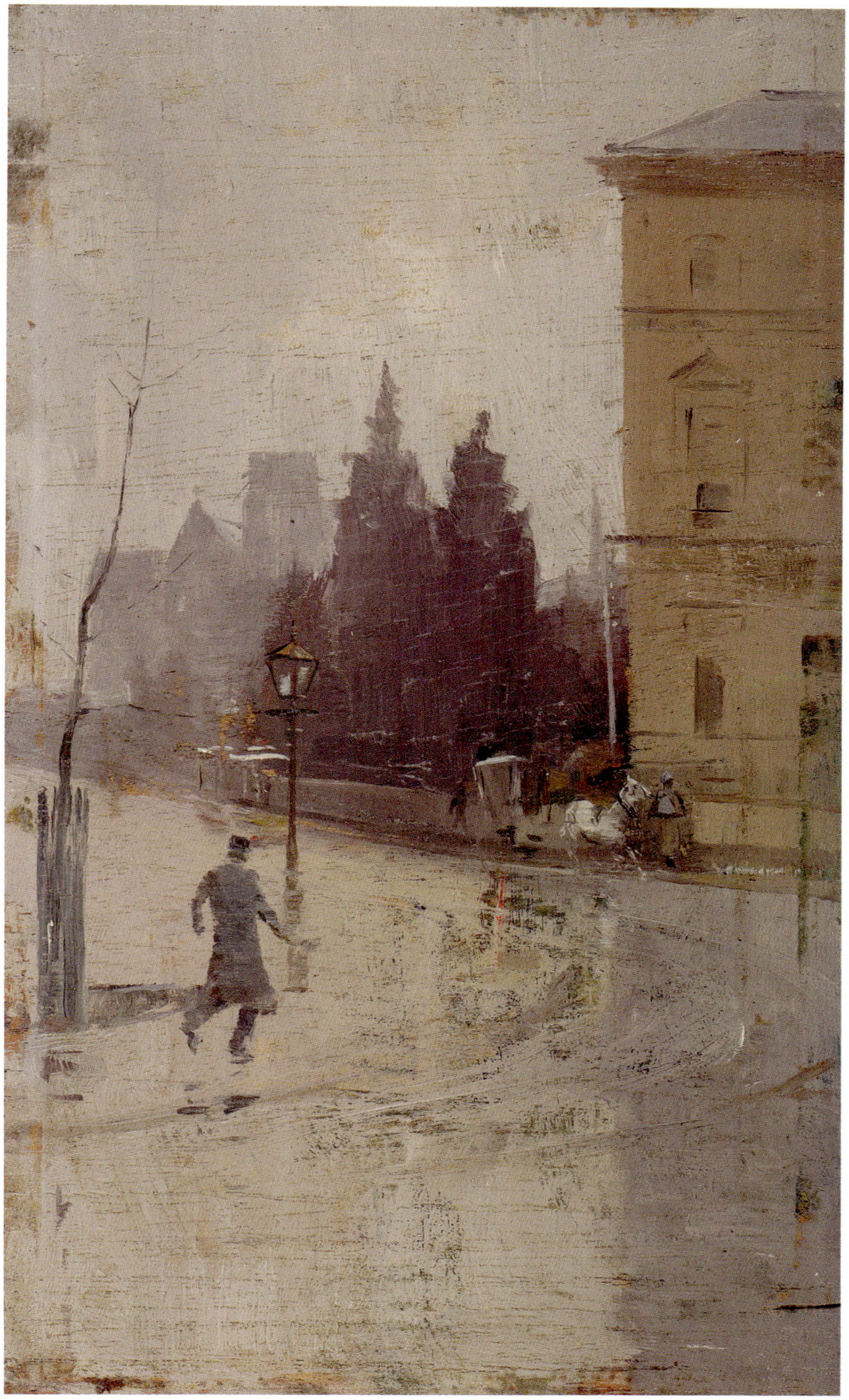

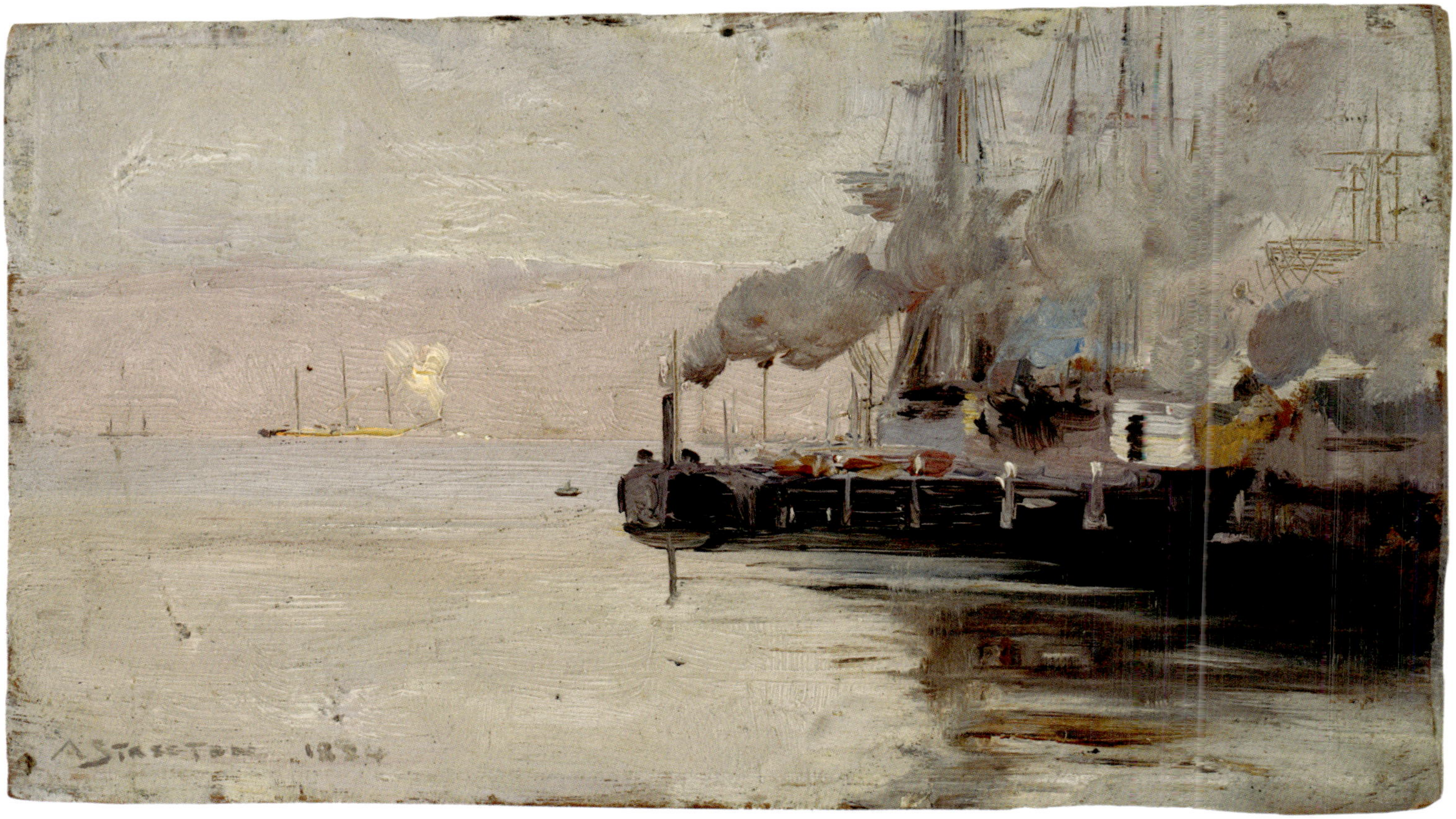

4
**Arthur Streeton** (1867–1943)
*Sandridge*, about 1888
Oil on wood panel, 12.8 × 23.3 cm
National Gallery of Australia, Canberra

Purchased 1969
(Accession No. NGA 69.47)

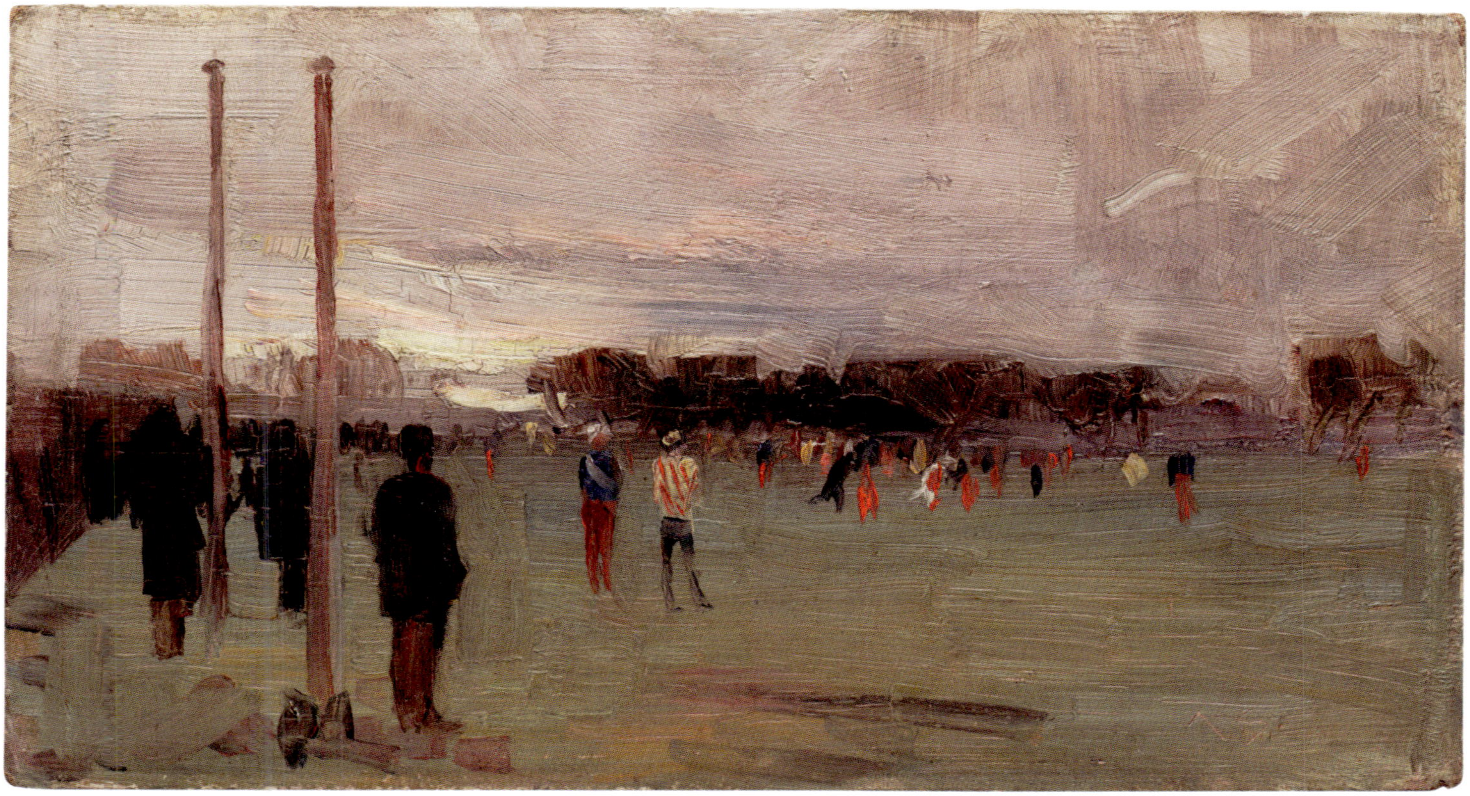

5
**Arthur Streeton** (1867–1943)
*The National Game*, 1889
Oil on cardboard, 11.8 × 22.9 cm
Art Gallery of New South Wales, Sydney

Purchased 1963
(Accession No. OA11.1963)

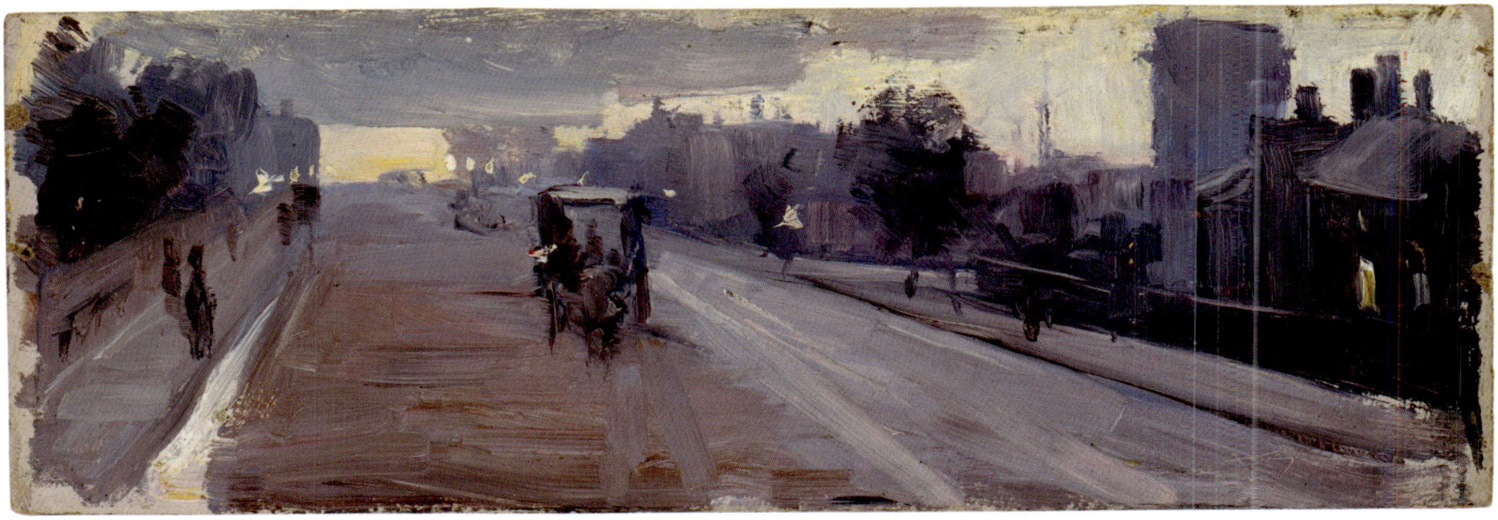

6
**Arthur Streeton** (1867–1943)
*Hoddle St.,10 pm*, 1889
Oil on cardboard, 7.9 × 23.3 cm
National Gallery of Australia, Canberra

Purchased 1974
(Accession No. NGA 74.138)

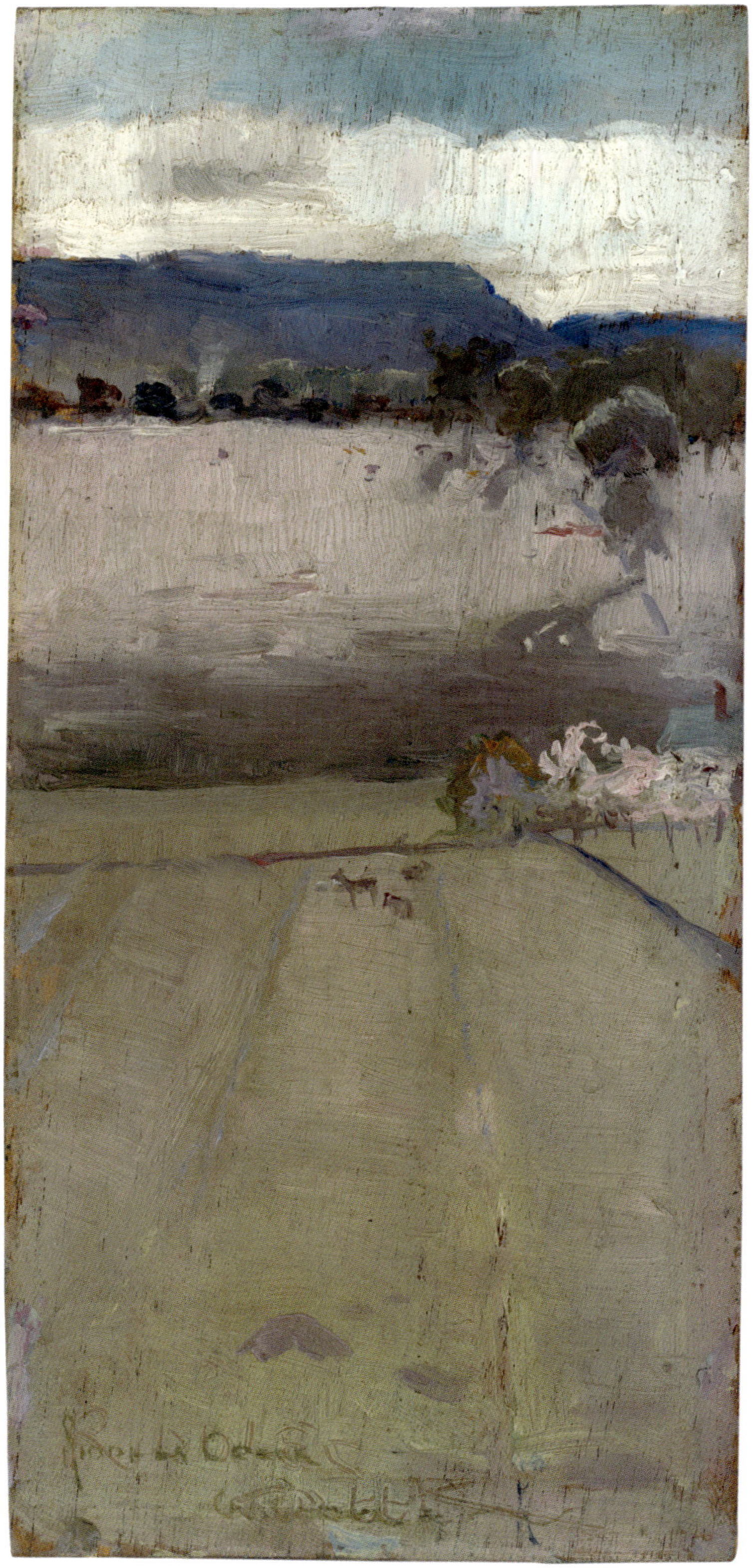

7
**Charles Conder** (1868–1909)
*Riddells Creek*, 1889
Oil on wood panel on paper on two layers of cardboard, 24.4 × 11.2 cm
National Gallery of Australia, Canberra

Purchased 1972
(Accession No. NGA 72.8)

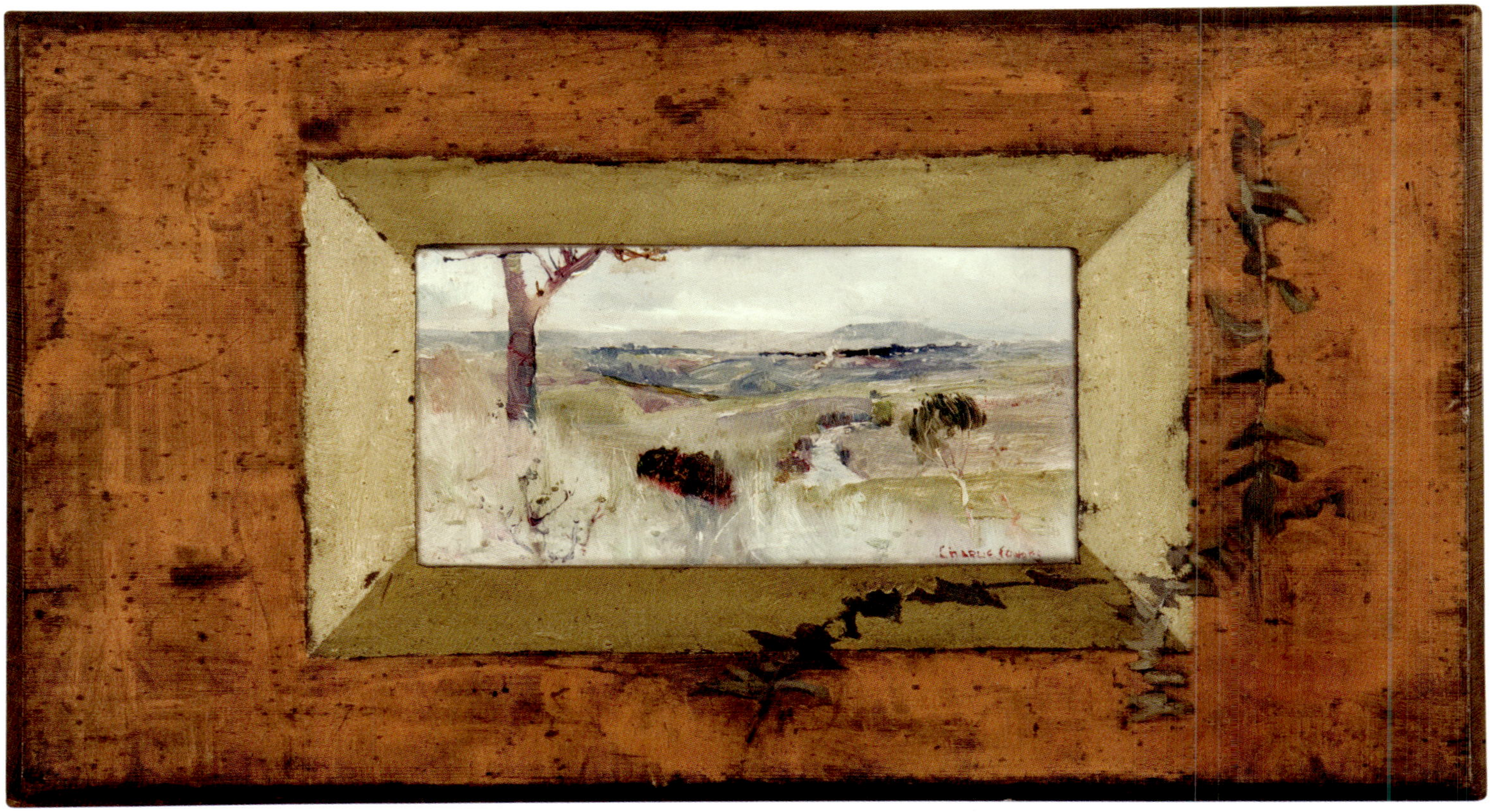

8
**Charles Conder** (1868–1909)
*Dandenongs from Heidelberg*, about 1889
Oil on wood panel, 11.5 × 23.5 cm
Art Gallery of South Australia, Adelaide

M.J.M. Carter AO Collection through the Art Gallery of South Australia Foundation 2012, to mark the 123rd anniversary of the '9 by 5 Impression Exhibition', August 1889. Donated through the Australian Government's Cultural Gifts Program (Accession No. 20124P12)

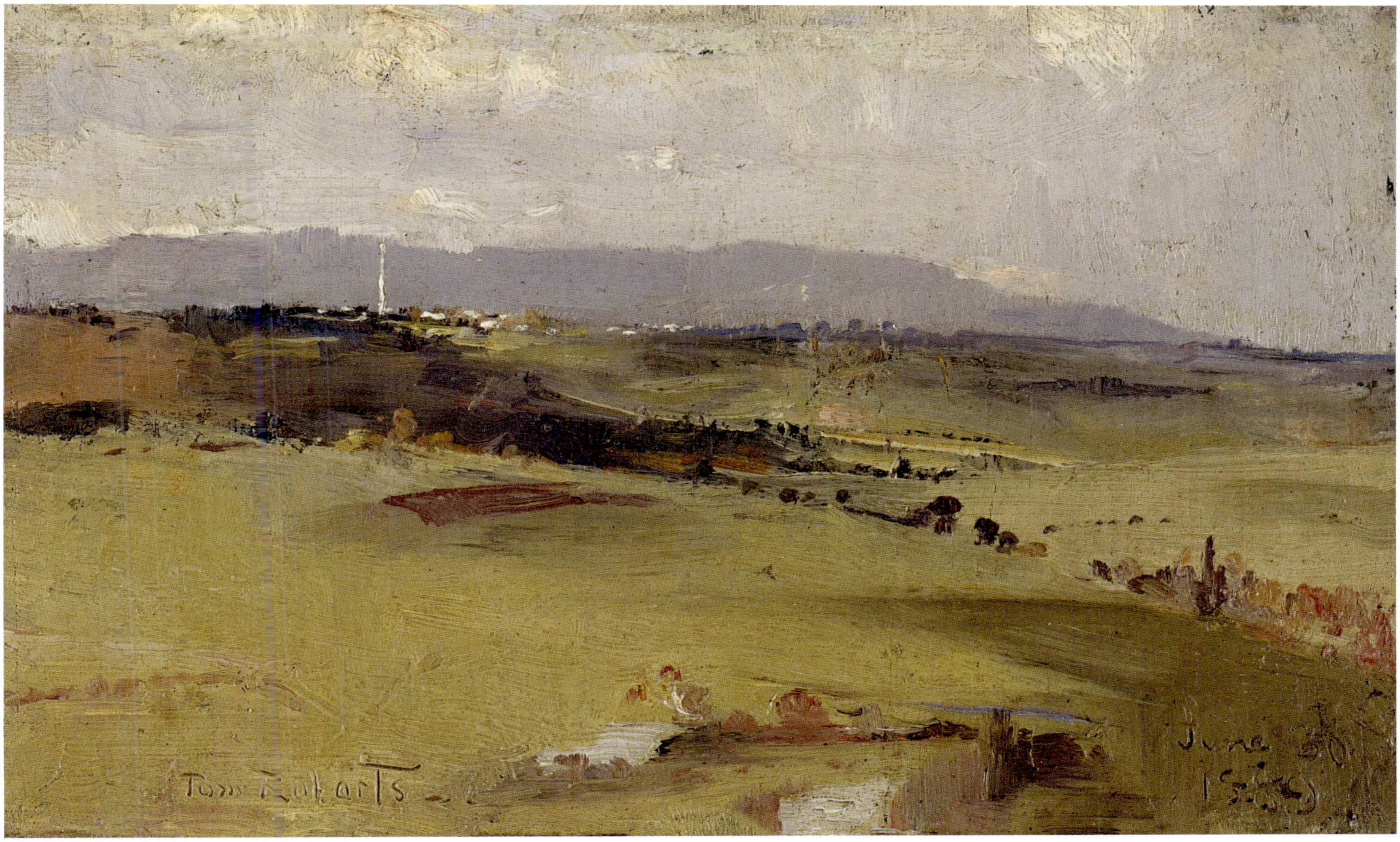


9
**Tom Roberts** (1856–1931)
*Across the Dandenongs*, 1889
Oil on wood panel, 13.7 × 23.2 cm
National Gallery of Victoria, Melbourne

Purchased 1962
(Accession No. 1207-5)

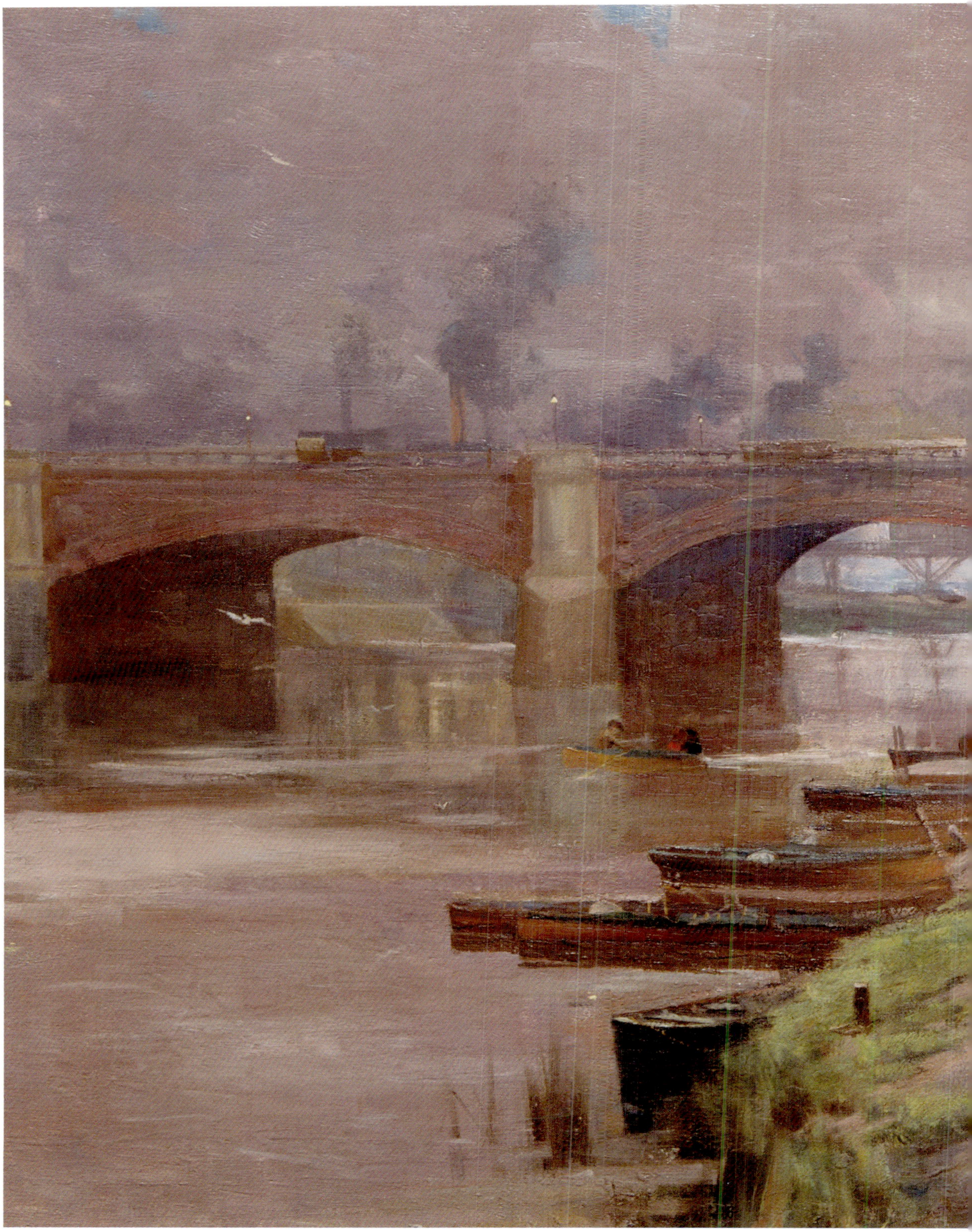

10
**Arthur Streeton** (1867–1943)
*Between the Lights –*
*Princes Bridge*, 1888
Oil on canvas, 82 × 152 cm
Private collection, London

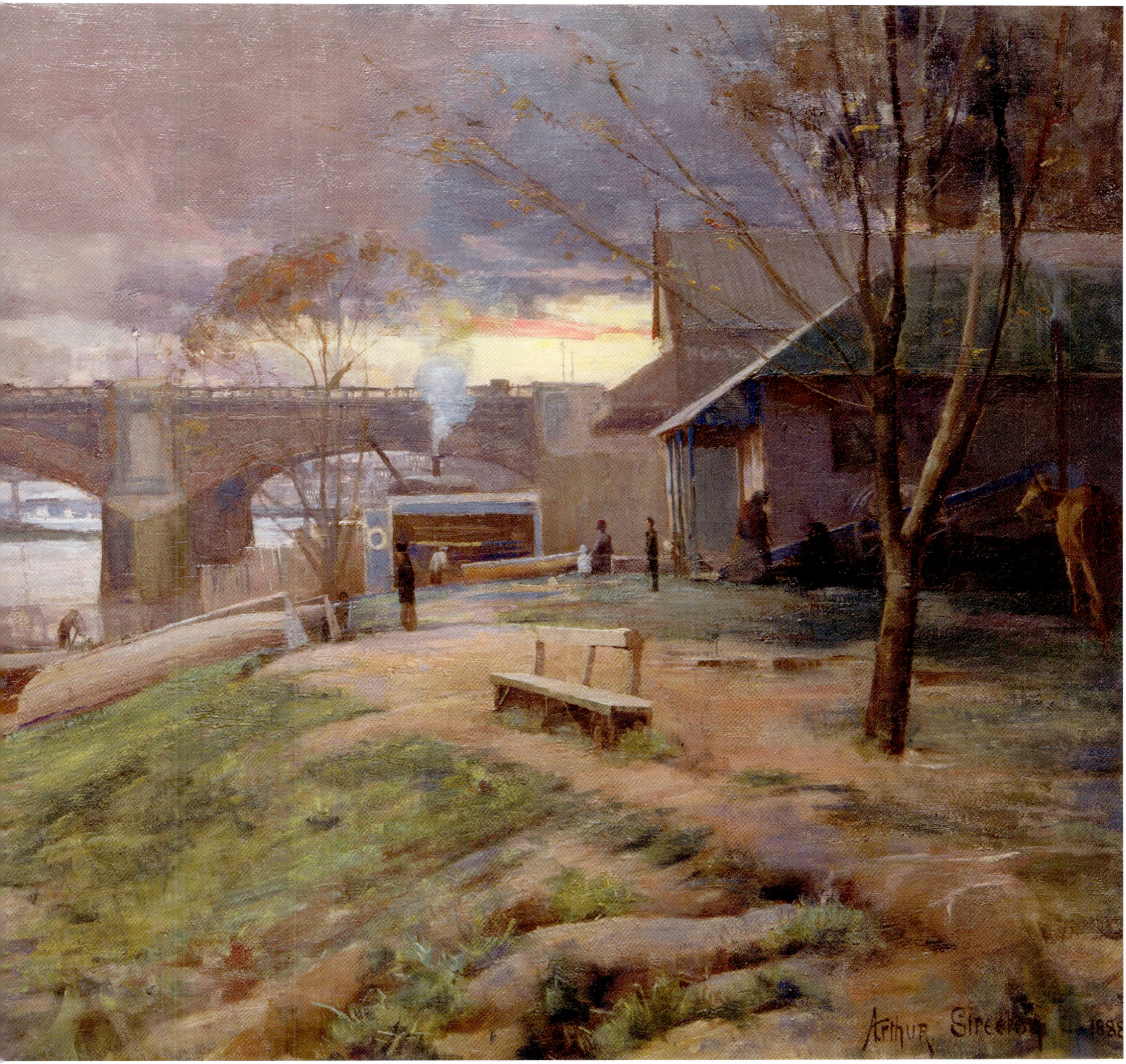
Arthur Streeton 1888

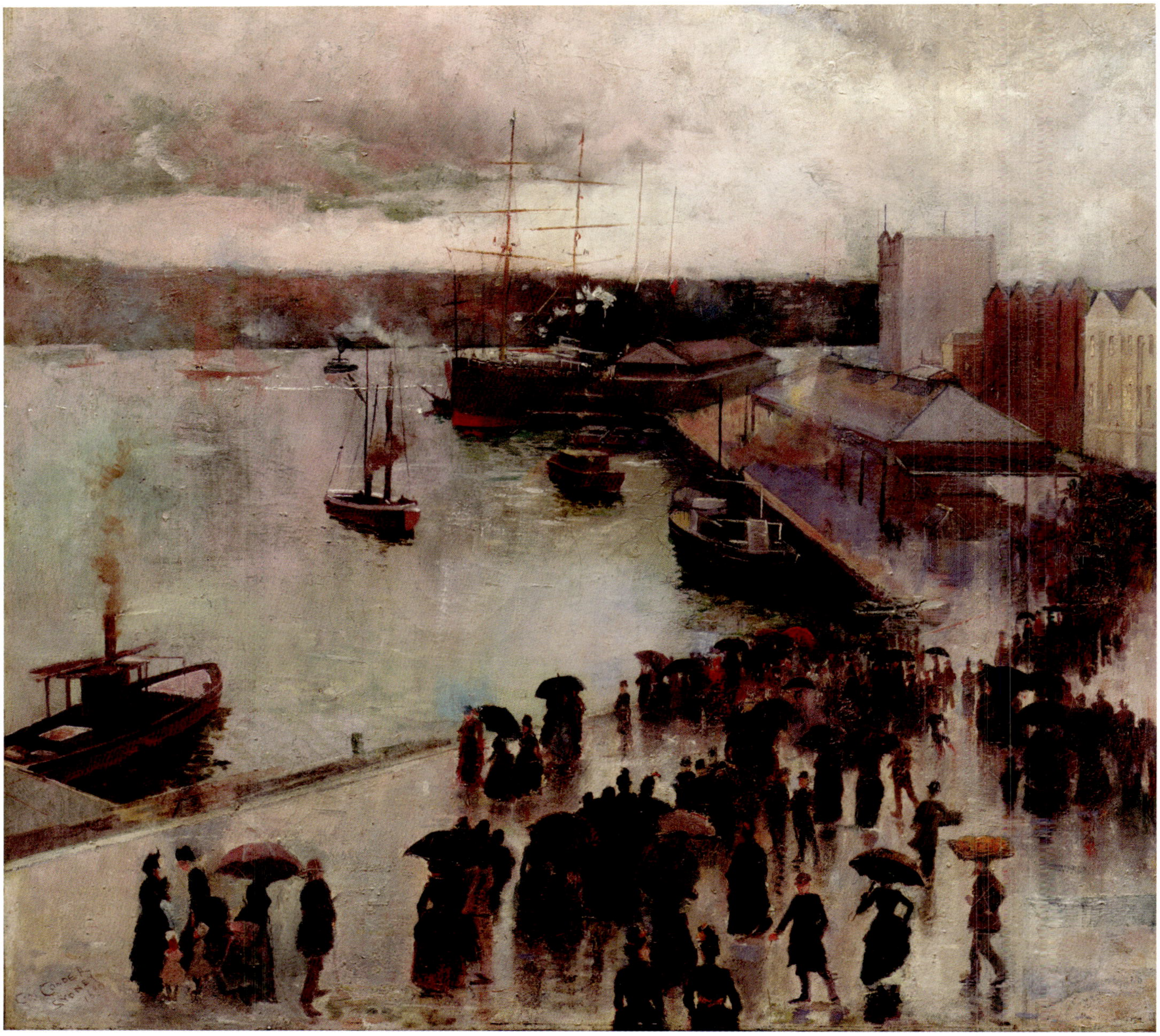

11
**Charles Conder** (1868–1909)
*Departure of the Orient – Circular Quay*, 1888
Oil on canvas, 45.1 × 50.1 cm
Art Gallery of New South Wales, Sydney

Purchased 1888
(Accession No. 829)

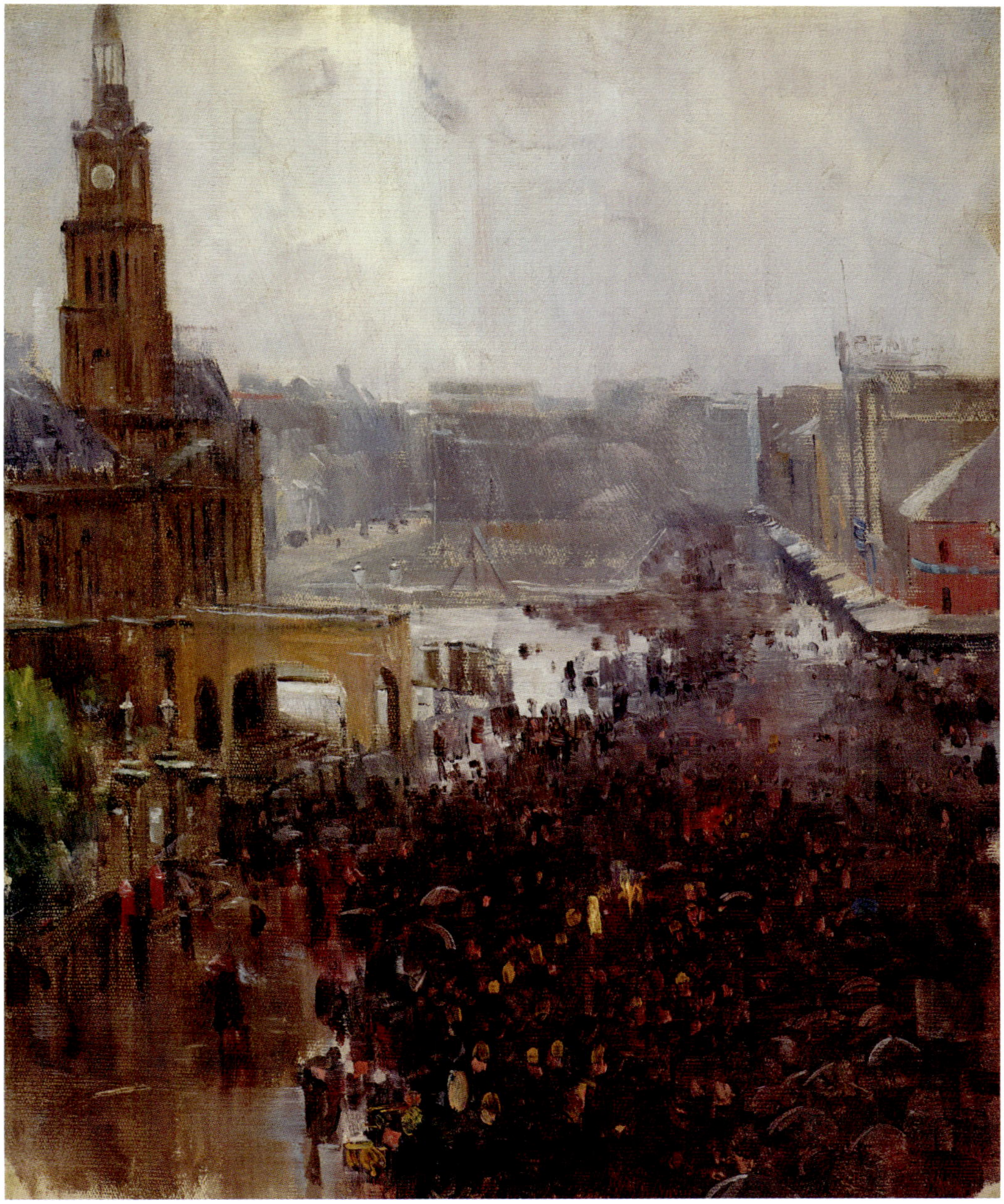

12
**Arthur Streeton** (1867–1943)
*Fireman's Funeral, George Street*, 1894
Oil on canvas, 45.3 × 38.2 cm
Art Gallery of New South Wales, Sydney

Purchased 1980
(Accession No. 43.1980)

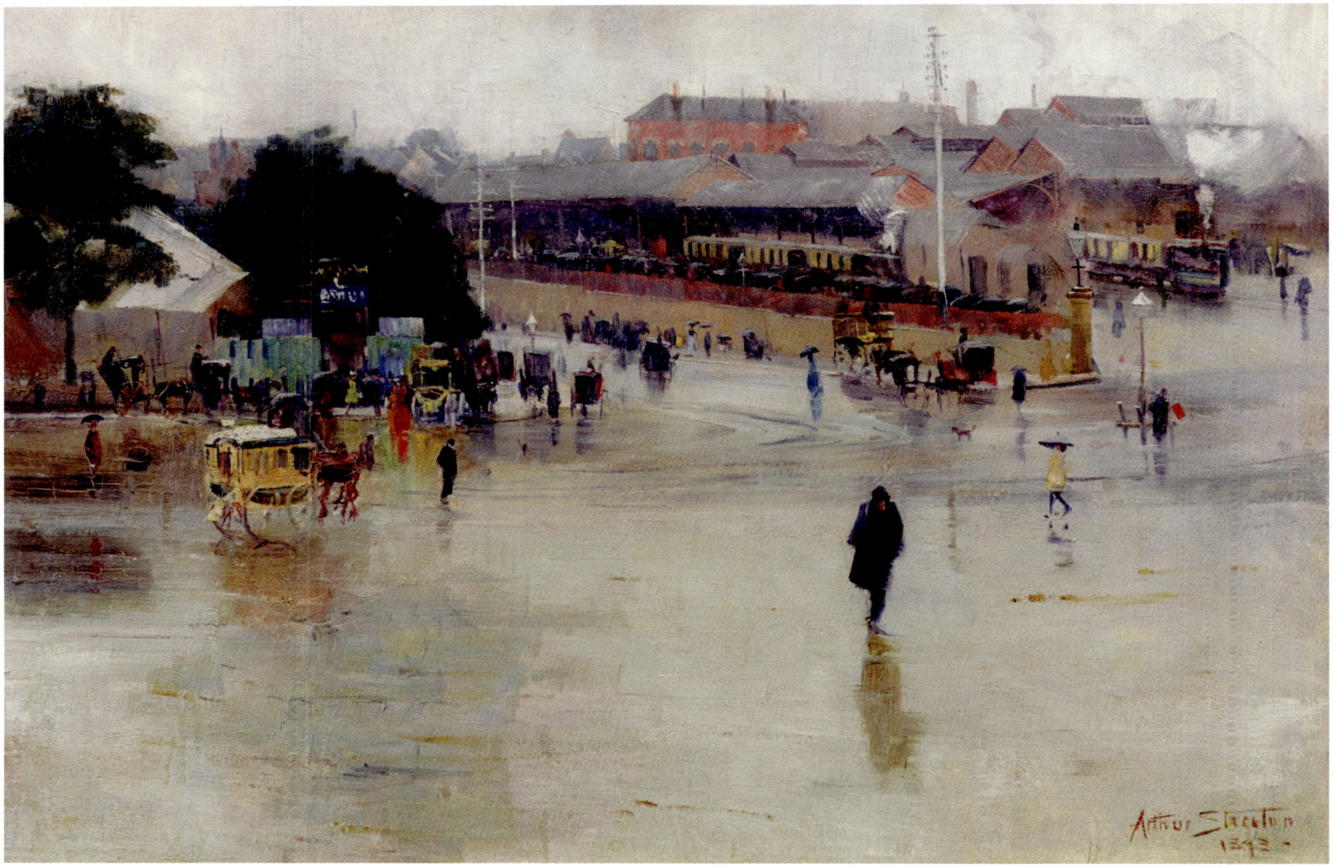


13
**Arthur Streeton** (1867–1943)
*The Railway Station, Redfern*, 1893
Oil on canvas, 40.8 × 61 cm
Art Gallery of New South Wales, Sydney

Gift of Lady Denison 1942
(Accession No. 7209)

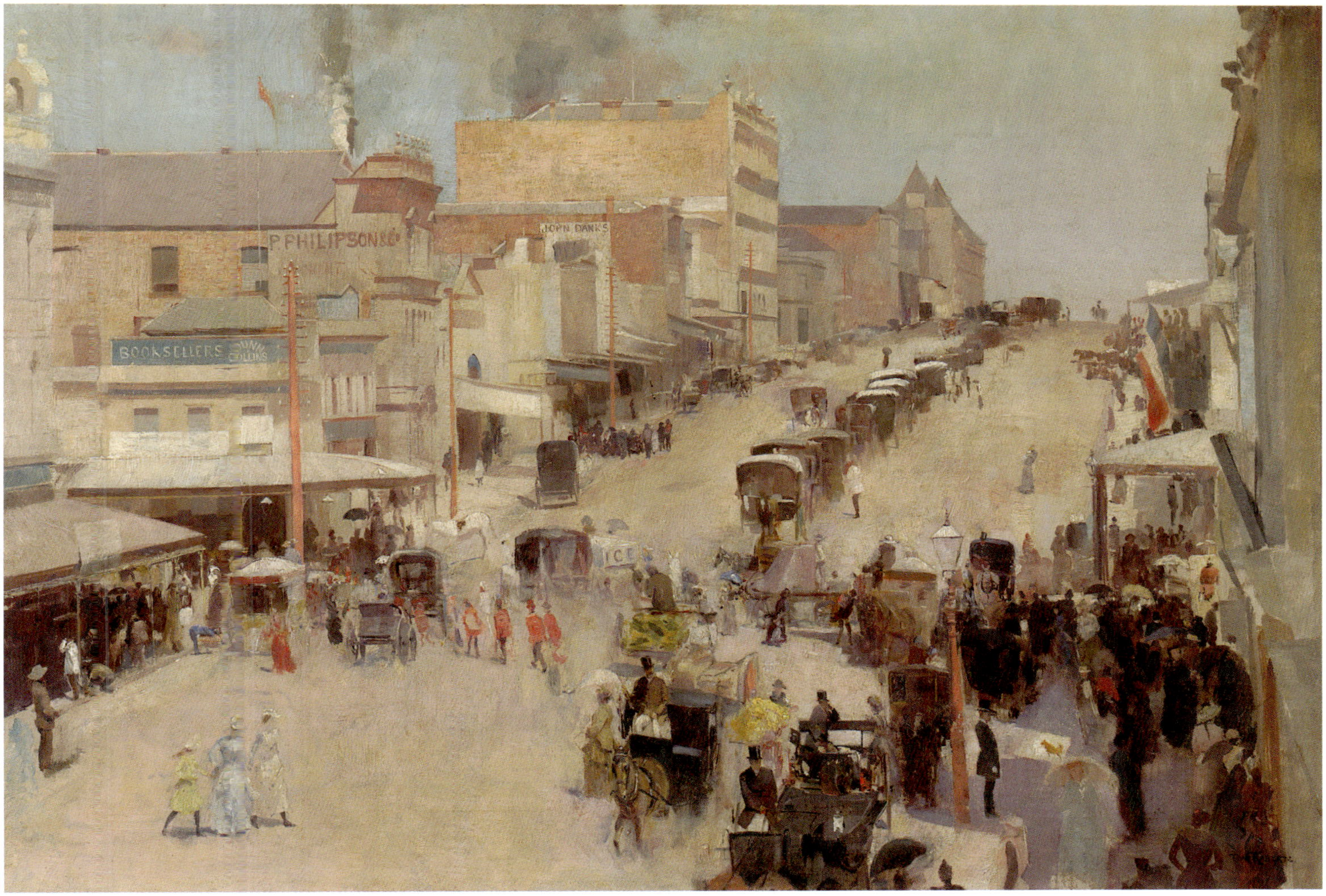

14
**Tom Roberts** (1856–1931)
*Allegro con Brio, Bourke Street West,*
about 1885–6, reworked 1890
Oil on canvas mounted on composition
board, 51.2 × 76.7 cm
National Gallery of Australia, Canberra and
the National Library of Australia, Canberra

Purchased 1920 by the Parliamentary
Library Committee

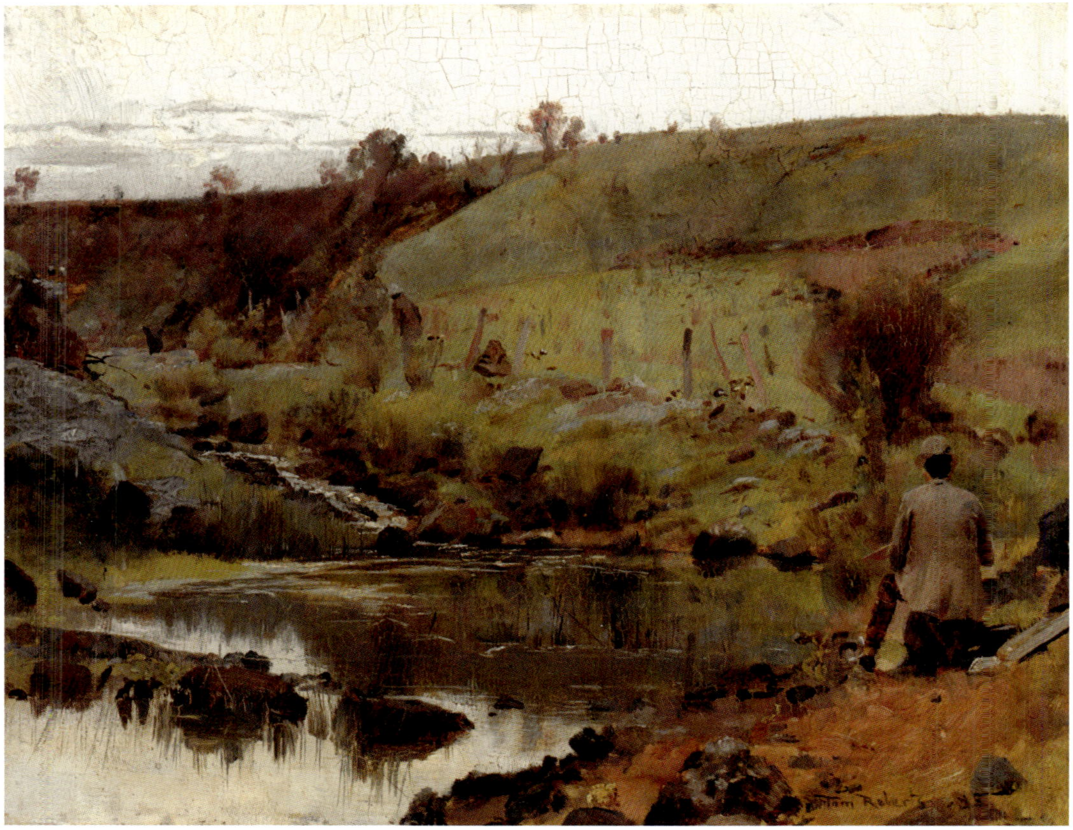

15
**Tom Roberts** (1856–1931)
*A Quiet Day on Darebin Creek*, 1885
Oil on wood panel, 26.4 × 34.8 cm
National Gallery of Australia, Canberra

Purchased 1969
(Accession No. NGA 69.4)

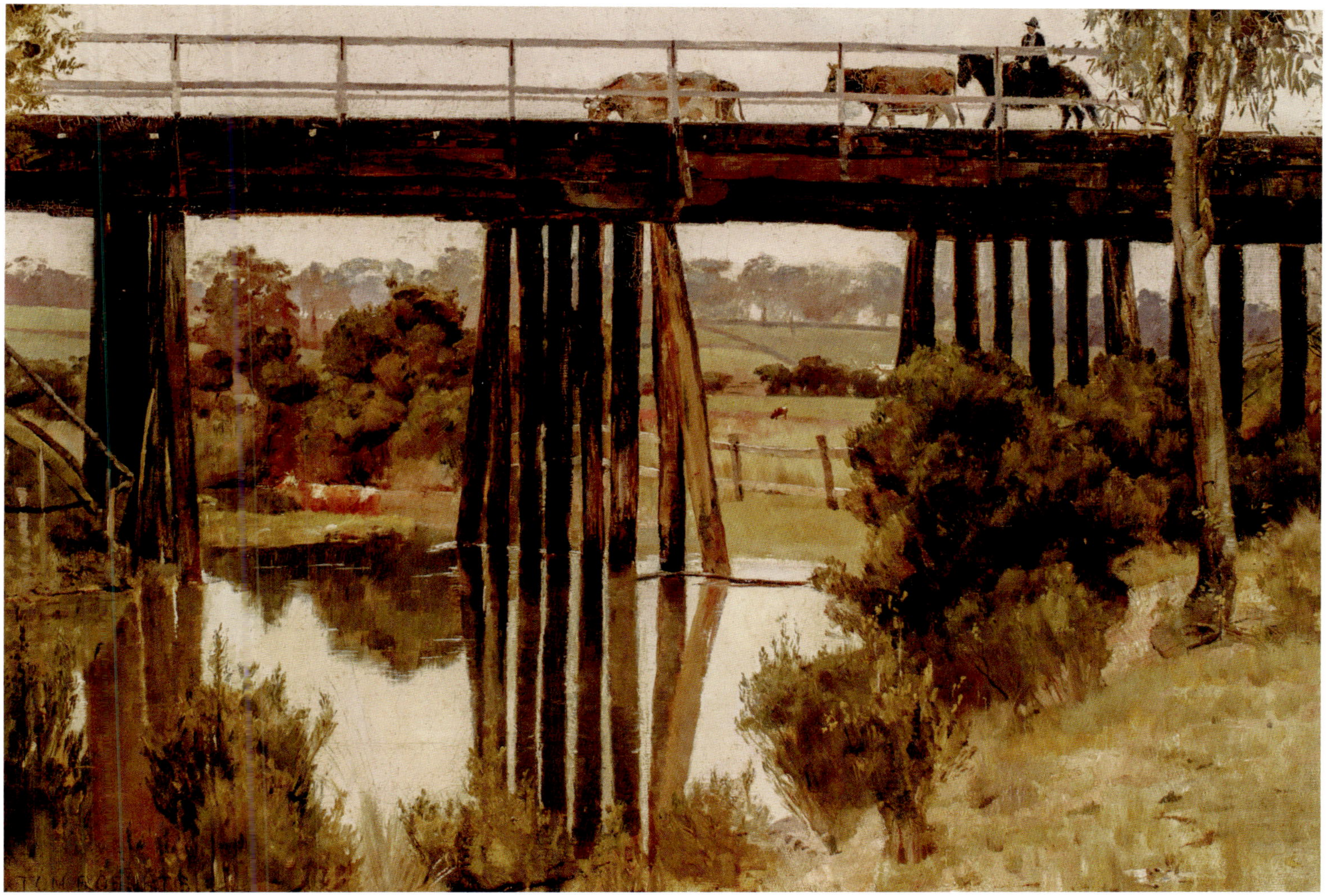

16
**Tom Roberts** (1856–1931)
*Winter Morning after Rain, Gardiner's Creek*, 1885
Oil on canvas, 47 × 66 cm
Art Gallery of South Australia, Adelaide

M.J.M. Carter AO Collection through the Art Gallery of South Australia Foundation to mark the 130th anniversary of the Gallery, 2011 (Accession No. 20111P14)

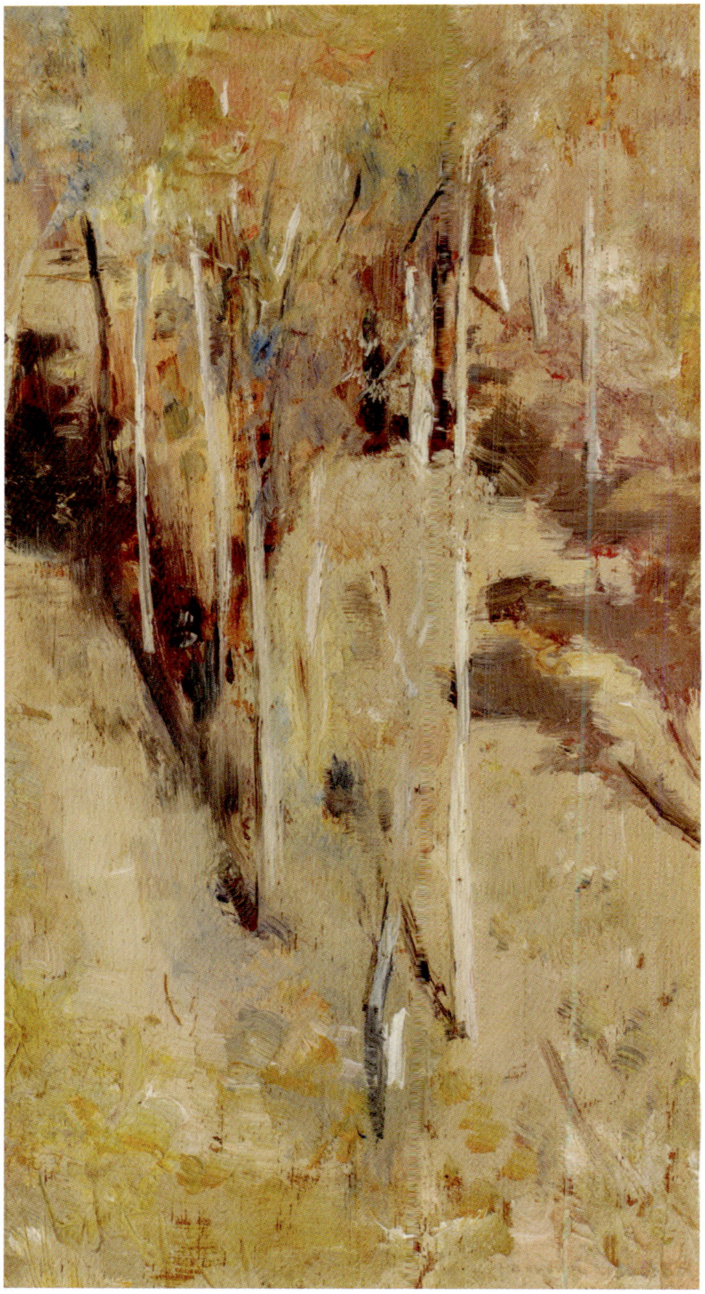

17
**Tom Roberts** (1856–1931)
*Saplings*, about 1889
Oil on cedar panel, 34.5 × 14.5 cm
Art Gallery of South Australia, Adelaide

Morgan Thomas Bequest Fund 1927
(Accession No. 0.707)

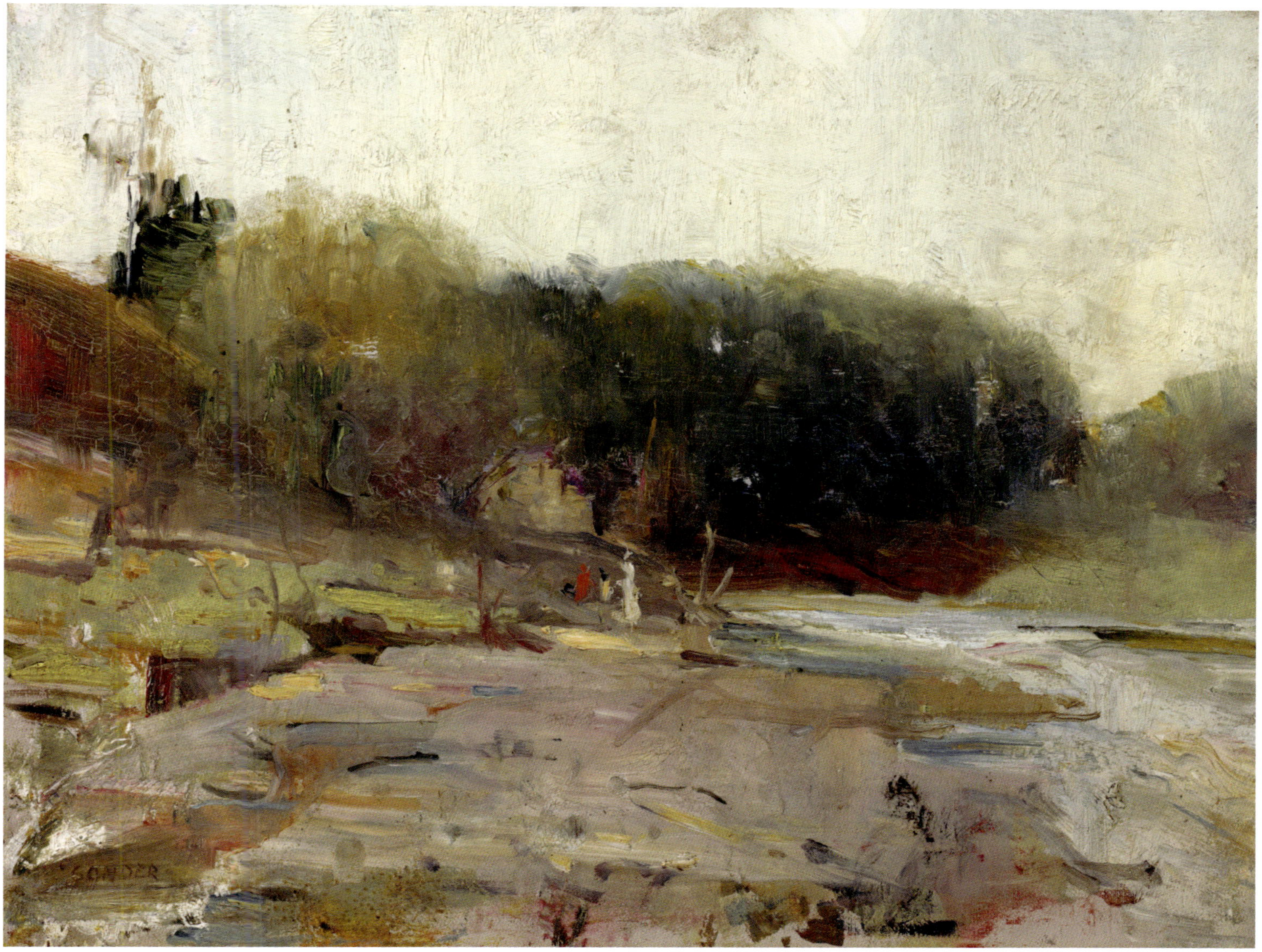

18
**Charles Conder** (1868–1909)
*On the River Yarra, near Heidelberg, Victoria*, about 1890
Oil on canvas 30.4 × 40.7 cm
Art Gallery of New South Wales, Sydney

Jean Cameron Gordon Bequest Fund in memory of her mother Mary Gordon 2002
(Accession No. 298.2002)

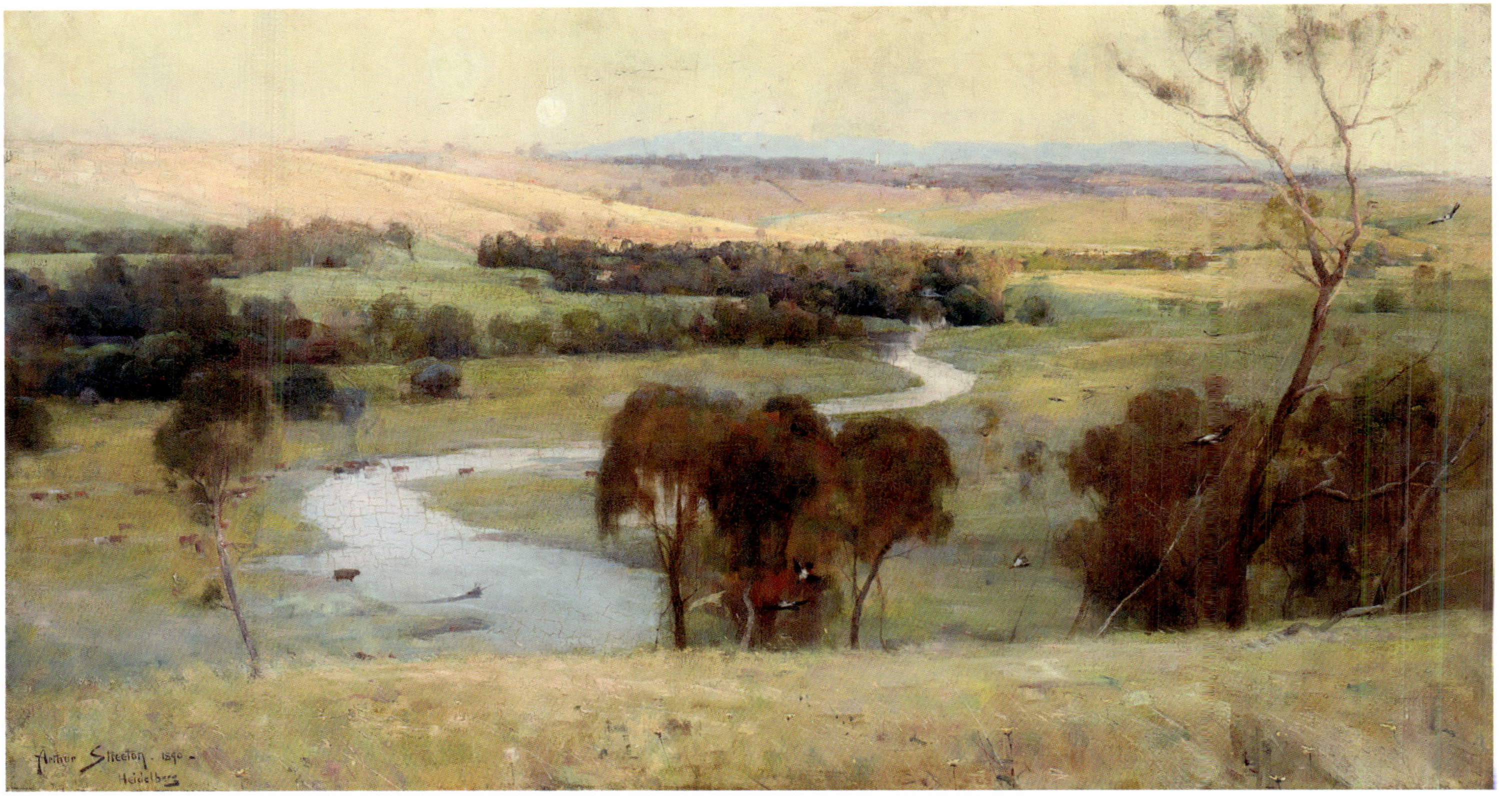


19
**Arthur Streeton** (1867–1943)
*'Still glides the stream, and shall for ever glide'*, 1890
Oil on canvas, 82.6 × 153 cm
Art Gallery of New South Wales, Sydney

Purchased 1890
(Accession No. 859)

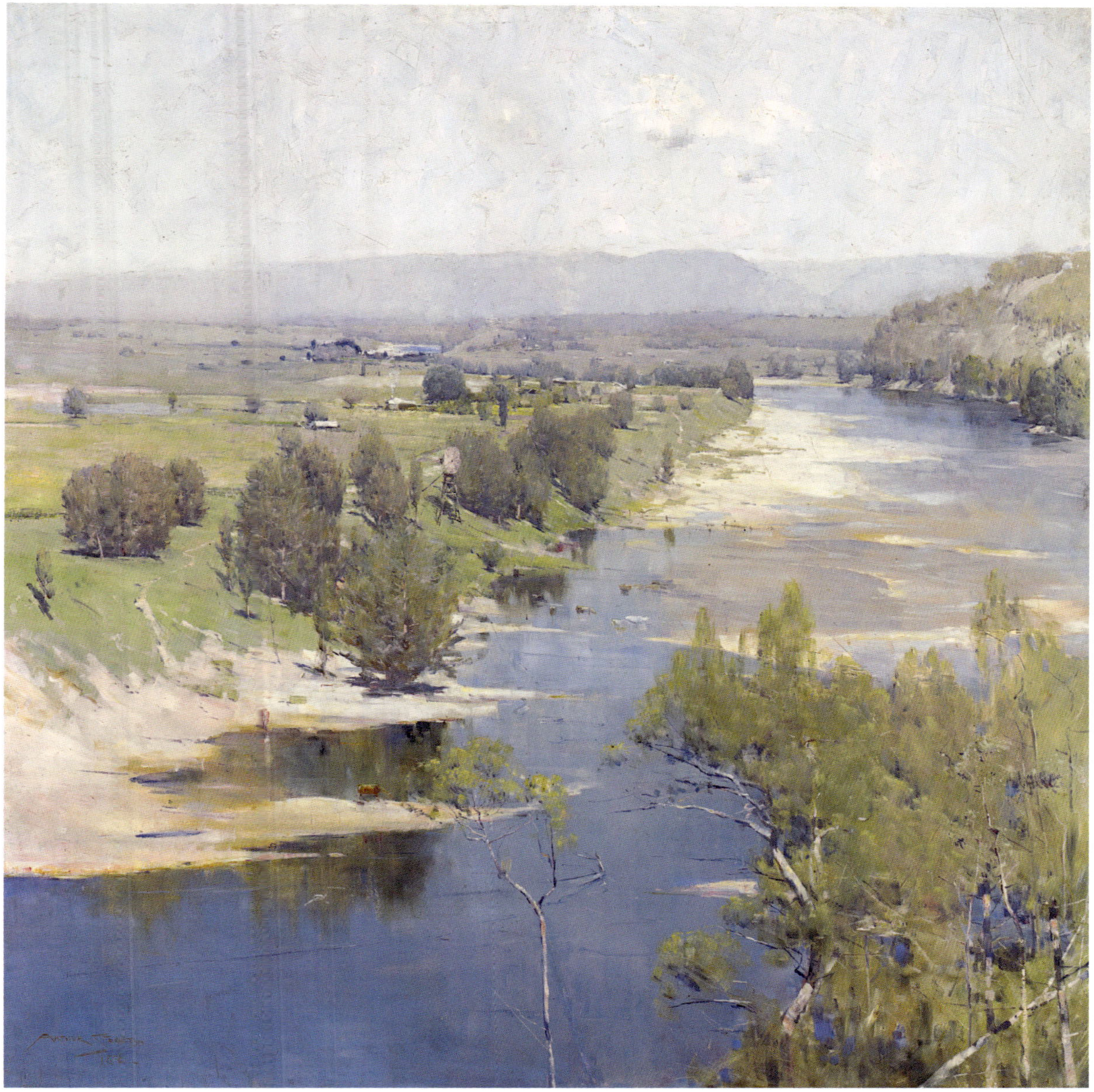

20
**Arthur Streeton** (1867–1943)
*'The purple noon's transparent might'*, 1896
Oil on canvas, 123 × 123 cm
National Gallery of Victoria, Melbourne

Purchased, 1896
(Accession No. 33-2)

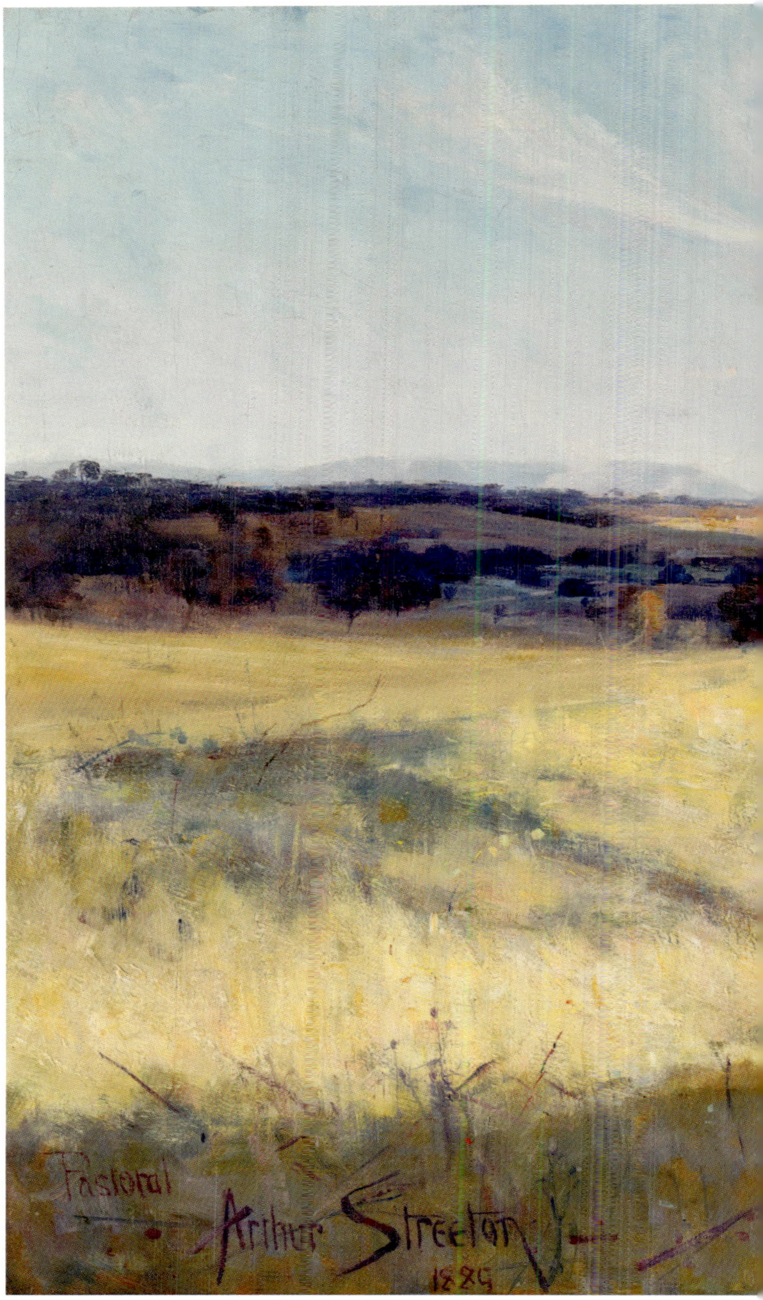


21
**Arthur Streeton** (1867–1943)
*Golden Summer, Eaglemont*, 1889
Oil on canvas, 81.3 × 152.6 cm
National Gallery of Australia, Canberra

Purchased 1995
(Accession No. NGA 95.604)

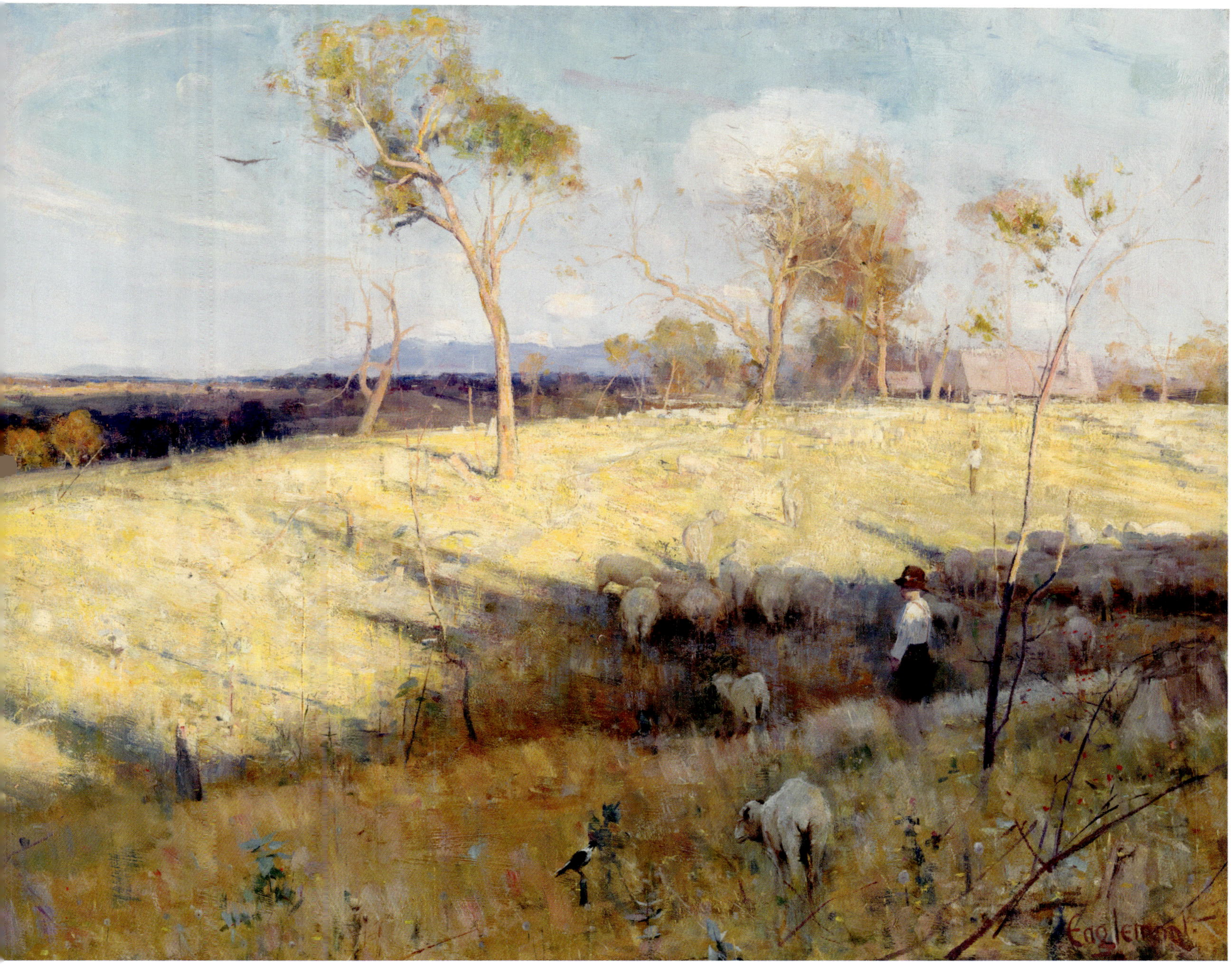

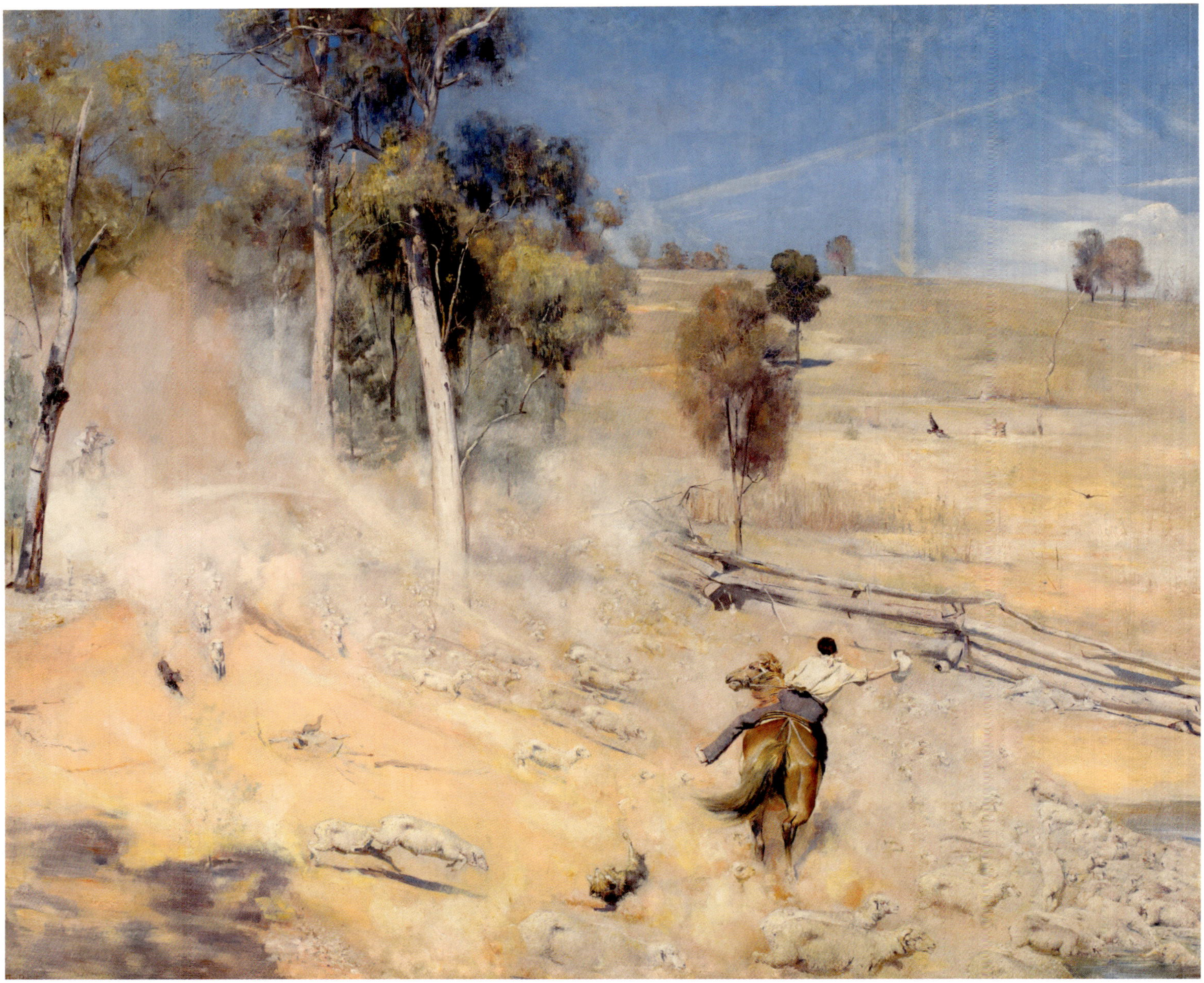

22
**Tom Roberts** (1856–1931)
*A Break Away!*, 1891
Oil on canvas, 137.3 × 167.8 cm
Art Gallery of South Australia, Adelaide

Elder Bequest Fund 1899
(Accession No. 0.139)

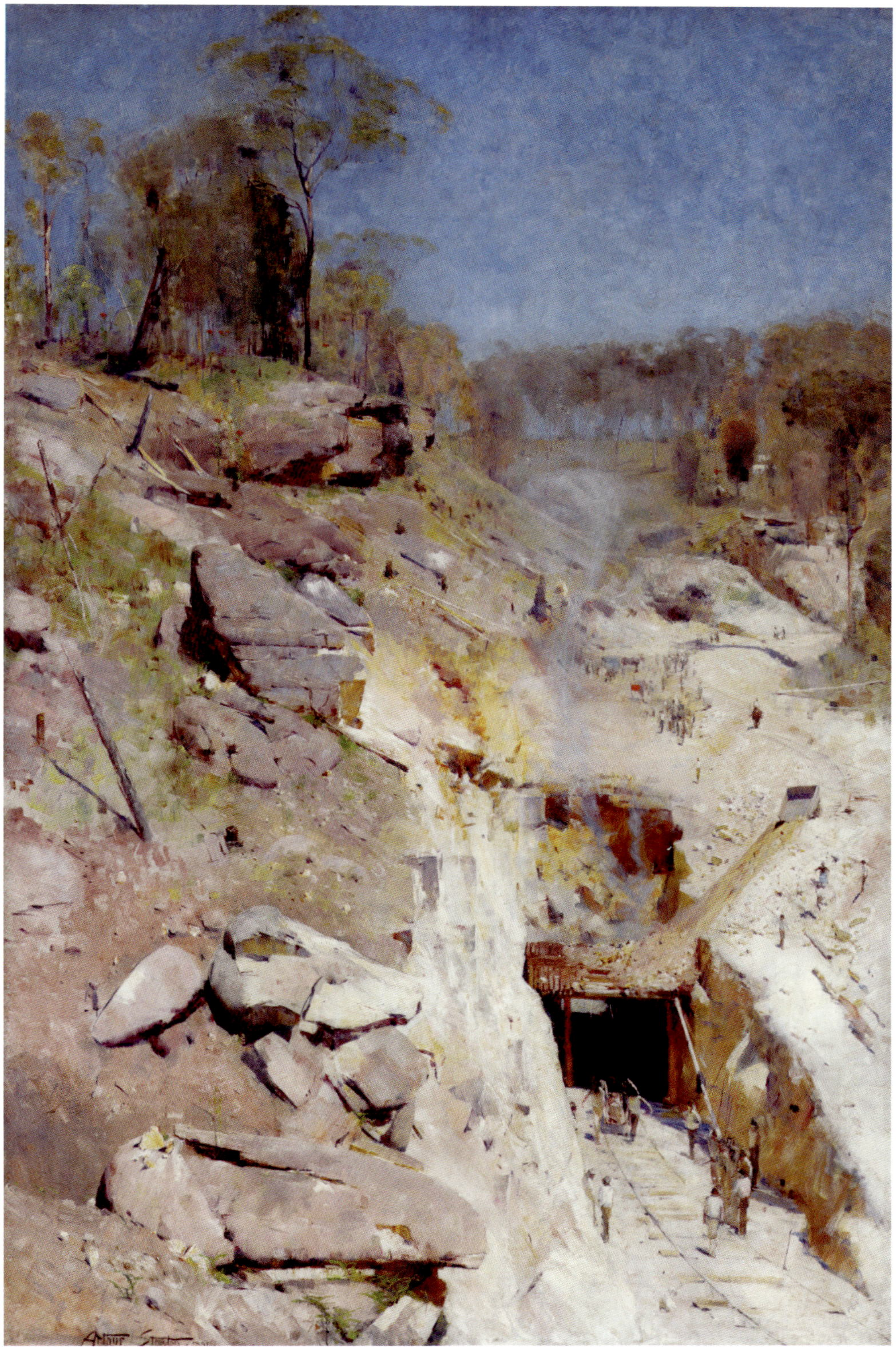

23
**Arthur Streeton** (1867–1943)
*Fire's On*, 1891
Oil on canvas, 183.8 × 122.5 cm
Art Gallery of New South Wales, Sydney

Purchased 1893
(Accession No. 832)

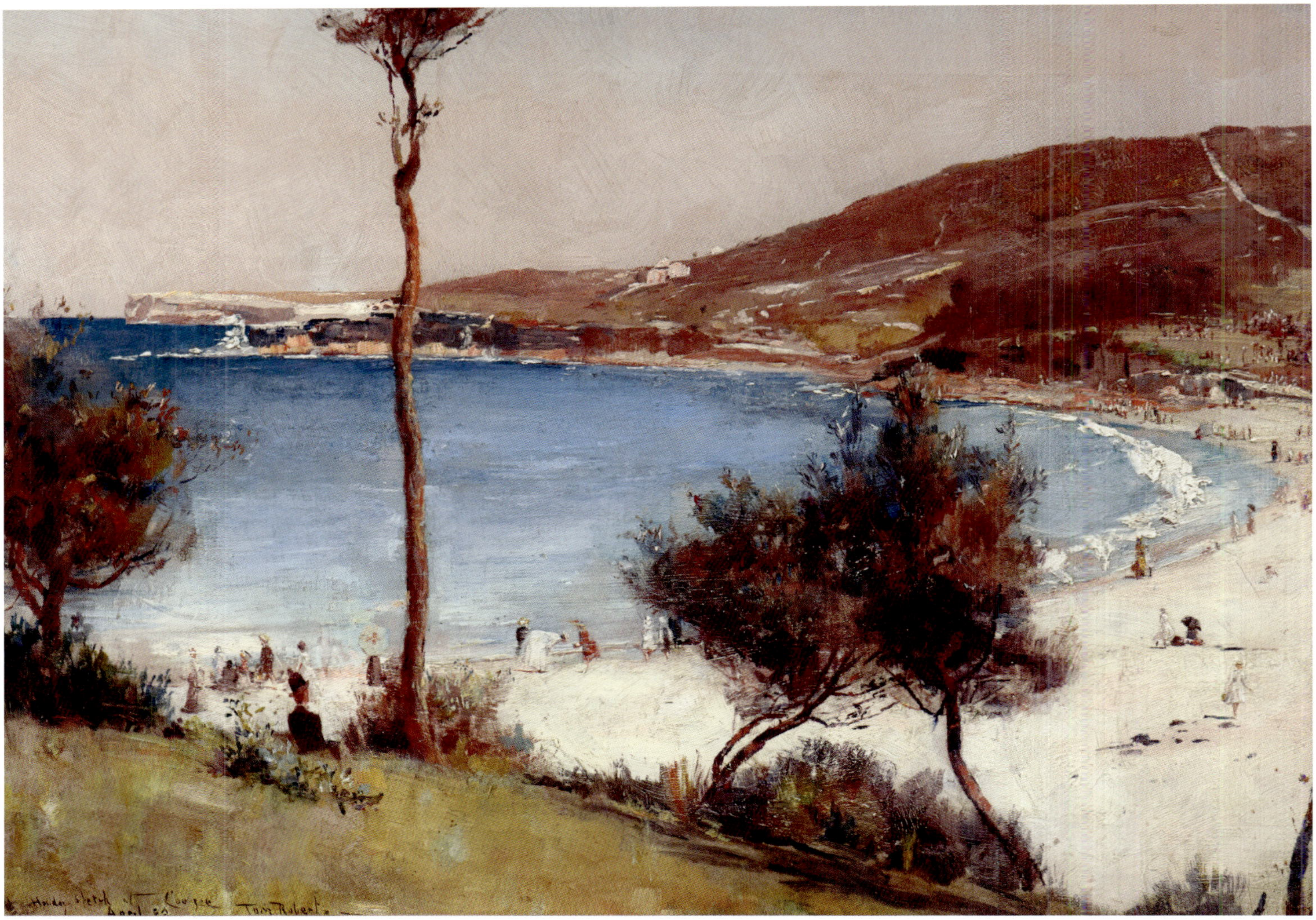

24
**Tom Roberts** (1856–1931)
*Holiday Sketch at Coogee*, 1888
Oil on canvas, 40.3 × 55.9 cm
Art Gallery of New South Wales, Sydney

Purchased 1954
(Accession No. 9078)

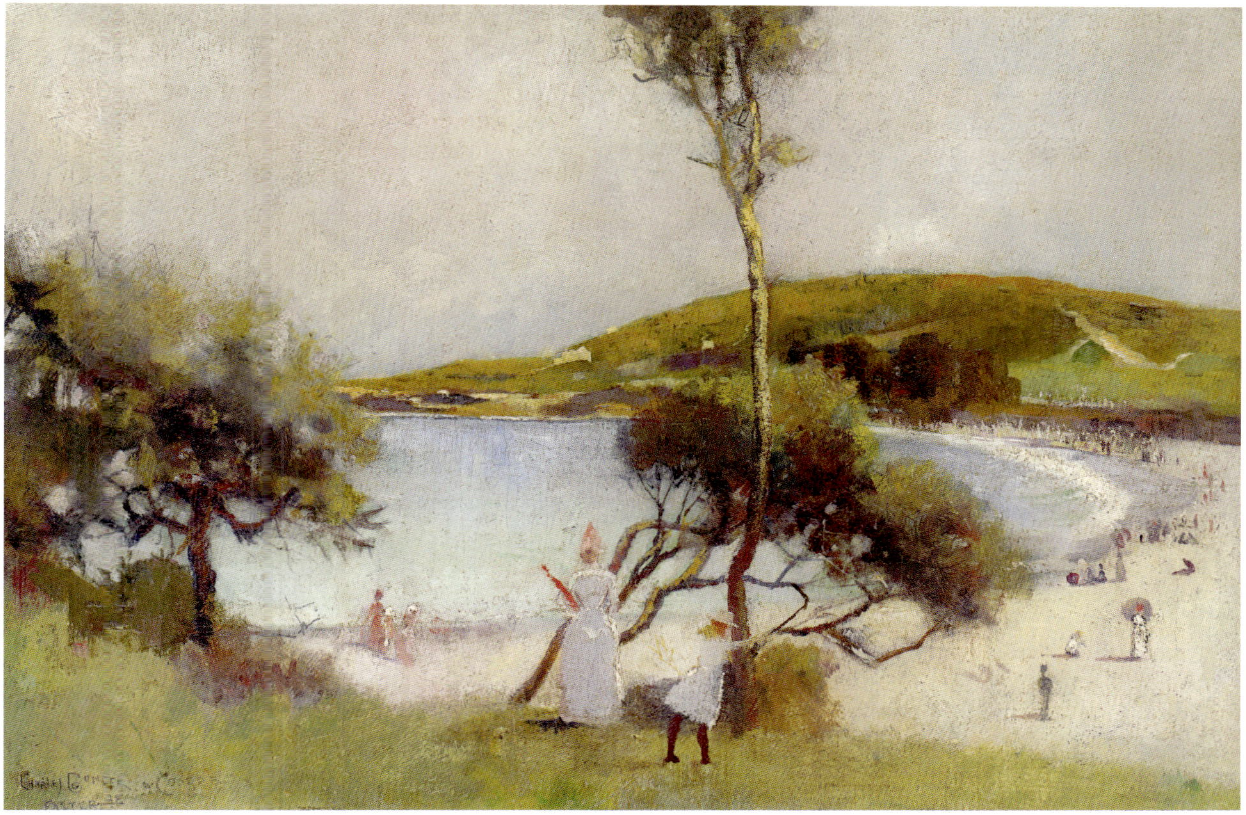

25
**Charles Conder** (1868–1909)
*Coogee Bay*, 1888
Oil on cardboard, 26.8 × 40.7 cm
National Gallery of Victoria, Melbourne

Purchased with the assistance of a special grant from the Government of Victoria, 1979 (Accession No. A41-1980)

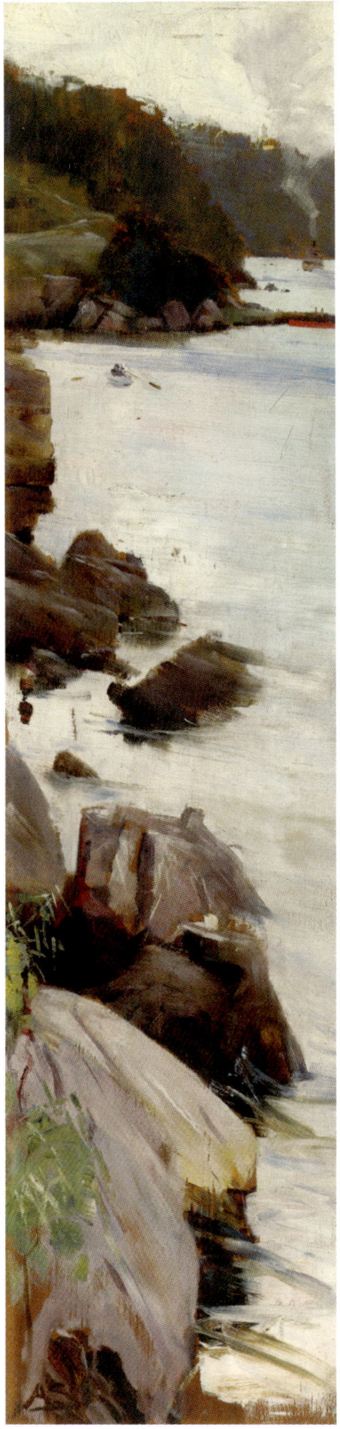

26
**Arthur Streeton** (1867–1943)
*Sirius Cove*, about 1895
Oil on wood panel, 68.8 × 16.8 cm
National Gallery of Australia, Canberra

Purchased 1973
(Accession No. NGA 73.1)

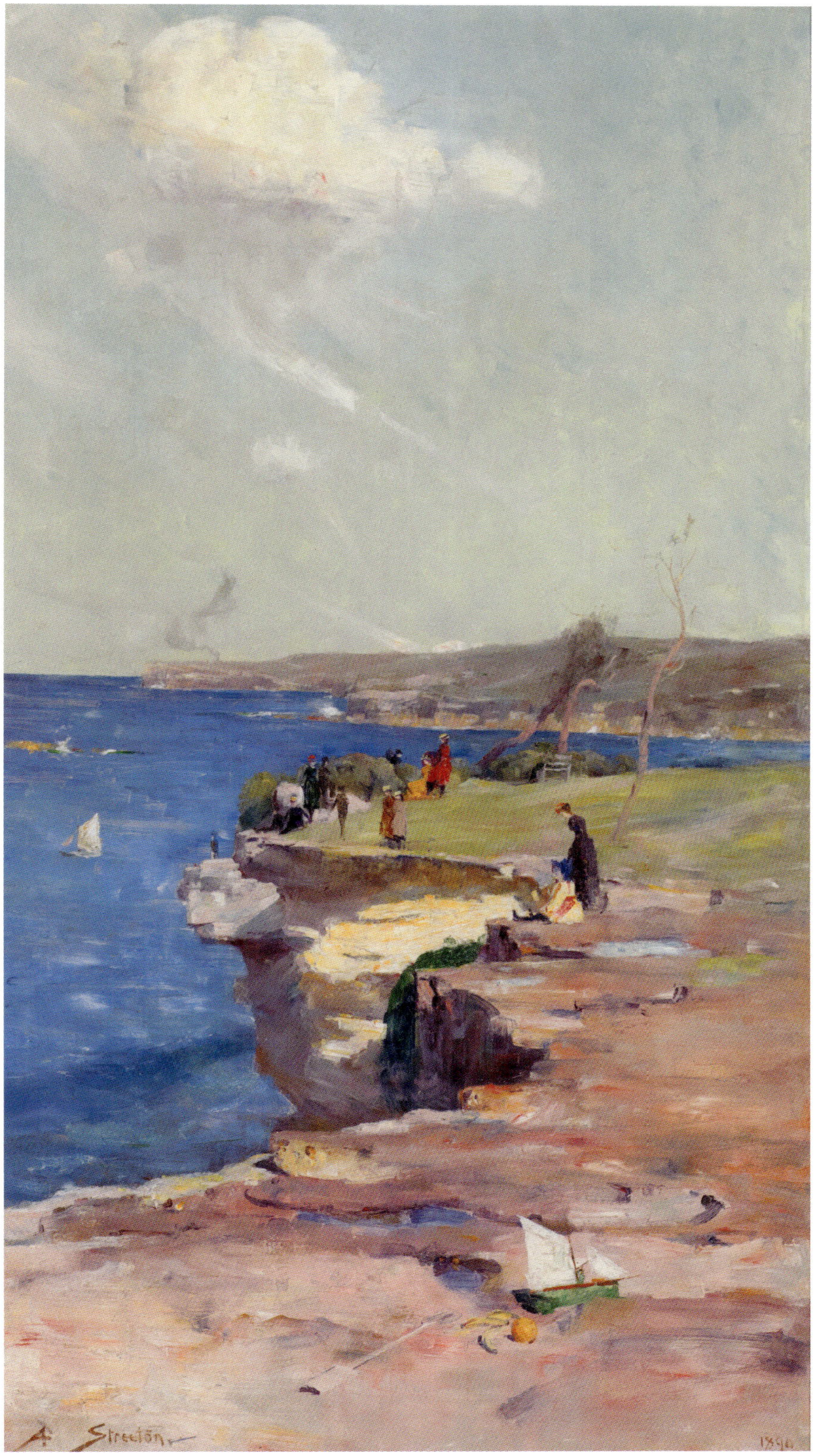

27
**Arthur Streeton** (1867–1943)
*Blue Pacific*, 1890
Oil on canvas, 91.4 × 50.8 cm
On loan to the National Gallery
from a private collection (L1177)

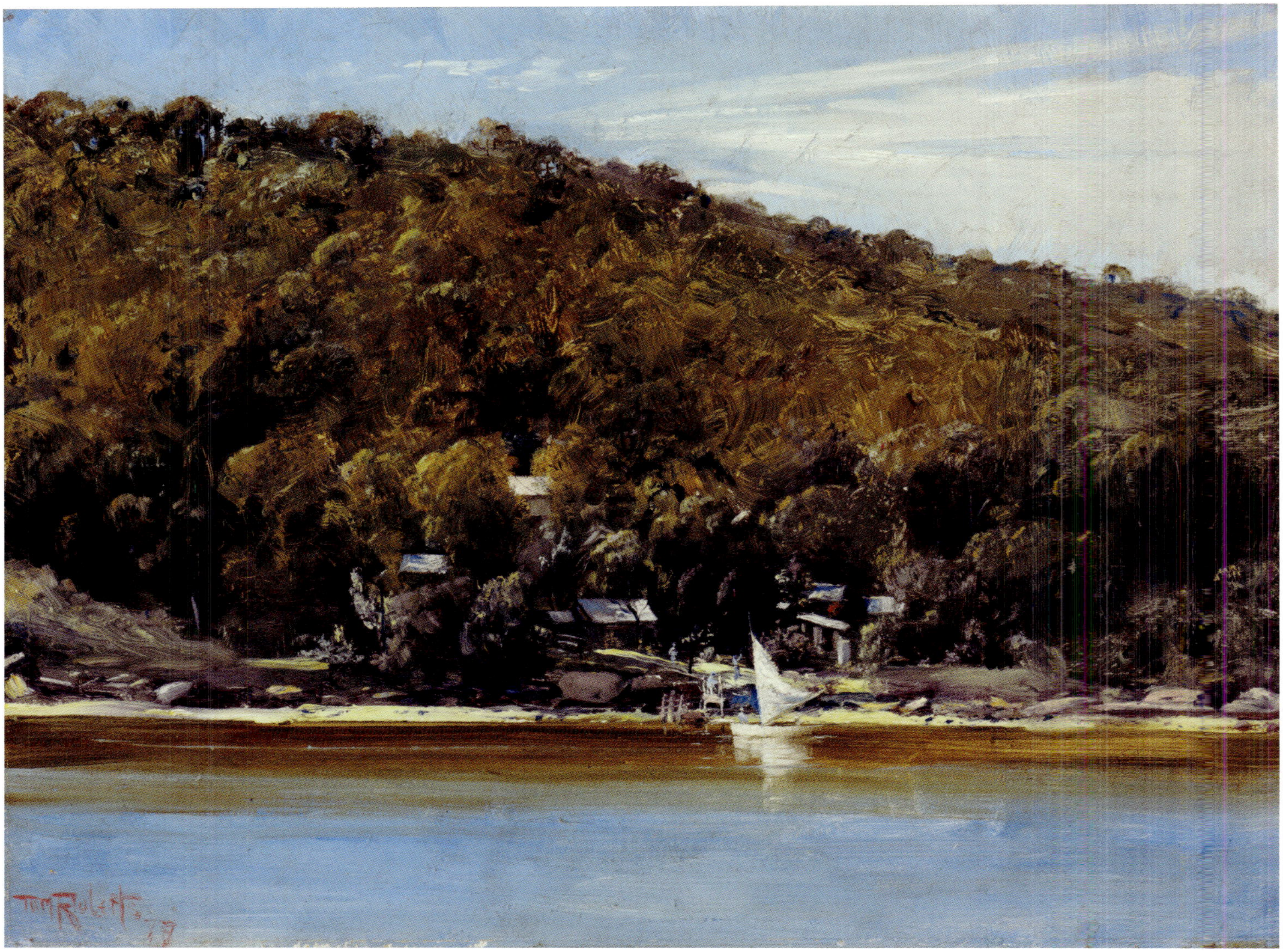

28
**Tom Roberts** (1856–1931)
*The Camp, Sirius Cove*, 1899
Oil on canvas on paperboard, 25.4 × 34.6 cm
Art Gallery of New South Wales, Sydney

Purchased 1940
(Accession No. 6928)

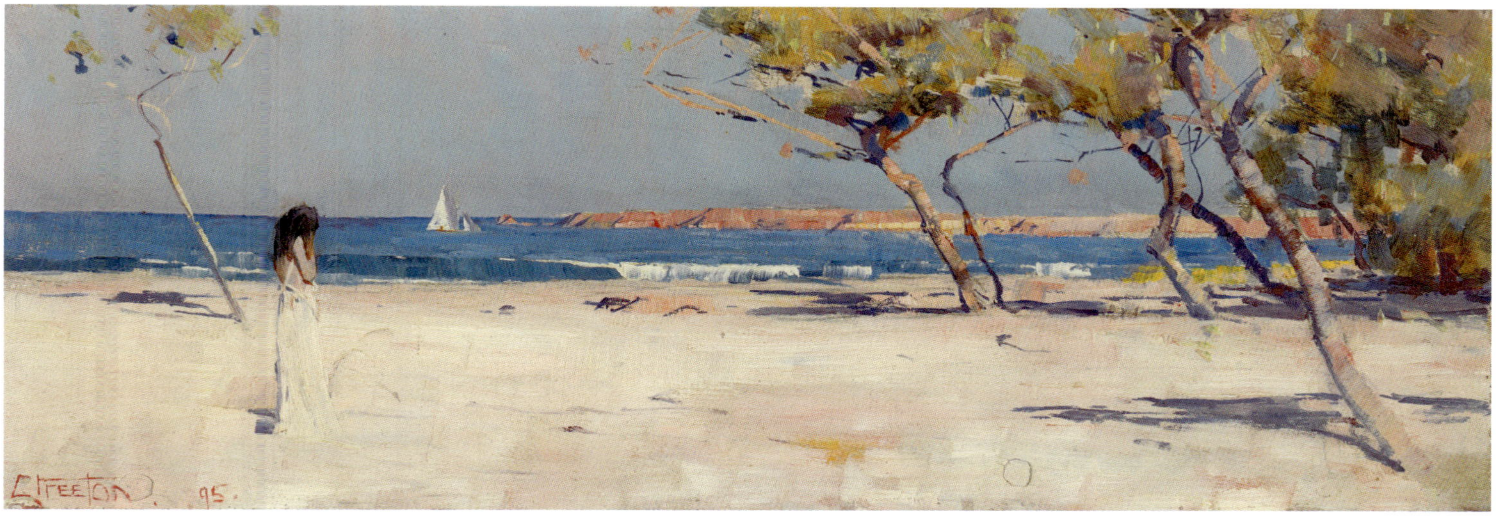

29
**Arthur Streeton** (1867–1943)
*Ariadne*, 1895
Oil on wood panel, 12.7 × 35.4 cm
National Gallery of Australia, Canberra

Members Acquisition Fund 2016
(Accession No. NGA 2015.1124)

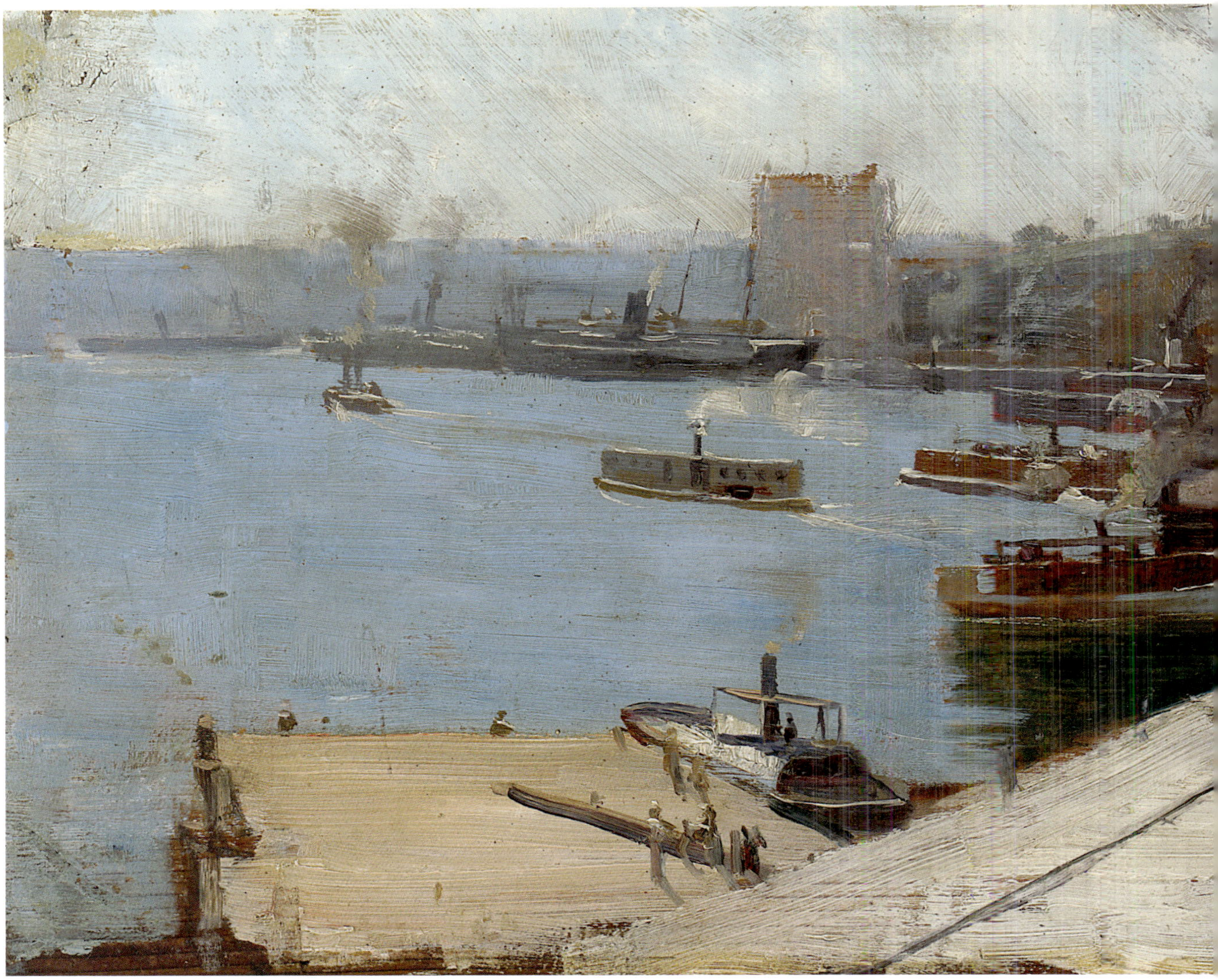

30
**Arthur Streeton** (1867–1943)
*Circular Quay*, 1892
Oil on wood panel, 19.3 × 47.6 cm
National Gallery of Australia, Canberra

Purchased 1959
(Accession No. NGA 59.222)

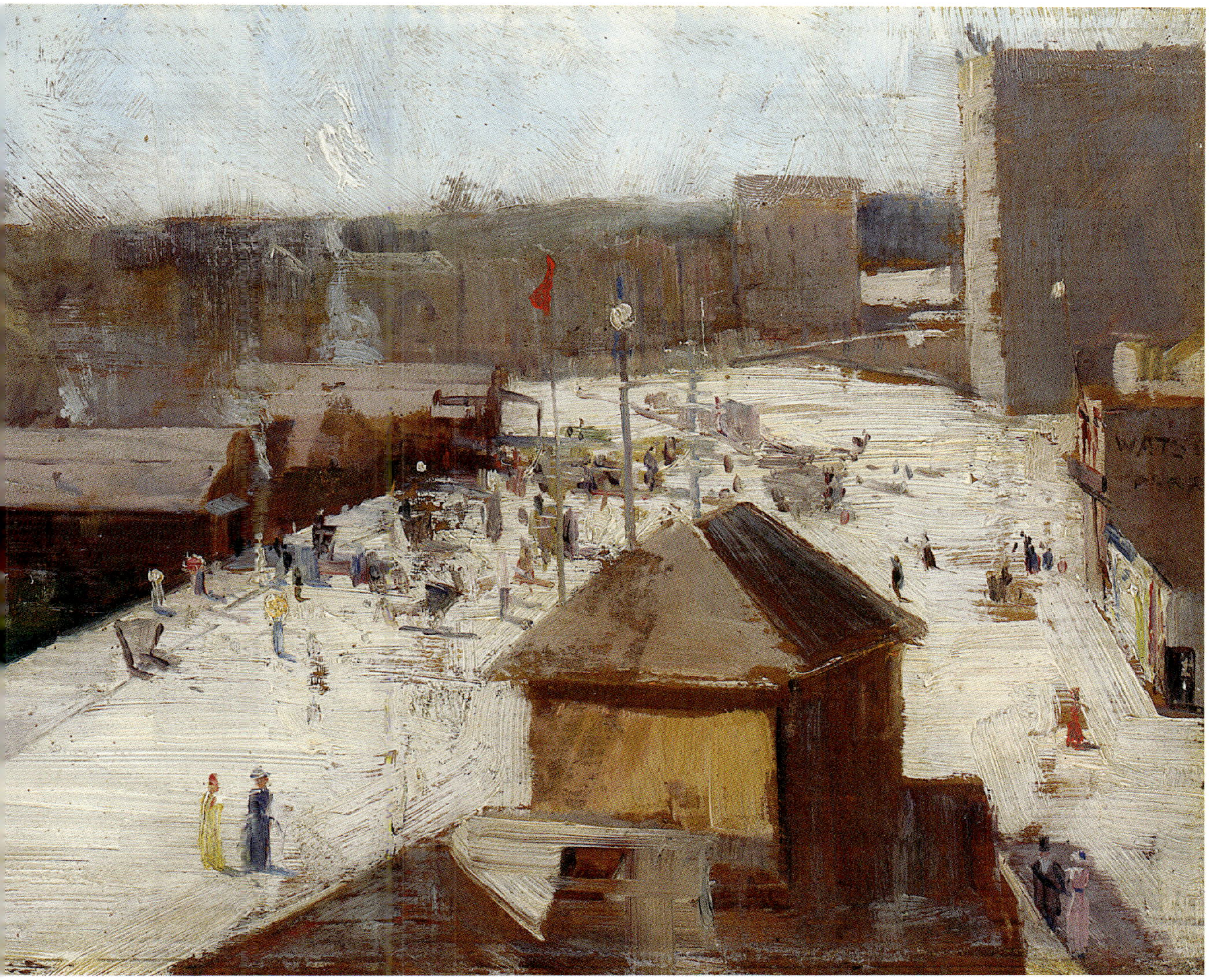

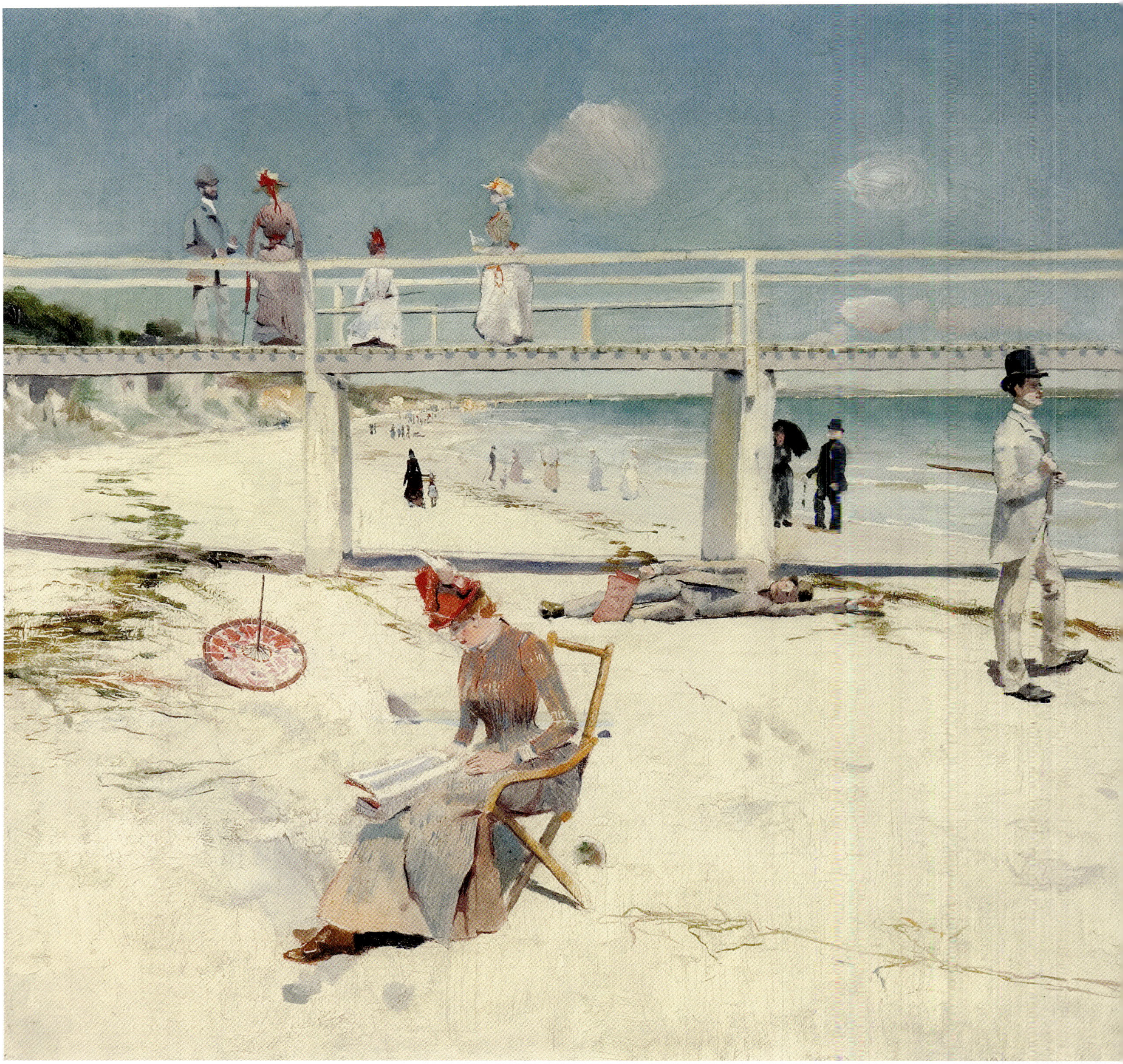

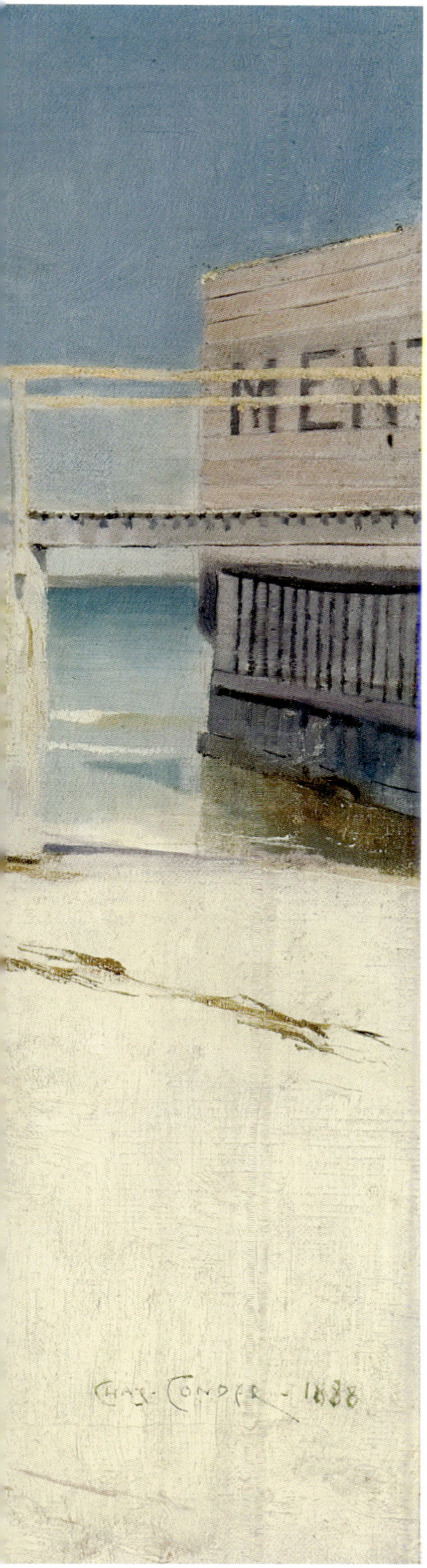

31
**Charles Conder** (1868–1909)
*A Holiday at Mentone*, 1888
Oil on canvas, 46.2 × 60.8 cm
Art Gallery of South Australia, Adelaide

South Australian Government Grant with the assistance of Bond Corporation Holdings Limited through the Art Gallery of South Australia Foundation to mark the Gallery's Centenary 1981 (Accession No. 815P14)

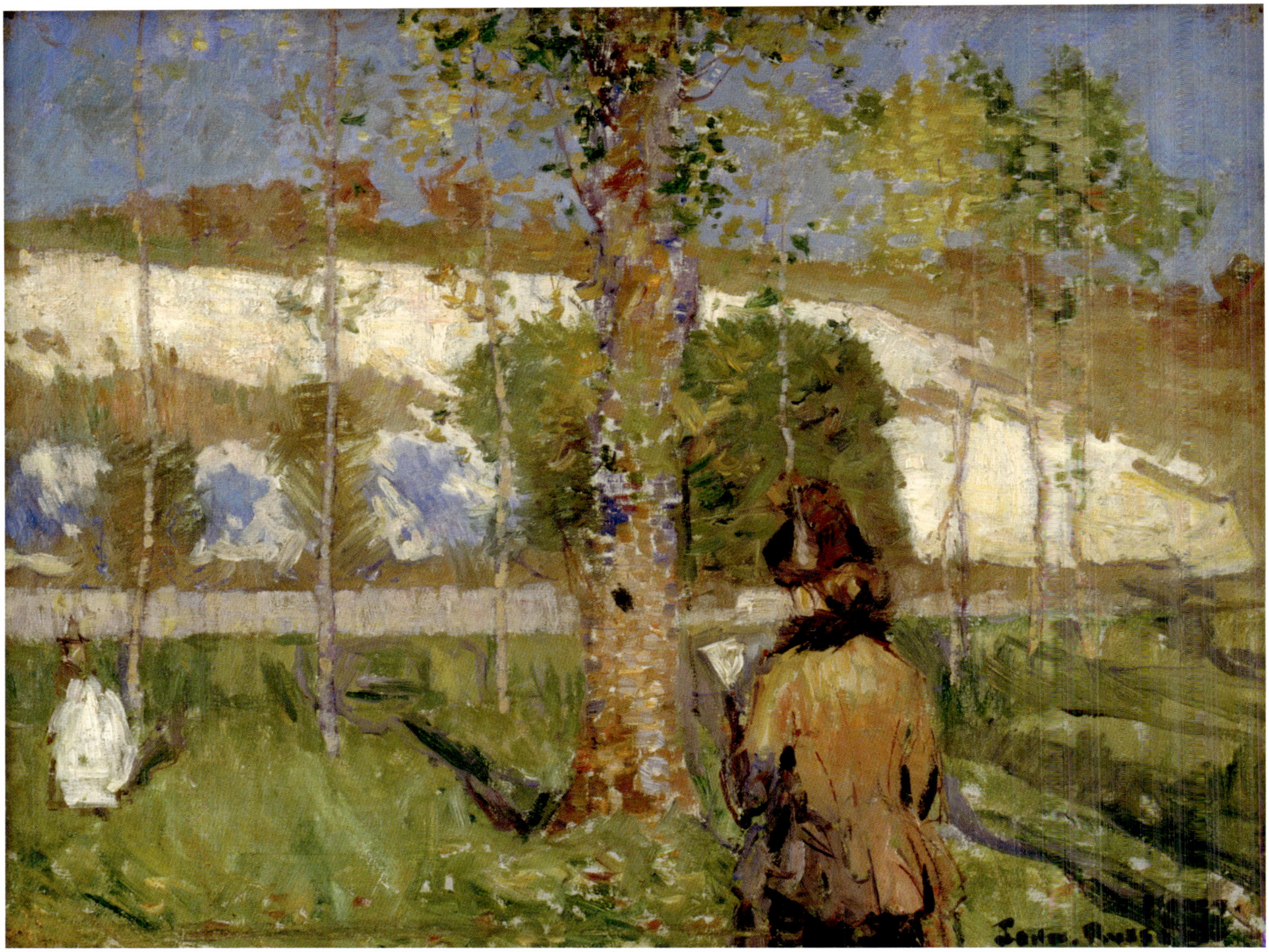

32
**John Russell** (1858–1930)
*Madame Sisley on the Banks of the Loing at Moret*, 1887
Oil on canvas, 45.7 × 60.9 cm
Art Gallery of New South Wales, Sydney

Purchased with assistance from the
Margaret Hannah Olley Art Trust 1996
(Accession No. 768.1996)

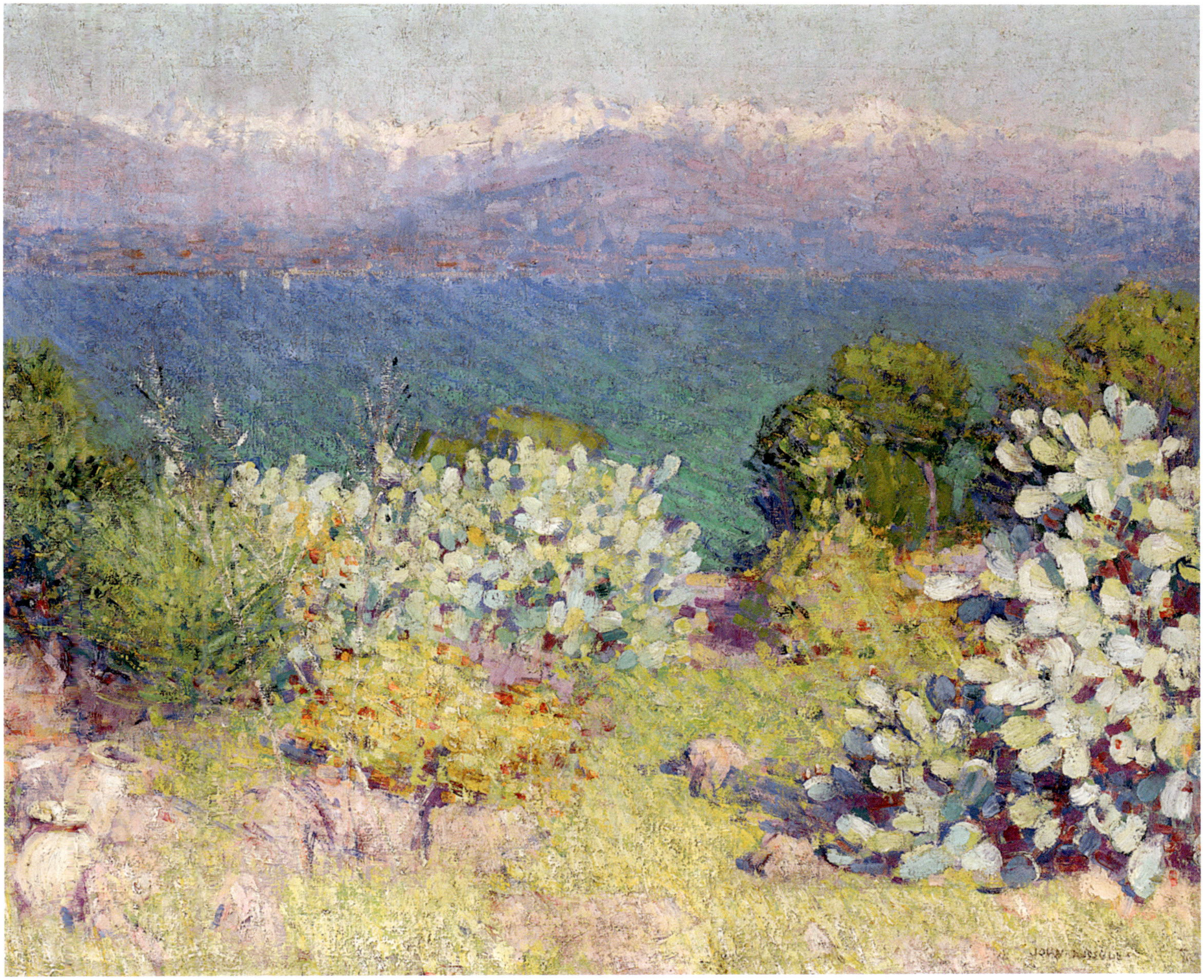

33
**John Russell** (1858–1930)
*In the Morning, Alpes Maritimes from Antibes*, 1890–1
Oil on canvas, 60.3 × 73.2 cm
National Gallery of Australia, Canberra

Purchased 1965
(Accession No. NGA 65.25)

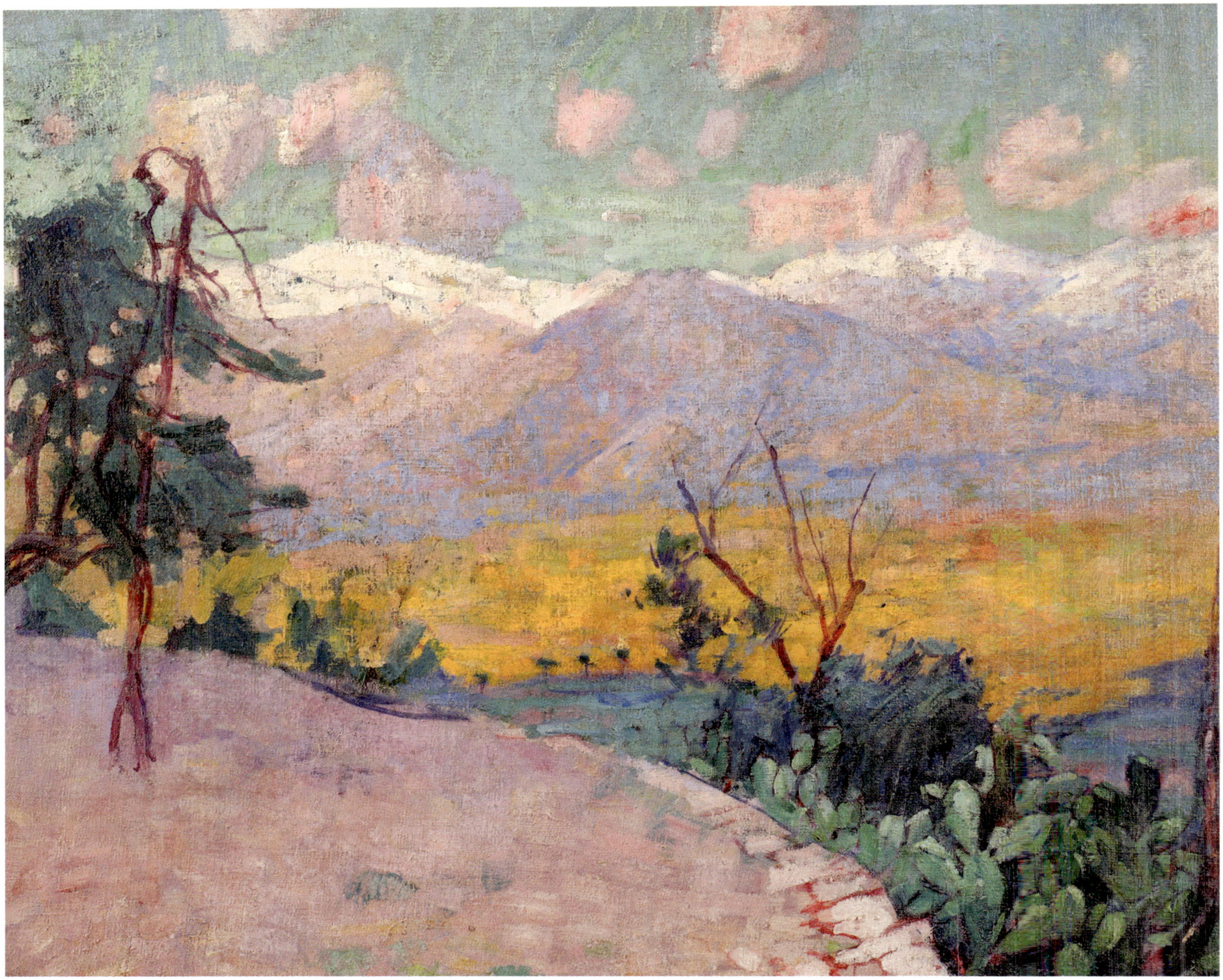

34
**John Russell** (1858–1930)
*Les Terrasses de Monte Cassino*, about 1889
Oil on canvas, 65 × 81 cm
Private Collection courtesy
of Nevill Keating Pictures

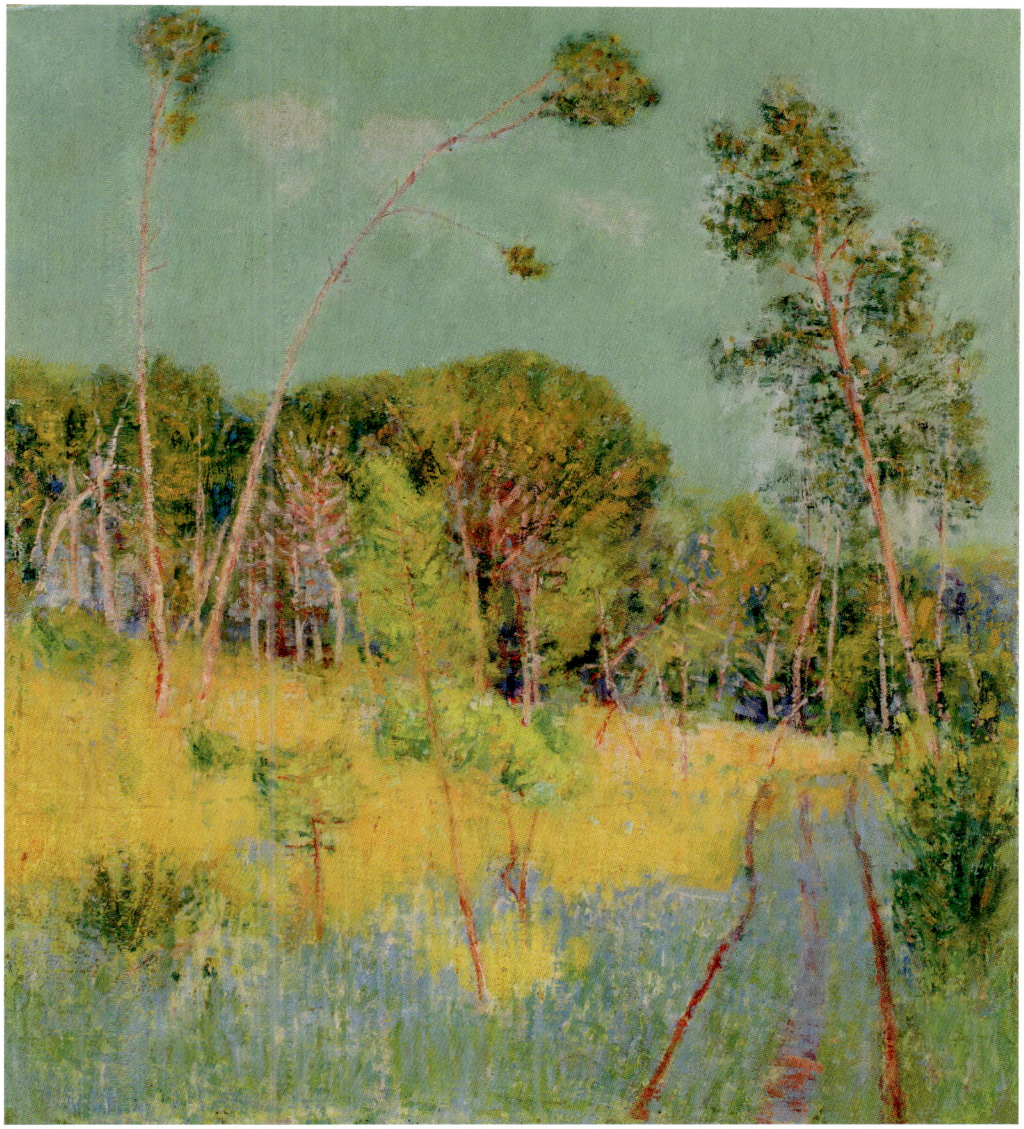

35
**John Russell** (1858–1930)
*A Clearing in the Forest*, 1891
Oil on canvas, 61 × 55.9 cm
Art Gallery of South Australia, Adelaide

A.M. & A.R. Ragless Bequest Funds 1968
(Accession No 6812P17)

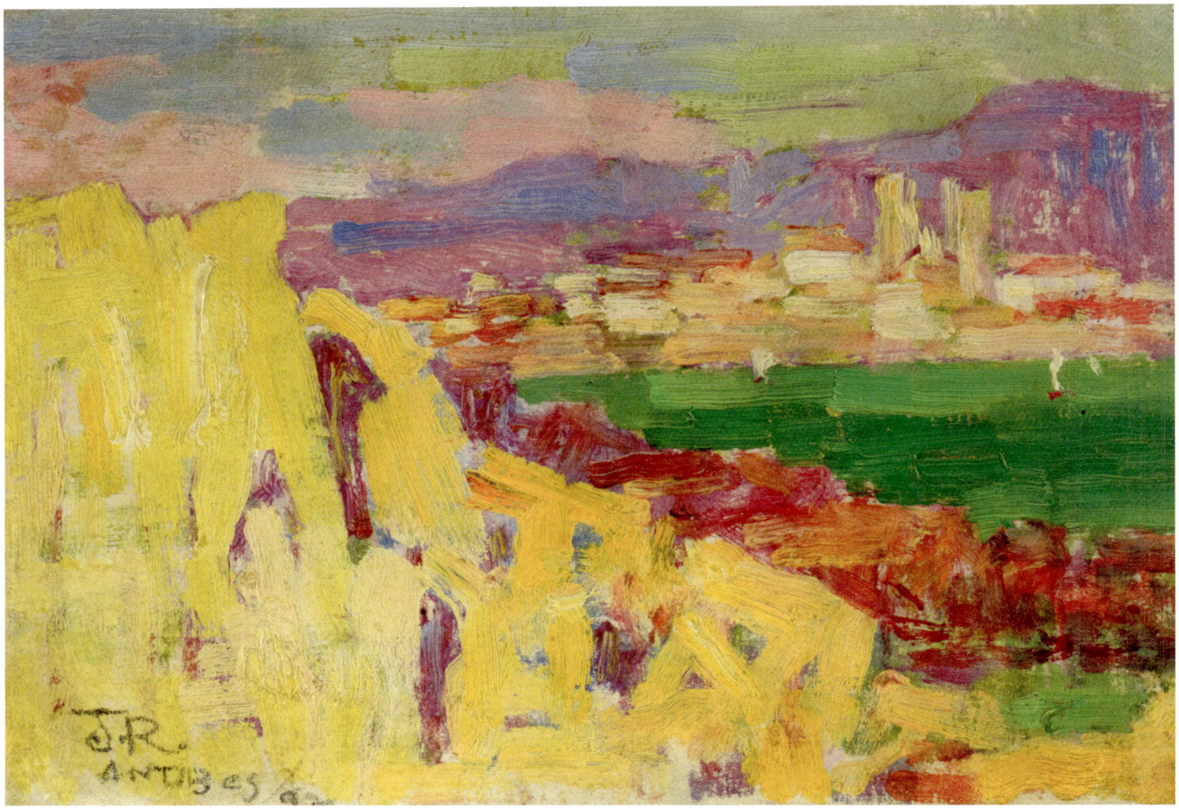


36
**John Russell** (1858–1930)
*Antibes*, about 1890–2
Oil on canvas, 16.5 × 24 cm
Art Gallery of New South Wales, Sydney

Gift of the Margaret Hannah Olley Art Trust 2012
(Accession No. 190.2012)

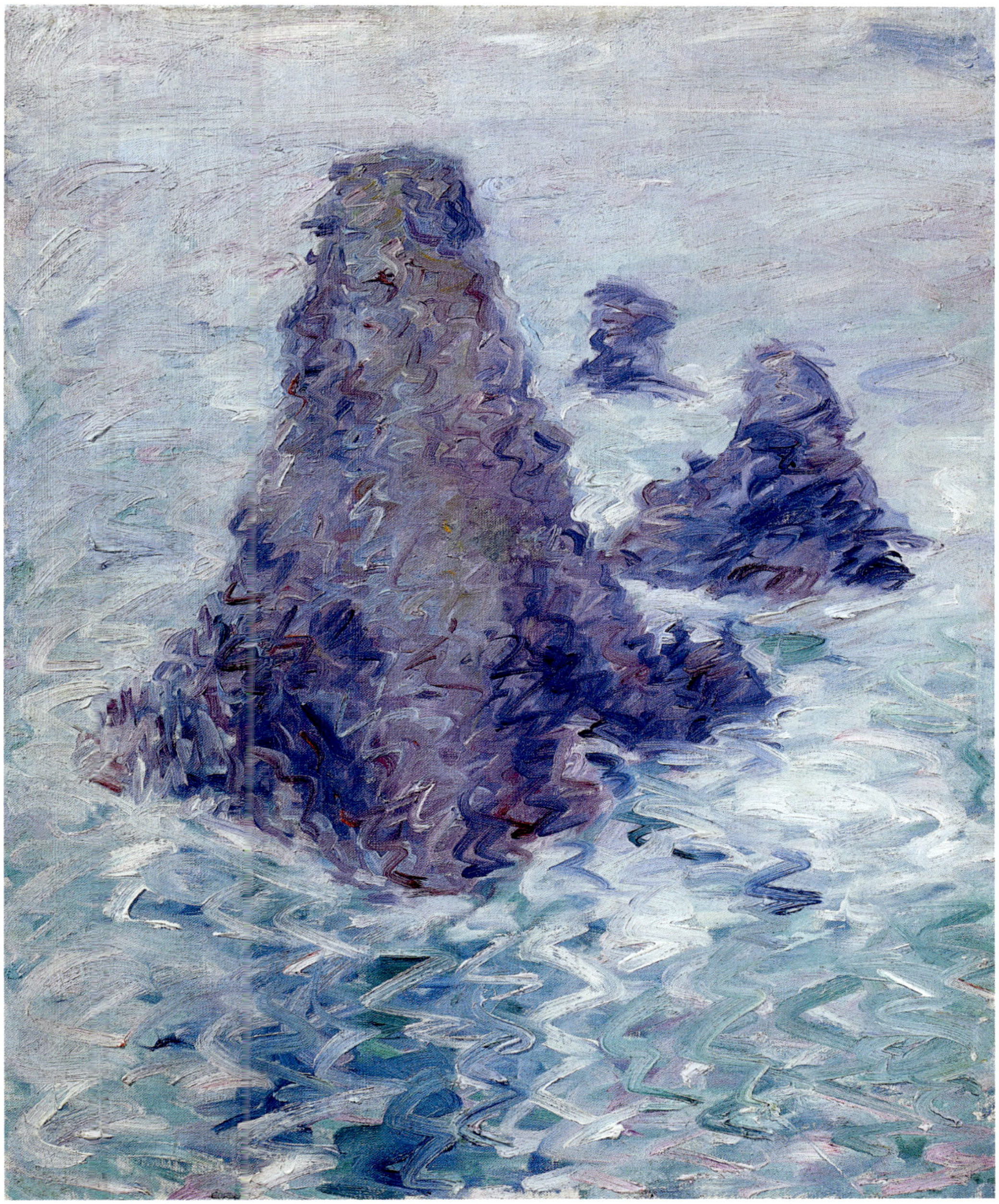

37
**John Russell** (1858–1930)
*Aiguille de Coton, Belle-Île*, about 1900
Oil on canvas, 60.8 × 50.5 cm
Kerry Stokes Collection, Perth
(Accession No. 1992.043)

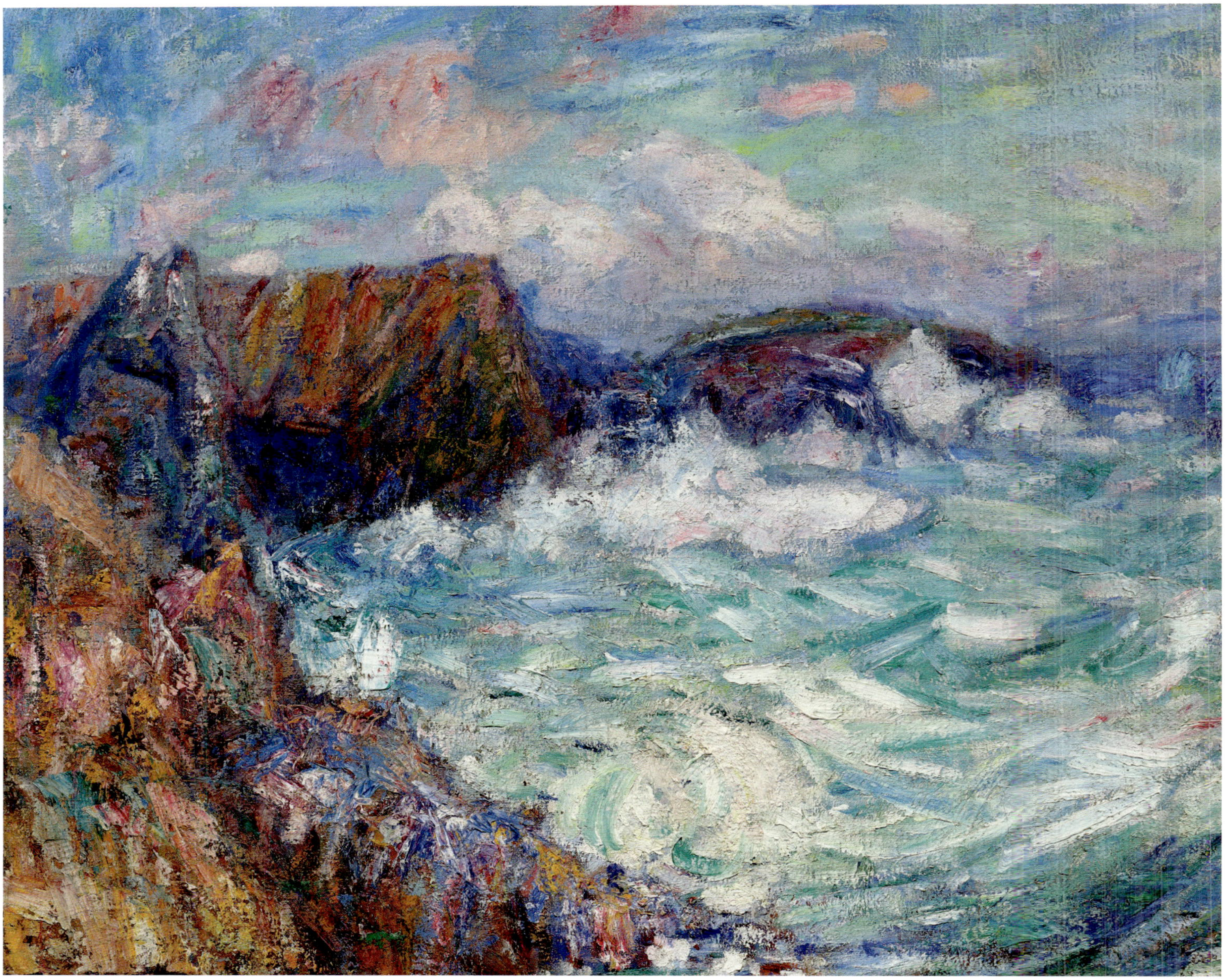

38
**John Russell** (1858–1930)
*Coucher de Soleil sur Morestil*, about 1904
Oil on hessian, 80.6 × 100.3 cm
Private collection, Switzerland

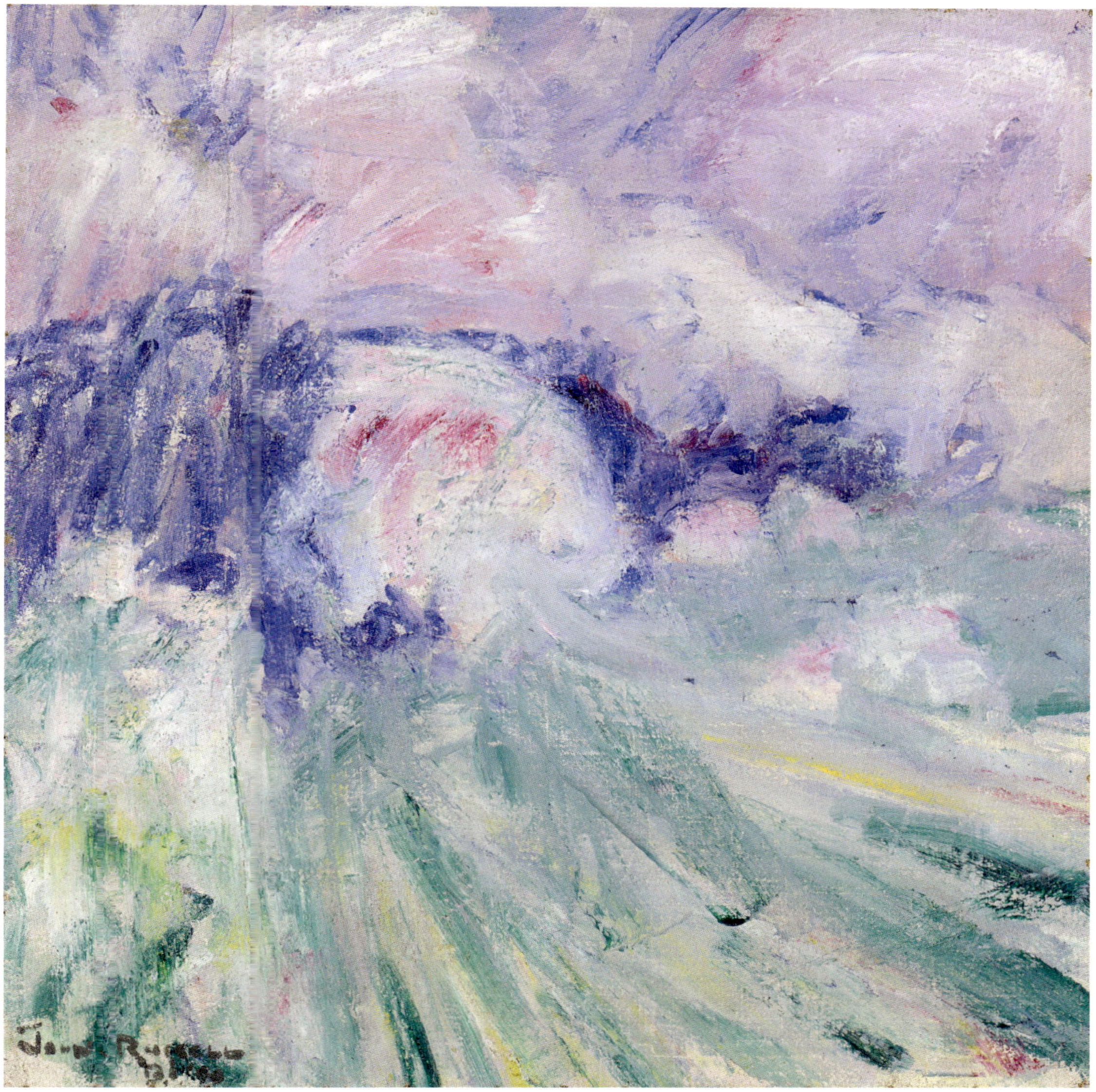

39
**John Russell** (1858–1930)
*Rough Sea, Belle-Île*, 1900
Oil on canvas, 63.2 × 63.1 cm
National Gallery of Victoria, Melbourne

The Joseph Brown Collection. Presented through the NGV Foundation by Dr Joseph Brown AO OBE, Honorary Life Benefactor, 2004
(Accession No. 2004.217)

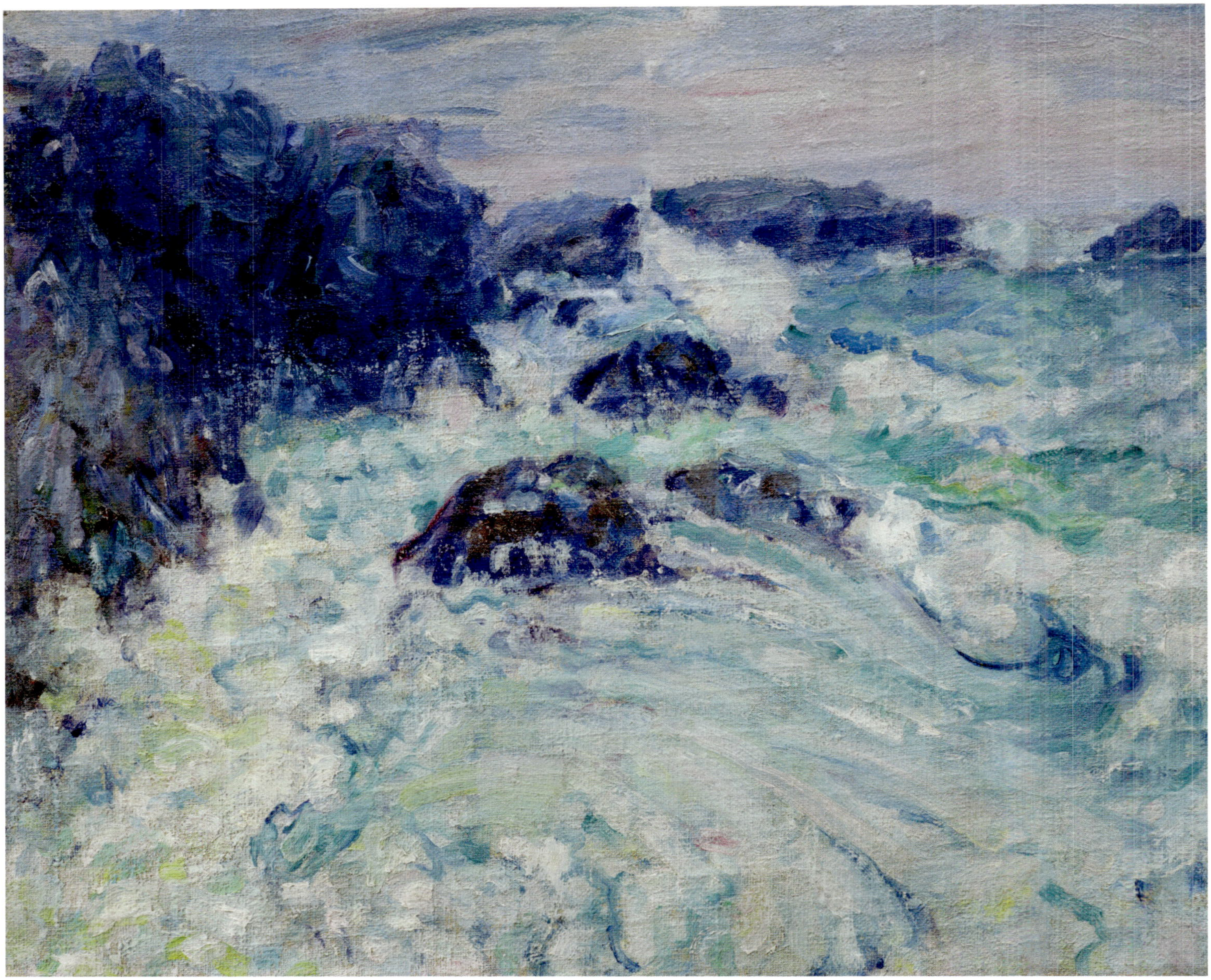

40
**John Russell** (1858–1930)
*Rough Sea, Morestil*, about 1900
Oil on canvas on hardboard, 66 × 81.8 cm
Art Gallery of New South Wales, Sydney

Purchased 1968
(Accession No. OA14.1968)

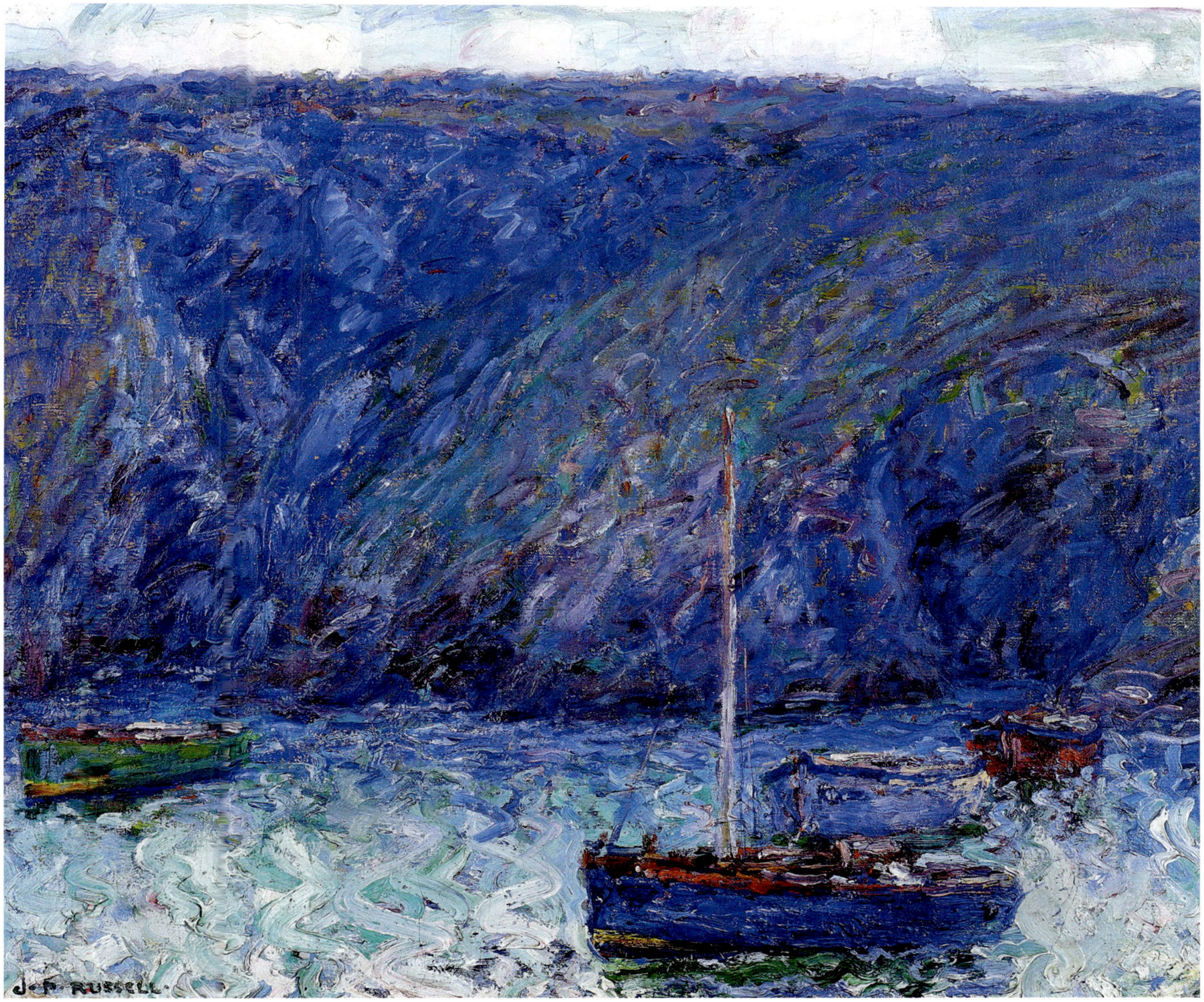


41
**John Russell** (1858–1930)
*Cruach en Mahr, Matin, Belle-Île-en-Mer*, about 1905
Oil on canvas, 60.4 × 73.5 cm
Private Collection courtesy
of Nevill Keating Pictures

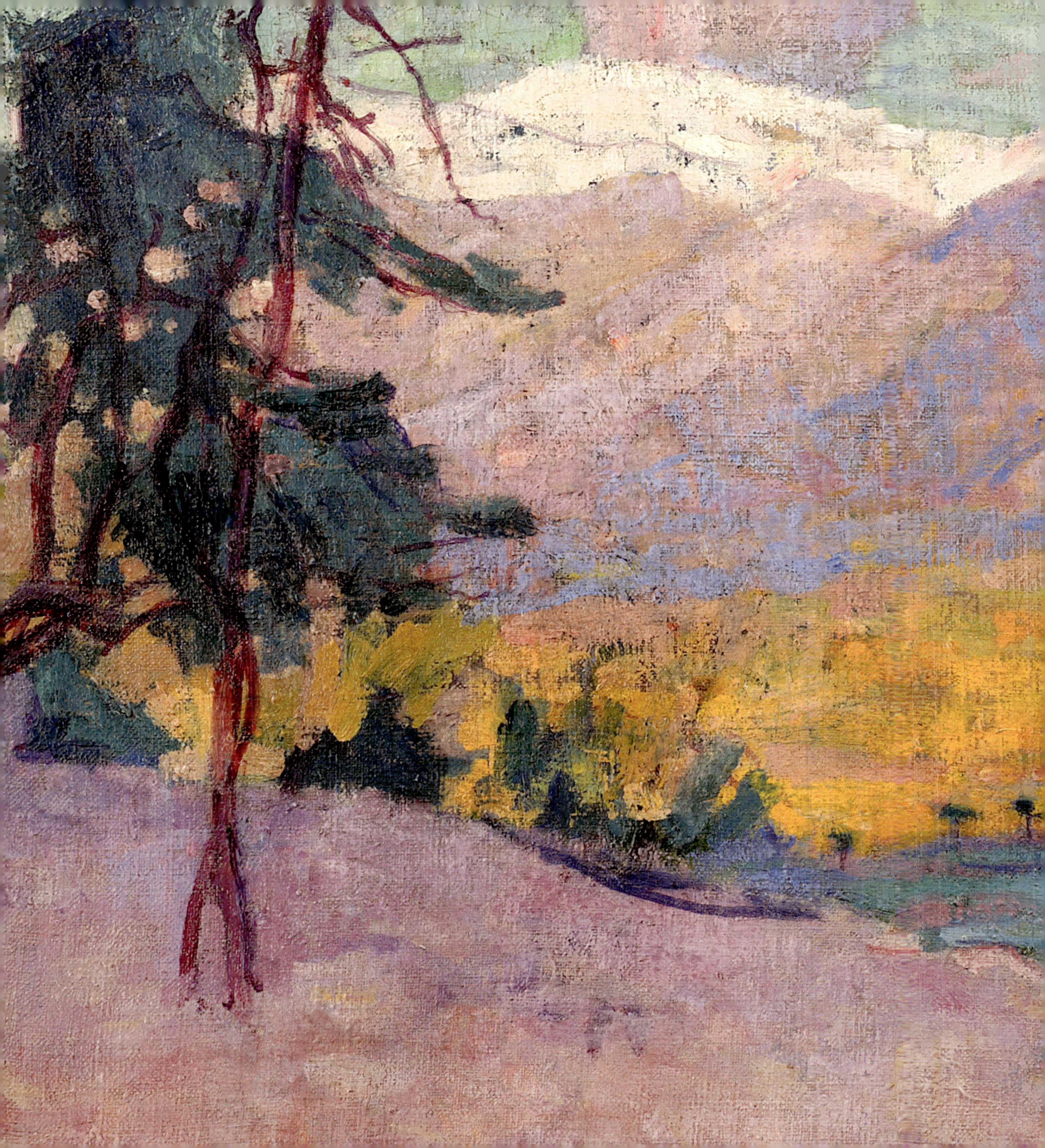

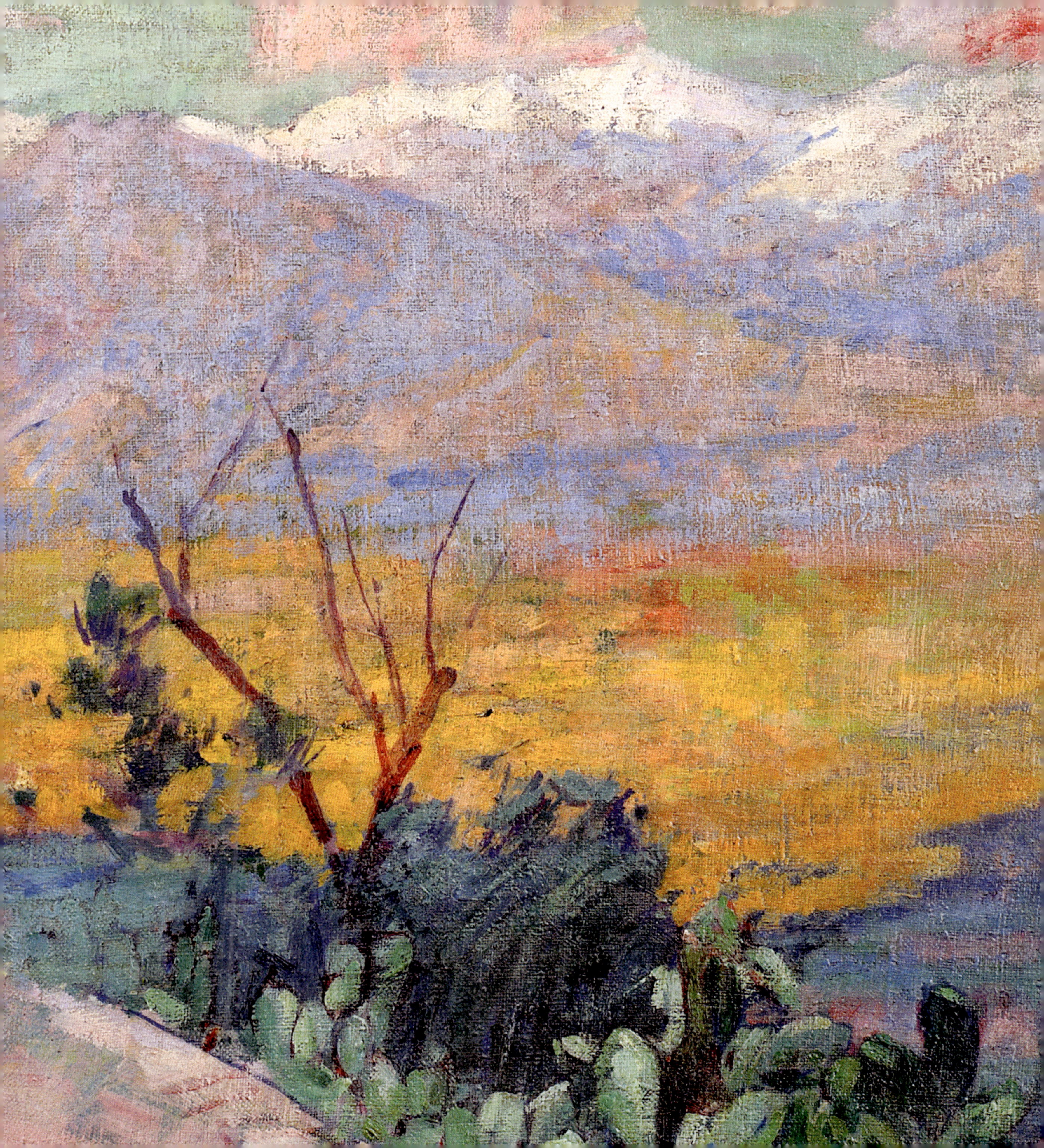

# PICTURE NOTES

Allison Goudie, Christopher Riopelle, Alex J. Taylor and Wayne Tunnicliffe

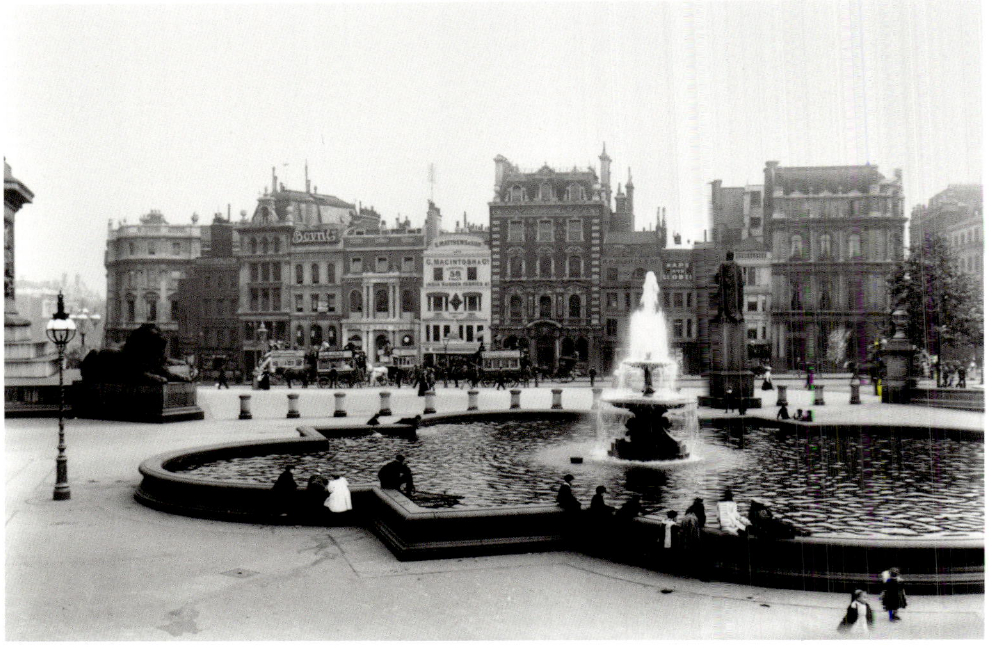

Fig. 37
Photograph of Trafalgar Square looking south, 31 July 1896.
London County Council Photograph Library, London Metropolitan Archives
(Accession no. SC PHL 01 537 393)

Cat. 1
**Tom Roberts** (1856–1931)
*Trafalgar Square*, 1904
Oil on cardboard, 14 × 28 cm
Art Gallery of South Australia, Adelaide

South Australian Government Grant 1988
(Accession No. 8810P45)

Once thought to date from Roberts's first visit to London in 1884, this oil sketch of the famous square at the heart of the imperial capital was more likely to have been painted on his second stay there early in the twentieth century. Nonetheless, it follows the format and diminutive scale of sketches exhibited at the 9 by 5 Impression Exhibition of 1889 while its silvery tonality recalls the works of Whistler which Roberts first admired in the 1880s. To the left – the south end of the Square – is the base of Nelson's Column and, facing west, two of Edwin Landseer's four mighty sculpted lions. To the right is the westernmost of the Square's two reflecting pools, as yet without the grander and more soaring fountain Edwin Lutyens would add after the Great War. The buildings in the distance stand on the south side of the square near Whitehall – not the east side as is sometimes said – the present site of Uganda House. The same view can be seen in a contemporary photograph (fig. 37). The artist stood on the north side of the Square as he worked, his back to the National Gallery. Thin streaks of light along the side of the column and lip of the pool establish that what little sunlight did eke through the fog came from the east; the sketch must have been made in the morning. CR

Cat. 2
**Tom Roberts** (1856–1931)
*Fog, Thames Embankment*, 1884
Oil on paperboard, 13.1 × 21.7 cm
Art Gallery of New South Wales, Sydney

Purchased with funds provided by the Gleeson O'Keefe Foundation 2008
(Accession No. 1.2008)

Painted in London in 1884, this ethereal oil sketch of the Thames looking towards a looming apparition of the Houses of Parliament is probably the work of the same name prominently positioned at the beginning of the catalogue for the 9 by 5 Impression Exhibition. Streeton later credited Roberts's London 'impressions' with having elicited an 'exciting revelation' among Australian artists, while Roberts reflected to a friend on one such work: 'You may remember a little thing... of the Embankment in fog – that always... held me, so I never parted with it... It's here and holds up with all my late stuff and they with it. A kind of touchstone and I didn't know it' (see p. 12). The spatial construction of the scene and the choppy brushstrokes used to render the bobbing waves make a compelling comparison with Monet's *The Thames below Westminster* (fig. 38) yet it is unlikely that Roberts would have seen it. AG

Cat. 3
**Tom Roberts** (1856–1931)
*By the Treasury*, 1889
Oil on wood panel, 23.5 × 14.2 cm
National Gallery of Victoria, Melbourne

Purchased through the NGV Foundation by The Hugh D.T. Williamson Foundation, Founder Benefactor, 2002
(Accession No. 2002.304)

This atmospheric urban scene was one of 62 small panels that Roberts exhibited in the 9 by 5 Impression Exhibition in August 1889. Like many of the works in the exhibition, it was painted on a cedar cigar box lid, whose visible grain furthers the effect of overcast light and winter drizzle. With a gentleman in a top hat dashing towards a Hansom cab, Roberts captures the top end of Melbourne's fashionable Collins Street. This was the view from outside Grosvenor Chambers, the recently built complex of artists' studios in which Roberts had established his own fashionably decorated rooms. A bold vertical shadow emphasises the scale of the imposing Old Treasury building, whose vaults held the gold that made Melbourne one of the world's richest cities. In the centre of the composition, tapered pine trees stand in for the unfinished central spire of St Patrick's Cathedral, a building that would – once boom turned to bust in the 1890s – remain uncompleted for decades. AJT

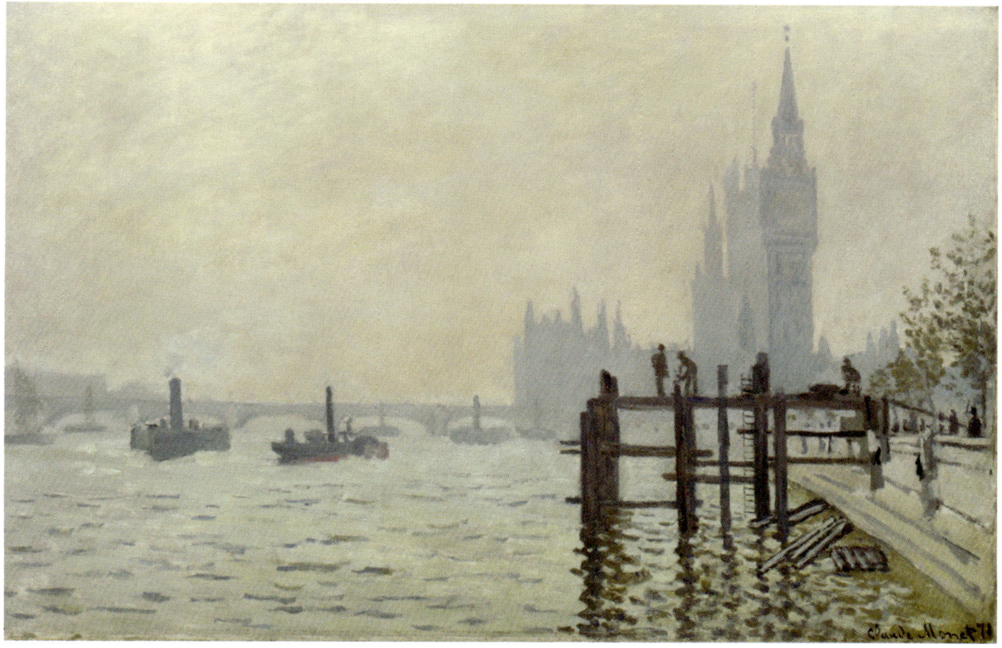

Fig. 38
**Claude Monet** (1840–1926)
*The Thames below Westminster* about 1871
Oil on canvas, 47 × 73 cm
The National Galley, London
Bequeathed by Lord Astor of Hever (NG 6399)

Cat. 4
**Arthur Streeton** (1867–1943)
*Sandridge*, about 1888
Oil on wood panel, 12.8 × 23.3 cm
National Gallery of Australia, Canberra
Purchased 1969 (Accession No. NGA 69.47)

Sandridge, now known as Port Melbourne, is on Port Phillip Bay to the south of Melbourne's central business district and near where the Yarra River enters the sea. The site offered an artist interested in plein-air sketching the constantly changing motifs of a bustling port. Here, Streeton juxtaposes steam transport in the foreground with the taller, older, masted ships at anchor beyond. The image, monochromatic except for discreet touches of blue and yellow, is painted with a bravura economy of means as Streeton establishes tonal unity at once true to a misty morning and to the silvery precedent of Whistler's riverside scenes. The artist added the date 1884 later; he would have been 17 in 1884 and, while a precocious painter, required the example of a mentor like Tom Roberts (who was in Europe until 1885), to pull off as confident a performance as this. More likely he executed it in anticipation of the 9 by 5 Impression Exhibition which he helped organise in 1889 and where it was first shown. CR

Cat. 5
**Arthur Streeton** (1867–1943)
*The National Game*, 1889
Oil on cardboard, 11.8 × 22.9 cm
Art Gallery of New South Wales, Sydney
Purchased 1963 (Accession No. NGA OA11.1963)

Streeton depicts the national game: Aussie rules football, played here at Richmond Paddock, Melbourne; actually it was twelve years before Australia really became an independent nation, in 1901. However, yearnings for national unity were in the air in the 1880s as were ideas of what constituted the national character. Sport was helping to forge a sense of oneness among autonomous colonies, and to shape an ethos of rugged, companionable Australian masculinity as well. Also under discussion was the role art would play in defining the national experience. For Streeton and his companions gathered around the oracular figure of Tom Roberts in late-1880s Melbourne, key to the breakthrough they sought was painting in a new, improvisatory manner they called Impressionism. In this sketch where brushwork is as quick and darting as the subject, Streeton forged an iconic image of that fusion of national and artistic aspiration. He would show it soon after, at the 9 by 5 Impression Exhibition of August 1889 where a thrilling new Australian art was introduced to a sceptical but intrigued public. CR

Cat. 6
**Arthur Streeton** (1867–1943)
*Hoddle St., 10 pm*, 1889
Oil on cardboard, 7.9 × 23.3 cm
National Gallery of Australia, Canberra
Purchased 1974 (Accession No. NGA 74.138)

'Two half hours are never alike, and he who tried to paint a sunset on two successive evenings, must be more or less painting from memory,' read the catalogue from the 9 by 5 Impression Exhibition, declaring works such as this as efforts to 'obtain records of effects widely differing, and often of a very fleeting character.' As its title indicates, this impression records the evening light on Hoddle Street, Melbourne, not far from where Streeton grew up in the suburb of Richmond. His attention here to the momentary effects of light extends to artificial illumination, including distant gas streetlights and a yellow slither that leaks from the window of the house in the foreground, all captured with assured brevity. Streeton's swift brushstrokes and limited palette of mauve, brown and cream brings to mind the work of Whistler, one of whose small panels had been exhibited in Melbourne in 1885. AJT

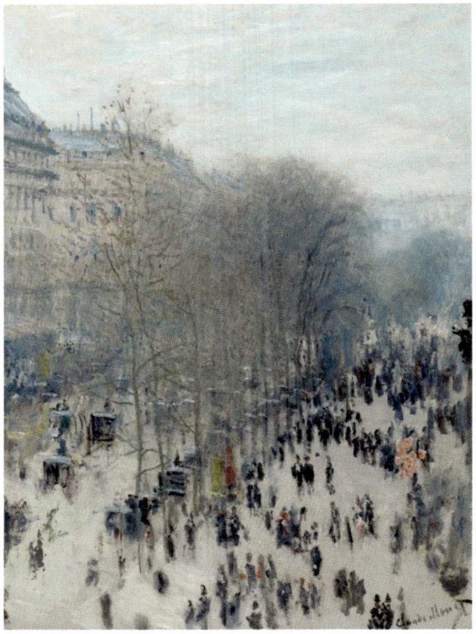

Fig. 39
**Claude Monet** (1840–1926)
*Boulevard des Capucines*, 1873–4
Oil on canvas, 79 × 59 cm
The Nelson-Atkins Museum of Art, Kansas City, Missouri

Purchased 1888 (Accession no. F72-35)

Cat. 7
**Charles Conder** (1868–1909)
*Riddells Creek*, 1889
Oil on wood panel on paper on two layers of cardboard, 24.4 × 11.2 cm
National Gallery of Australia, Canberra

Purchased 1972 (Accession No. NGA 72.8)

With barely a few weeks to go before the 9 by 5 Impression Exhibition was due to open, Conder accepted an invitation from Kathleen Caffyn – the wife of a patron and a Bohemian novelist whose portrait Conder had previously painted – to visit her in Riddells Creek, north-west of Melbourne. Here, the newspaper *Table Talk* reported, Conder would 'study the scenery' and 'prosecute his search for likely subjects' for the exhibition. This picture was probably still wet when it came to be hung. Having splashed bronze paint over it while decorating the frame after fitting, Conder appears to have wiped back the area around the now blurred vestiges of a signature, exposing more of another inscription, 'Riddles [*sic*] Creek', scraped into the paint with the end of a brush in larger lettering, and revealing hints of the warm wood beneath. AG

Cat. 8
**Charles Conder** (1868–1909)
*Dandenongs from Heidelberg*, about 1889
Oil on wood panel, 11.5 × 23.5 cm
Art Gallery of South Australia, Adelaide

M.J.M. Carter AO Collection through the Art Gallery of South Australia Foundation 2012, to mark the 123rd anniversary of the '9 by 5 Impression Exhibition', August 1889. Donated through the Australian Government's Cultural Gifts Program (Accession No. 20124P12)

This is one of the few pictures from the 9 by 5 exhibition that retains its original frame – roughly hewn from Queensland Kauri Pine and decorated with sprigs of foliage painted by Conder. Frames such as this were integral to the exhibition: a union of art and decoration that made use of Liberty draperies, carved furniture, art pottery and floral arrangements. Here, the simple gilding of the frame's chamfered edge serves to extend the blonde tonality of the work. Conder manipulates his oily medium with rough bristles and sgraffito highlights to reveal the pale ground, producing delicate textures that convincingly suggest the sun-bleached dazzle of grassy fields without compromising the work's self-consciously rough handling. Conder admired an equivalent lack of finish in other art forms too, once criticising the poet who 'polishes up an idea and so leaves no suggestion'. AJT

Cat. 9
**Tom Roberts** (1856–1931)
*Across the Dandenongs*, 1889
Oil on wood panel, 13.7 × 23.1 cm
National Gallery of Victoria, Melbourne

Purchased 1962 (Accession No. 1207-5)

This verdant view from Heidelberg towards the blue Dandenong Ranges was first exhibited in the 9 by 5 Impression Exhibition in 1889. The darker green passage of the picture underlines a slim but deliberate flick of white paint – an unmistakable landmark for period viewers that would have instantly located Roberts's dashed-off panel. The white stroke represents the Doncaster Tower, an 87-metre high structure erected by an enterprising hotelier as a scenic outlook for tourists. 'The tower that was erected before the days of Eiffel rises there, and is at least as light and airy and free of all assertiveness of solidity and strength as that of the great French architect,' reads one newspaper account of the attraction. 'The view, however, must be as broad as from Eiffel, and as all good Australians who have made the ascent know, infinitely more beautiful.' Roberts's painting equally participates in the growing national zeal for Australian scenery. AJT

Cat. 10
**Arthur Streeton** (1867–1943)
*Between the Lights – Princes Bridge*, 1888
Oil on canvas, 82 × 152 cm
Private collection, London

This ambitious painting of Melbourne's Princes Bridge nearing completion immediately attracted the attention of critics who eagerly followed the development of the 21-year-old Streeton. One wrote: 'It is not the finished work which Mr Streeton will exhibit in a year or two, but it is a picture alike showing the patience and earnestness of this talented young artist.' Another saw in the perceived 'unfinish' evidence of Streeton belonging 'to the school of French Impressionists', his pictures possessing 'a certain clever vagueness that leaves something to the imagination' and allowing the viewer to 'people the bridge as one will'. Revealing for what it says about the reception of contemporary French painting by the Australian critical eye, what was meant here by 'French Impressionism' was much less the broken colour of Monet than the naturalism of Bastien-Lepage in which this indomitable symbol of urban expansion, 'by no means a picturesque object per se, is made to look almost poetical'. AG

Cat. 11
**Charles Conder** (1868–1909)
*Departure of the Orient – Circular Quay*, 1888
Oil on canvas, 45.1 × 50.1 cm
Art Gallery of New South Wales, Sydney

Purchased 1888 (Accession No. 829)

The flattened, elevated view of Conder's bustling Sydney dockside scene has prompted comparisons with Japanese prints, but one might equally detect Conder's experience working on a trigonometrical survey for the Lands Department in its carefully plotted geometry. Period critics of the picture noted that Conder had 'studied the Impressionist school', an attention to the fugitive effects of light that suggests the influence of émigré artists he knew in Sydney, such as the British-born Alfred Daplyn, who had painted at Barbizon, France, in the 1870s, and the Italian-born Girolamo Nerli, whose work assimilated the dashing brushstrokes of Italy's *Macchiaoli* painters. Conder's bruised palette achieves a silvery, almost iridescent effect, with touches of aqua and fiery red that recall the precious opals so fashionable around this time. Purchased by the Art Gallery of New South Wales when Conder was just 19, this was among the Australian works exhibited at the World's Columbian Exposition in Chicago in 1893. AJT

Cat. 12
**Arthur Streeton** (1867–1943)
*Fireman's Funeral, George Street*, 1894
Oil on canvas, 45.3 × 38.2 cm
Art Gallery of New South Wales, Sydney

Purchased 1980 (Accession No. 43.1980)

Abutted by the imposing, Second Empire-inspired Sydney Town Hall, this is New South Wales's answer to the wintry, Hausmannian Paris depicted by Monet in 1873 in his seminal *Boulevard des Capucines* (fig. 39), which he exhibited the following year at the First Impressionist Exhibition. With its bold, off-centre perspective funnelling the blurred maelstrom of a crowd northwards down George Street past the gaping excavations for what would become the Queen Victoria Building, it is hard to conceive that Streeton did not have *Boulevard des Capucines* in mind, and yet he completed the picture having never left Australia and without having seen the Monet. Observed through a curtain of heavy rain, the individuals in the crowd, gathered for the funeral of a heroic fireman, recall what one critic of Monet's picture described as his 'tongue-lickings'; indeed, they are as close as Streeton comes to a French Impressionist idiom of broken brushstrokes. AG

Cat. 13
**Arthur Streeton** (1876–1943)
*The Railway Station, Redfern*, 1893
Oil on canvas, 40.8 × 61 cm
Art Gallery of New South Wales, Sydney

Gift of Lady Denison 1942 (Accession No. 7209)

This depiction of the approaches to a railway station just south of what is today Sydney's gargantuan Central Station is among Streeton's most audacious compositions. Reportedly, he completed it in just three hours. The bottom half is taken up entirely with the rain-slicked approaches to the station populated most prominently by a single, angular figure ambling across the gusty plaza. The interest here lies in the fluid brushwork, subtle in its depiction of shadows and slippery surfaces. It is hard to think of such a composition, with its conjunction of emptiness in the foreground and precise detail beyond, without the precedent of the Italian Giuseppe de Nittis. He was a friend of Degas and Whistler, among the most evocative painters of London in its unrelieved wet misery, and a fixture of the 1890s European avant-garde. Could Streeton have known his work, perhaps through the Italian emigré Nerli? The canvas shows Streeton's mastery of tonal painting and his pleasure in defying expectation by depicting the opposite of the sun-blasted, rural canvases for which he was gaining fame. CR

Cat. 14
**Tom Roberts** (1856–1931)
*Allegro con Brio, Bourke Street West*,
about 1885–6, reworked 1890
Oil on canvas mounted on composition board, 51.2 × 76.7 cm
National Gallery of Australia, Canberra
and National Library of Australia, Canberra

Purchased 1920 by the Parliamentary Library Committee

Roberts's captivating record of a Melbourne street life embraces the kind of urban anecdote – a crouching bootblack here, a sun-baking dog there – that so delighted late nineteenth-century audiences. Such details remain endlessly fascinating. Scholars have debated, for instance, the identity of the tricolour flag on the right of the picture, while Roberts's biographer points to the ice cart in the centre of the composition as a paradoxical sign for the sweltering summer heat. But it is the ambiguous and even illegible passages of the picture that are the most evocative: moving figures evaporate into the dusty ground, denser crowds are swallowed by purple shadows. The bewildering patchwork of terracotta buildings, awnings and telegraph poles that march up the street barely provides any more stability. With its shifts in focus and disorienting blurs, Roberts conjures the distracting buzz of modern urban life in a way that the empty streets of early long-exposure photography was unable to capture. AJT

Cat. 15
**Tom Roberts** (1856–1931)
*A Quiet Day on Darebin Creek*, 1885
Oil on wood panel, 26.4 × 34.8 cm
National Gallery of Australia, Canberra

Purchased 1969 (Accession No. NGA 69.4)

Two artists explore the countryside about an hour from Melbourne; one is seated by the edge of a shallow, reedy creek already at work on a sketch as the other, further off, searches for a distinctive motif. This is one of four paintings Roberts sent to the Colonial and Indian Exhibition, a celebration of Empire held in South Kensington in 1886. With it, Roberts provided a lesson in what the ambitious young painters of Melbourne, himself in the lead, were up to at the moment. They were committed to plein-air painting in order to capture the uniquely muted tones and fleeting atmosphere of the Australian landscape. Visitors to the London exhibition would have seen that Australian painters were entirely *au courant* with European trends in informal, improvisatory, naturalistic painting, and Roberts would have demonstrated that his time in Europe, from which he had just returned, had proved useful in importing new approaches to painting capable of rejuvenating Australian art. CR

Cat. 16
**Tom Roberts** (1856–1931)
*Winter Morning after Rain, Gardiner's Creek*, 1885
Oil on canvas, 47 × 66 cm
Art Gallery of South Australia, Adelaide

M.J.M. Carter AO Collection through the Art Gallery of South Australia Foundation to mark the 130th anniversary of the Gallery, 2011 (Accession No. 20111P14)

Like *A Quiet Day on Darebin Creek* (cat. 15), Roberts sent this work to the 1886 Colonial and Indian Exhibition in London. Like that painting, it too served to demonstrate his sophisticated and confident appropriation of motifs and strategies from avant-garde European art. Here, a horseman drives his cattle across a high wooden bridge. Reflected in the still creek, the uprights of the bridge frame distant views of the countryside.

An obvious source for the image is Whistler's recent paintings and etchings of bridges, much admired by Roberts. Many dramatic images of bridges, often seen from below, as in this painting, were experimented with by French Impressionists like Claude Monet in the 1870s. If the high horizon and strict architectonics of the composition bespeak European influence, still thrillingly new to Roberts, the muted tonalities specific to the countryside near Melbourne demonstrate the artist's skill in intuiting how he could use such influences to shape an image entirely true to Australian visual experience. CR

Cat. 17
**Tom Roberts** (1856–1931)
*Saplings*, about 1889
Oil on cedar panel, 34.5 × 14.5 cm
Art Gallery of South Australia, Adelaide

Morgan Thomas Bequest Fund 1927
(Accession No. 0.707)

Painted on a cedar cigar-box lid, and probably exhibited in the 9 by 5 Impression Exhibition, this bravura sketch has everything of the drama of the Australian bush that Roberts would work up into his grander 'history' paintings such as *A Break Away!* (cat. 22), distilled into a tightly cropped flash of a steep, forested hillside. The almost abstract 'all-over' composition, dispensing entirely with the sky, emphasises the vertiginous landscape, combined with the portrait format and the sleek white parallels of the tree trunks to create a compelling downward thrust and injecting the scene with a sense of speed. The rapid, agitated brushstrokes evoke a landscape glimpsed from a careering horse or hurtling train in the quivering midday heat, while the restrained, arid palette is relieved by smudges of blue that conjure up the cool scent of eucalyptus. AG

Cat. 18
**Charles Conder** (1868–1909),
*On the River Yarra, near Heidelberg, Victoria*, about 1890
Oil on canvas, 30.4 × 40.7 cm
Art Gallery of New South Wales, Sydney

Jean Cameron Gordon Bequest Fund
in memory of her mother Mary Gordon 2002
(Accession No. 298.2002)

During the two years he spent in Melbourne, 1888–90, Conder placed himself at the heart of the emerging group of young painters, including Roberts and Streeton who, working in the new European manner, made quick and vibrant landscape oil sketches in the suburbs of the city, particularly at Heidelberg. (They came to be known as the Heidelberg School but Australian art historians today shy from the term; see p. 25)
A particularly creative moment came in the summer of 1889–90 – Britain's winter, of course – when Conder produced this quick and animated sketch, a kind of manifesto of what the painters were hoping to achieve by a direct engagement with the local landscape and by the application of paint in immediate and unpremeditated response to visual stimuli. Conder gave this sketch to another artist working with the group, Walter Withers, as if to underline that their endeavours there were a shared and mutually sustaining pursuit. Leaving Australia in April 1890, Conder never returned. CR

Cat. 19
**Arthur Streeton** (1867–1943)
*'Still glides the stream, and shall for ever glide'*, 1890
Oil on canvas, 82.6 × 153 cm
Art Gallery of New South Wales, Sydney

Purchased 1890 (Accession No. 859)

Depicting Melbourne's Yarra River at dusk, this painting's title was drawn from William Wordsworth's *River Duddon Sonnets*. Wordsworth imagined his subject as a 'glistering snake', and Streeton's silver river achieves a similarly serpentine quality as it winds towards the distant Dandenong Ranges. While its handling suggests the style of Corot, whose work Streeton had admired in reproduction, the scene still records the particulars of the Heidelberg topography. Streeton even repainted the foreground when it was alleged that its grass did not sufficiently resemble local species. The dense vegetation in the middle distance marks the Bolin Bolin Billabong, a small oxbow lake that was an important gathering place for the local Wurundjeri people. The Yarra's name was itself a mistranslation of an indigenous word for 'ever-flowing', and Streeton's landscape (like Wordsworth's poem) presents a romantic paean to the timeless cycles of nature – even if these pastures were only cleared 50 years earlier. AJT

Cat. 20
**Arthur Streeton** (1867–1943)
*'The purple noon's transparent might'*, 1896
Oil on canvas, 123 × 123 cm
National Gallery of Victoria, Melbourne

Purchased, 1896 (Accession No. 33-2)

Using a line from a Percy Bysshe Shelley poem to suggest the strong, clear heat of the midday sun, this muscular Hawkesbury River scene seems barely contained by its bold square format. The picture's compositional sweep leads the eye up the sapphire torrent and around to a glimpse of the next reach of river, and then back across the fertile land with signs of agricultural productivity – farmhouses, cattle and a windmill – that dot the summer landscape. The golden fields on the left suggest the maize planted on the Richmond lowlands, whose frequent flooding is hinted at by the river's turbulent sand banks. Of his time in this area of New South Wales, Streeton recalled that the 'glory of river and plain spread before me', and this work's elevated perspective bolsters its sense of visibility and possession. Exhibited at London's Grafton Gallery in 1898, Streeton's vista was indeed described by one local critic as a 'record of imperial tracts' in which the 'remotest distances seem almost in touch'. AJT

Cat. 21
**Arthur Streeton** (1867–1943)
*Golden Summer, Eaglemont*, 1889
Oil on canvas, 81.3 × 152.6 cm
National Gallery of Australia, Canberra

Purchased 1995 (Accession No. NGA 95.634)

'The wind seems sunburnt and fiery as it runs through my beard,' recalled Streeton of his time painting in Eaglemont, in a typically intimate letter to Roberts. The intense currents of summer heat are palpable in Streeton's squally, smeared handling of the sun-drenched hill, his dry brushwork emphasising the parched conditions. A shepherd boy and his flock may strike a sentimental note, but they also support Streeton's designation of the picture as a 'pastoral' scene – personifying the ideals of youthful self-sufficiency so prevalent amid the centenary celebrations of 1888. Streeton's ambitious canvas was exhibited at the Royal Academy in 1891 (under the title of *Golden Summer, Australia,* suggesting the national status that this painting would indeed acquire) and at the Paris Salon in 1892. The work may record the landscape of Melbourne's soon-to-be subdivided suburban fringe, but the picture did eventually make its way to sheep country: in 1924, the work was bought for the homestead of a grazier. AJT

Cat. 22
**Tom Roberts** (1856–1931)
*A Break Away!*, 1891
Oil on canvas, 137.3 × 167.8 cm
Art Gallery of South Australia, Adelaide

Elder Bequest Fund 1899 (Accession No. 0.139)

In *A Break Away!*, a lunging horseman attempts to control a mob of bolting sheep as they dash towards a waterhole in the Riverina district of New South Wales. Dense billows of dust cut across the sharp realism of Roberts's rider, almost subsuming a second horseman, and emphasising the high speed (and high stakes) of the picture's action. The dramatic episode corresponds with the kind of black and white illustrations and 'bush ballads' by which a burgeoning popular press was developing a national imagery of hardworking men struggling to tame the land, even if the majority of Australians already lived in cities. In a small but deliberate detail on the tree on the left of the composition, Roberts depicts the gum to have been 'ring barked' – the technique by which native trees were removed to promote grass growth, causing great swathes of fertile land to turn to dust during the droughts of the 1880s. AJT

Cat. 23
**Arthur Streeton** (1867–1943)
*Fire's On*, 1891
Oil on canvas, 183.8 × 122.5 cm
Art Gallery of New South Wales, Sydney

Purchased 1893 (Accession No. 832)

As well as depicting the dramatic terrain of the Blue Mountains, *Fire's On* also records a more human drama. Streeton painted his scene as a new tunnel was being blasted through the mountain at Lapstone, west of Sydney, to replace the slow and perilous network of zig-zag railway crossings. As one worker yelled 'Fire's On' to warn of each dynamite explosion, Streeton described in a letter to artist Frederick McCubbin, 'all the men drop their tools and scatter... A deep hush is everywhere – then... what a boom of thunder shakes the rock and me.' It was dangerous work, and after several days painting the site, Streeton witnessed the death of the young 'navvy' Edward Brown. 'I was only speaking to him yesterday', the shaken artist wrote to Roberts that evening. In *Fire's On,* his body is taken out on a stretcher, the tragedy framed by a solemn square of crimson and black (see pp. 23–4). AJT

Cat. 24
**Tom Roberts** (1856–1931)
*Holiday Sketch at Coogee*, 1888
Oil on canvas, 40.3 × 55.9 cm
Art Gallery of New South Wales, Sydney

Purchased 1954 (Accession No. 9078)

With the mirrored curve of its two hills, and its tall tree positioned according to the classic 'rule of thirds', *Holiday Sketch at Coogee* is a carefully composed picturesque scene. Roberts's heavy sky in warm grey helps accentuate the jewel-like intensity of the Pacific Ocean, its deep cerulean blue softening as it reaches the impasto white crest of the breaking surf. Roberts painted the popular beach on a day trip with Conder in April 1888, and the naming of this work as a 'holiday' sketch as much describes his own brief visit to Sydney, as it does the swarms of sightseers he depicts buzzing along the shore. A quick trip from the city by tram, the popular leisure spot had become especially busy since the opening of the Coogee Palace Aquarium in December 1887, luring tourists with its swimming baths, skating arena, toboggan rides and ever-changing program of displays and concerts. AJT

Cat. 25
**Charles Conder** (1868–1909)
*Coogee Bay*, 1888
Oil on cardboard, 26.8 × 40.7 cm
National Gallery of Victoria, Melbourne

Purchased with the assistance of a special grant from the Government of Victoria, 1979 (Accession No. A41-1980)

Eschewing Roberts's darker, naturalist tones, Conder adopts a more delicate palette of high-keyed pastels for his depiction of Coogee Bay. Diffuse foliage and softer colour suggest the kinds of techniques that the young artist learnt in Julian Ashton's 'sketch club', working alongside accomplished watercolourists such as Benjamin Minns, with whom he briefly shared a studio. In taking Roberts to Coogee, Conder selected a site he knew well: in late 1887, he had produced black and white vignettes of the popular beach for the *Illustrated Sydney News*. Although his emphasis here is colour rather than line, one can detect something of the whiplash curves of his later *art nouveau* illustrations – such as his cover design for the 9 by 5 exhibition catalogue – in his treatment of the central windswept tree, its boughs further tortured by a frolicking child. A small figure profiled against an umbrella on the beach strikes an equally fashionable *japonisme* note. AJT

Cat. 26
**Arthur Streeton** (1867–1943)
*Sirius Cove*, about 1895
Oil on wood panel, 68.8 × 16.8 cm
National Gallery of Australia, Canberra

Purchased 1973 (Accession No. NGA 73.1)

The National Gallery in Streeton's native Victoria collected Asian art from the year of his birth, 1867. He grew up with it. He would have been open to the news friends like Tom Roberts brought back from overseas that Asian, particularly Japanese, influence was sweeping the European avant-garde. The Australian Mortimer Menpes would exhibit his charming exercises in *japoniserie* soon after. The oil sketches Streeton and his Melbourne friends painted from the second half of the 1880s, like his own *Hoddle St., 10 pm* (cat. 6) or Conder's *Riddells Creek* (cat. 7), often employed exaggeratedly horizontal or vertical formats distantly indebted to precedents in Asian painting. Streeton relocated to Sydney late in 1892, soon joining Roberts at Curlew Camp, Sirius Cove. This view of the tranquil site pushes *japonisme* further still; as with a Japanese hanging scroll, deep space is daringly established by rock piled upon rock upon hillside, one atop another. They intersect with limpid blue water the junction creating a jagged, almost calligraphic line, full of nervous energy, running the height of the panel. CR

Cat. 27
**Arthur Streeton** (1867–1943)
*Blue Pacific*, 1890
Oil on canvas, 91.4 × 50.8 cm

On loan to the National Gallery from a private collection (L1177)

Writing to Roberts in 1890, shortly after arriving in Sydney for the first time, Streeton described his experience of painting a picture, perhaps even this one, at Coogee: 'Worked in the morning at an upright canvas. The ocean is a big wonder Bulldog [Roberts's nickname]!... You're made to clutch the rocks & be delighted, a dreadful heaving & soft eternity.' In choosing Coogee as one of his first Sydney subjects, Streeton was nostalgically retracing the steps of Roberts and Conder, who had painted side-by-side on this headland two years earlier (see cats 24 and 25). Here, Streeton has ventured slightly north, around the coastline, selecting a vantage point that obscures the beach in favour of the golden sandstone cliffs silhouetted against the ocean. A flicker of paint suggests a small figure perched on an overhang at the centre-left of the scene, introducing a sense of the sublime Streeton so revelled in at Coogee. AG

Cat. 28
**Tom Roberts** (1856–1931)
*The Camp, Sirius Cove*, 1899
Oil on canvas on paperboard, 25.4 × 34.6 cm
Art Gallery of New South Wales, Sydney

Purchased 1940 (Accession No. 6928)

Bucolic Sirius Cove looks now much as it did then. Today, however, a visitor turning 90 degrees to the right confronts across the noisy harbour the soaring skyscrapers of central Sydney. In the 1890s Roberts and his companions reached the relative seclusion of Sirius Cove easily. They merely rowed across from town and turned Curlew Camp into a rustic artists' colony where they painted out-of-doors, roughed it in tents, and slipped home for dinner parties. The tranquility and easy-going charm of the place inspired Roberts to one of his most beguiling small-scale masterpieces, a work of limpid freshness and simplicity. The composition could not be more straightforward: a band of water, a wedge of densely wooded hillside slanting down from the left and a countervailing bank of clouds moving in from the right. A pure white sailing boat floats on the still water – perfect innocence. Roberts added to this a sparking sense of high summer sunlight to evoke an Eden thrillingly close at hand. CR

Cat. 29
**Arthur Streeton** (1867–1943)
*Ariadne*, 1895
Oil on wood panel, 12.7 × 35.4 cm
National Gallery of Australia, Canberra

Members Acquisition Fund 2016
(Accession No. NGA 2015.1124)

The subject of the Greek goddess, Ariadne, occupied Streeton around the turn of the century, though perhaps nowhere with such exquisite results as in this panel, depicting the heroine at the moment when her lover Theseus, denoted by a sailboat piercing the horizon, abandons her on the island of Naxos. This quintessential beach landscape, trees almost dissolving in the glare of the sun and waves softly unfurling across the horizontal panel, strikes a Symbolist note, Ariadne's drapery fusing with the white-hot sand. Writing from his studio in London's Chelsea, not long after his arrival some two years later, a 'pale and melancholy' (read 'homesick') Streeton reported to a friend: 'Have just commenced a little decorative picture of Ariadne .. she shall have a lovely background of gum trees and quiet harbour water.' The fact that Streeton was re-imagining a distinctly Australian Ariadne despite all London had to offer suggests the notion, popular among some Australian Impressionists, of their home as a new Arcadia. AG

Cat. 30
**Arthur Streeton** (1867–1943)
*Circular Quay*, 1892
Oil on wood panel, 19.3 × 47.6 cm
National Gallery of Australia, Canberra

Purchased 1959 (Accession No. NGA 59.222)

'Circular Quay with many steamers busy & bright – towering behind are Metropole [Hotel] and Morts [warehouse] & beautiful Sydney all glowing and oriental – little steamers puffing hard & skipping over the blue water,' was how Streeton described this location in an 1891 letter to his patron, Theodore Fink. A year later, Streeton realised such impressions in this vivid scene of harbourside bustle, with broad horizontal brushstrokes and an elongated format emphasising the panoramic spectacle. Describing the work in a letter to the artist Frederick McCubbin, Streeton noted that Circular Quay looked 'like Venice', an idea buoyed perhaps by the grand Neo-Renaissance architecture of Mort and Co.'s woolshed, included in the upper right-hand corner of this panel. Critics somehow picked up on Streeton's Venetian fantasy: when this painting was exhibited in Melbourne the following year, one critic thought the broad dockside to be 'almost St Mark's', a scene 'one would mistake for a bit of Venice'. AJT

Cat. 31
**Charles Conder** (1868–1909)
*A Holiday at Mentone*, 1888
Oil on canvas, 46.2 × 60.8 cm
Art Gallery of South Australia, Adelaide

South Australian Government Grant with the assistance of Bond Corporation Holdings Limited through the Art Gallery of South Australia Foundation to mark the Gallery's Centenary 1981 (Accession No. 815P14)

Keen to make a splash on the Victorian art scene, Conder put his hand to that most fashionable of motifs, favoured by Whistler, the French Impressionists, and a staple of the woodcuts of Hokusai and Hiroshige: the bridge. Conder had seen Roberts's *Winter Morning after Rain, Gardiner's Creek* (cat. 16) in his studio, and like that work, Conder's is a kaleidoscope of smaller compositions folded into the primary one, the background served up into individual landscapes by the framework of the boardwalk bridge leading to the baths at Mentone, near Melbourne. A true artefact of plein-air painting, grains of sand have been trapped in the paint, and yet Conder's eye for the decorative is all pervasive, from the fine red striations used to pick out the stripes and contours of the ladies' dresses, to the dotted lines – one larger and in grey blue, the other smaller and in black – that articulate the shadows cast by the planks along the boardwalk. All these details give the picture a clarity that enhances its midday, springtime luminosity – a luminosity so intense as to render the suit of the gentleman on the bridge almost transparent with its glare. AG

Cat. 32
**John Russell** (1858–1930)
*Madame Sisley on the Banks of the Loing at Moret*, 1887
Oil on canvas, 45.7 × 60.9 cm
Art Gallery of New South Wales, Sydney

Purchased with assistance from the Margaret Hannah Olley Art Trust 1996
(Accession No. 768.1996)

Russell's painting of Madame Sisley at Moret-sur-Loing, south of Paris, is one of his first forays into Impressionism. The highly keyed colour, loose and obvious multi-directional brushstrokes and the unusual composition all betray his recent interest in Impressionist painting, fostered by observing Monet paint on Belle-Île in 1886. Russell travelled to Moret-sur-Loing in October 1887, writing to Roberts that he was going to 'have a slap at the autumn colour'. He is likely to have stayed with his friend American artist Dodge McKnight who lived near the English born Impressionist Alfred Sisley. Russell has depicted Sisley's companion Eugénie Lescouezec, known as Madame Sisley though they did not marry until 1897, reading a letter in the landscape near the river banks with white limestone cliffs in the background, while a woman enters the view from the left carrying washing. The unusual placement and cropping of the figures betrays the influence of Japanese prints and the work of Edgar Degas. WT

Cat. 33
**John Russell** (1858–1930)
*In the Morning, Alpes Maritimes from Antibes*, 1890–1
Oil on canvas, 60.3 × 73.2 cm
National Gallery of Australia, Canberra

Purchased 1965 (Accession No. NGA 65.25)

If on the isolated island of Belle-Île Russell confronted pounding waves, extravagant natural formations like the needles of rock that jut menacingly from the rolling ocean (cat. 37), and a still-primitive society, it was not the same at Antibes. He was following Monet's lead in heading south to the Mediterranean but what he found there was tranquility and a chic and worldly resort newly popular with wealthy tourists. The sophisticated and superficial Parisians he had fled from to Brittany in 1888 were thick on the ground. He didn't much like it but nonetheless saw in the conjunction of water, exotic foliage and the distant peaks of the Alpes Maritimes rich possibilities for picture-making. The composition here is simple: foreground grasses and cacti, limpid blue sea, purple hills and snow-capped peaks line up in horizontal striations across the canvas. Only the top sixth is given over to sky. Suffused in sunlight, the colours are muted, pastel, but the aerial perspective – the suggestion of depth and distance achieved by tonal modulation – is masterfully achieved. CR

Cat. 34
**John Russell** (1858–1930)
*Les Terrasses de Monte Cassino*, about 1889
Oil on canvas, 65 × 81 cm
Private Collection courtesy
of Nevill Keating Pictures

Known as a view of the Italian countryside near Cassino and thought to have been painted on a trip Russell and his wife Marianna took there to visit her family in 1889, this painting likewise recalls the landscape near Antibes, framed by the Alpes Maritimes, which Russell visited for the first time in 1890–1. Either way, Russell's attraction to the unmistakable Mediterranean light is palpable, and it is no coincidence that this period coincided with a turning point in Russell's work characterised by bold chromatic experimentation. Shocking pinks and shimmering turquoise vibrate here with golden yellow and rich emerald in an almost Symbolist construction of the landscape. Russell's approach to evoking the dry, sun-bleached Mediterranean landscape through intense, pure colour makes an instructive comparison with the 'glare aesthetic' favoured by Streeton and Roberts at the same moment in time in their rendering of the Australian light (see p. 22). AG

Cat. 35
**John Russell** (1858–1930)
*A Clearing in the Forest*, 1891
Oil on canvas, 61 × 55.9 cm
Art Gallery of South Australia, Adelaide

A.M. & A.R. Ragless Bequest Funds 1968
(Accession No. 6812P17)

Russell here references key components of painterly Modernism as practised by his French contemporaries; the use of an almost-square canvas – the format neatly signals that everything is of equal pictorial value – a high horizon line, evident brushwork and, most important, broad areas of intense, almost artificial colour. As he moved on from academic training and, under the influence of Monet, increasingly allowed himself to experiment, he also wanted to understand exactly how, technically, he achieved the surprising effects he did. He explained to Roberts back in Australia that his idol Monet spent countless sittings perfecting his paintings as if to underline that the path he was now on was not an easy one. Streeton, for one, was unimpressed remarking that Russell seemed 'to bother too much about the ways and means'. And yet, it was in works such as this unprepossessing forest scene, executed at Antibes but with senses finely attuned to developments in Paris, that Russell achieved a breakthrough that for a decade put him at the forefront of formal developments in avant-garde painting. CR

Cat. 36
**John Russell** (1858–1930)
*Antibes*, about 1890–2
Oil on canvas, 16.5 × 24 cm
Art Gallery of New South Wales, Sydney

Gift of the Margaret Hannah Olley Art Trust 2012
(Accession No. 190.2012)

Russell's paintings of Antibes are usually highly worked, painted over several sessions and showing great attention to layered colour and interwoven brushwork. Surprisingly Russell concurrently painted a group of highly experimental small oils. While their size and freely painted nature suggests they could be studies, they do not relate to any known finished paintings and are in themselves dazzling exercises in colour painting. The subject of *Antibes* is a familiar view of the old town with the Alpes Maritimes behind; what was unfamiliar at this time was the highly expressive broad brushstrokes of pure colour almost entirely freed from depicting naturalistic form. Russell has chosen brightly coloured pigments including the intense cadmium yellow, emerald green, cobalt violet and lead white that are the focus of this painting. It is in such highly expressive and individual works as this that Russell's subsequent influence on Matisse later in the decade can be discerned, seeding the colour experimentation in Matisse's art that culminated in his Fauve canvases in the new century. WT

Cat. 37
**John Russell** (1858–1930)
*Aiguille de Coton, Belle-Île*, about 1900
Oil on canvas, 60.8 × 50.5 cm
Kerry Stokes Collection, Perth

(Accession No. 1992.043)

Framed in portrait format and with the horizon line pushed right up to the top of the canvas, this unconventional seascape evokes the vertiginous cliffs upon which Russell precariously positioned himself to paint the iconic Port-Coton needles, and records something of the derring-do that he embodied in his highly personal engagement with the Belle-Île coastline. In the tangled zig-zags of teals, violets, indigos and flashes of pure white, Russell brings a lyricism to his depiction of the rocky outcrops reflected in the rolling sea. The hurried strokes with which Russell has built up the tones – smaller and tighter on the rocks, broader and more loose in the sea – evokes a sense of glittering sunlight dancing on the water and of the surge of the swell reverberating in the shadows of the needles. AG

Cat. 38
**John Russell** (1858–1930)
*Coucher de Soleil sur Morestil*, about 1904
Oil on hessian, 80.6 × 100.3 cm
Private collection, Switzerland

This painting, one of Russell's largest, is ambitious not only in scale, but in technique. With its alternating passages of chromatic harmony and dissonance created through heavily layered pure colour, this is Russell in full force as a colourist, combined here with a vigorous exploration of the physical qualities of the medium of paint. Switching between short, punchy strokes of the brush and lashes of the palette knife as he moves across the canvas, Russell then scratches back into the paint with the hard end of the brush to build up an almost sculptural evocation of the solidity of the rocky cliffs. This is set off by the longer, more lyrical swirls of the brush with which the choppy sea is rendered, topped with rough pats of white that capture the foam as the waves crash against the coastline. AG

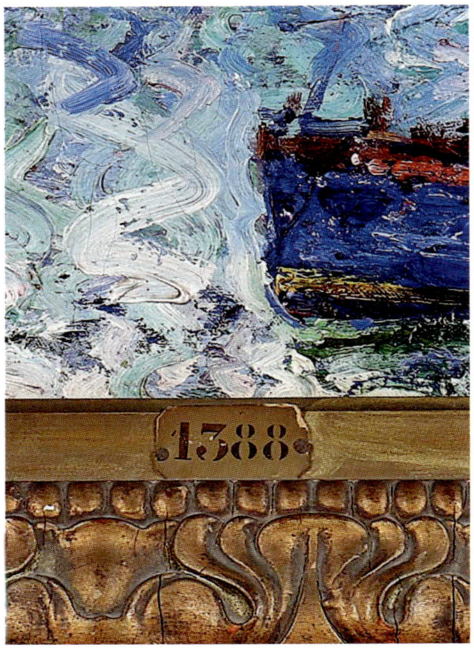

Fig. 40
Exhibition ticket, attached to centre of the frame, lower edge, of cat. 41

Cat. 39
**John Russell** (1858–1930)
*Rough Sea, Belle-Île*, 1900
Oil on canvas, 63.2 × 63.1 cm
National Gallery of Victoria, Melbourne

The Joseph Brown Collection. Presented through the NGV Foundation by Dr Joseph Brown AO OBE, Honorary Life Benefactor, 2004 (Accession No. 2004.217)

Foreign artists in London flocked to the National Gallery to see the paintings of J.M.W. Turner which had come to the nation by bequest in 1851. Russell certainly would have seen them during his four years there in the 1880s, just as Monet had done in 1870 and 1871 and was doing so again on his painting trips to London in 1899, 1900 and 1901. By then it was Turner's late, indistinct and highly atmospheric land and seascapes, skeins of muted colour washed across the canvas, which particularly intrigued him. Russell too might have been thinking about such works when he painted this view of pounding waves along the rocky coast at Belle-Île. Turner offered a precedent for the thrillingly free and improvisatory manner of painting here, which flirts with the very limits of representation, and a way for a daring young artist like Russell to think through the aesthetic potential of what, in a letter to Rodin of 1903, he called the 'terrible...fury of the sea... the diabolical noise'. CR

Cat. 40
**John Russell** (1858–1930),
*Rough Sea, Morestil*, about 1900
Oil on canvas on hardboard, 66 × 81.8 cm
Art Gallery of New South Wales, Sydney

Purchased 1968 (Accession No. OA14.1968)

Early in the new century Russell wrote to his friend Auguste Rodin saying that after 15 years of studying the Belle-Île coastline he had found a sheltered spot from which he could paint the ferocious storms that periodically battered the island. He continued: 'The fury of the sea has visited terrible weather upon us at the moment... Not without danger, certainly, the noise is diabolical and extraordinary and hard to get used to. This morning there was, near me, a whirlwind of foam, like big snowflakes, that rose up a good 80 feet. But the poor painter is no match.' Despite his hesitation in confidence, Russell captured in rhythmic form the ever-changing phenomena of wind and waves sweeping onto the coastline in a series of paintings that are amongst his most energetic and expressive. *Rough Sea, Morestil* shows an interest in extreme dynamism that characterised some avant-garde painting in the early twentieth century, though Russell continued to focus on natural subjects rather than the mechanistic city that was embraced later by modernist painters. WT

Cat. 41
**John Russell** (1858–1930)
*Cruach en Mahr, Matin, Belle-Île-en-Mer*, about 1905
Oil on canvas, 60.4 × 73.5 cm
Private Collection courtesy of Nevill Keating Pictures

With his complex layering of intense, contrasting colour, veiled with the dominant key of electric blue, Russell revels in exploring the dense chromatic modulations of shadow in this view of the coastline of Port-Goulphar not yet fully illuminated by the rising sun. Russell himself surely recognised the significance of this work, as it is one of only a relatively small number that he chose to exhibit publicly (fig. 40) during his lifetime. The catalogue number '1388' still attached to the frame is a record of its place in the Salon d'Automne of 1905; it was in response to the audacious colouring adopted by artists in this exhibition such as Henri Matisse, André Derain and Maurice de Vlaminck that the term 'Fauvist' was coined. This was fitting company and testament to Russell's place among the most daring and talented colourists of his day. AG

# BIOGRAPHIES

**Charles Conder** (London 1868–1909 Surrey)

Following a childhood spent in India and then in Eastbourne, the 15-year-old Conder arrived in Sydney in 1884, apprenticed to his uncle, the Chief Trigonometrical Surveyor of New South Wales. Conder's father had hoped that this would distract his son from his artistic ambitions, but by 1886 Conder was working as a lithographer with a local publisher and contributing drawings to the *Illustrated Sydney News*. He immersed himself in the local art scene and was elected to the newly founded Art Society of New South Wales. He sought tutelage from prominent local plein-air painters, Julian Ashton (1851–1942) and Alfred Daplyn (1844–1926). In 1888 the Art Gallery of New South Wales acquired his *Departure of the Orient* (cat. 11). Having already met Roberts when he visited Sydney in early 1888, Conder moved to Melbourne later that year, initially sharing Roberts's studio. Conder was soon drawn to Europe, however, and in 1890 departed for Paris, never to return to Australia. He became a prominent figure in Anglo-French fin-de-siècle circles, associating with Henri de Toulouse-Lautrec, Aubrey Beardsley and Oscar Wilde. Conder suffered from ill-health for much of his adult life, and died aged 40 in a sanatorium in Surrey.

**Tom Roberts** (Dorchester, England 1856–1931 Kallista, VIC, Australia)

Roberts migrated to Melbourne with his family as a teenager. He juggled work as a photographer's assistant with studies at the National Gallery School in Melbourne, before returning to London in 1881 and enrolling at the Royal Academy Schools. During the summer of 1883 Roberts travelled around south-west France and Spain with John Russell. In Spain he started experimenting with plein air painting, and on returning to Melbourne in 1885, Roberts championed this approach to landscape art, becoming a figurehead for Australian Impressionism. During the 1880s and 1890s Roberts's large-scale compositions met with a mixed reaction from the Melbourne artistic establishment, but he enjoyed success as a portrait painter, culminating in his 1901 commission to depict the ceremony of Federation (a painting now at Parliament House, Canberra). This monumental canvas was completed in London, where Roberts lived from 1903 to 1923, serving as a hospital orderly during the First World War.

**John Russell** (Sydney 1858–1930 Sydney)

John Russell was born and died in Sydney, but spent some 40 years as an expatriate in Europe, closely connected to the avant-garde. Having come into a substantial inheritance, in 1881 he enrolled in art school in London before continuing his studies in Paris alongside Henri de Toulouse-Lautrec and Vincent van Gogh, who remained a close friend until his death in 1890. Russell settled on Belle-Île with his first wife Marianna Mattiocco, whose features Auguste Rodin later used in numerous sculptures. On a previous trip to the island he had encountered and befriended Claude Monet, observing Monet at work and learning his techniques. Henri Matisse visited the island in the second half of the 1890s and Russell, in turn, tutored the young artist in Impressionist technique and colour theory. Russell left Belle-Île following Marianna's death in 1908, and eventually returned to Australia, where he died in relative obscurity. Despite his connections to some of the most important artists of his time, Russell was only rediscovered, as 'Australia's lost impressionist', later in the twentieth century.

**Arthur Streeton** (Mt Duneed, VIC, Australia 1867–1943 Olinda, VIC, Australia)

Streeton's artistic training began at the age of 15, with night classes in design at Melbourne's National Gallery School, while he worked as an office clerk, and later, as an apprentice lithographer. He read amateur painting manuals imported from Europe and America that encouraged painting en plein air. While painting at Mentone Beach, south of Melbourne, Streeton met Tom Roberts, who invited him to join artists' camps Roberts had founded with Frederick McCubbin and Louis Abrahams at Box Hill. Streeton moved to Sydney in 1890, after the Art Gallery of New South Wales purchased *'Still glides the stream, and shall for ever glide'* (cat. 19). He was the first Australian-born artist to have a work exhibited at the Royal Academy (*Golden Summer, Eaglemont*, cat. 21, in 1891), but when he moved to London in 1897 he struggled to gain recognition. Nonetheless, he stayed in England for around thirty years, sending work back to Australia. During the First World War he served as a hospital orderly alongside Roberts, and then as an official war artist with the Australian Army. He was awarded a knighthood in 1937, by which point he had become a pillar of the Australian art establishment.

# Notes

## AUSTRALIA'S IMPRESSIONISTS IN A WORLD CONTEXT

Christopher Riopelle

1. A month before the 9 by 5 Impression Exhibition opened in August 1889, the newspaper *Table Talk* reported that preparation 'is now occupying the attention of our artists, more particularly of Mr Tom Roberts, Mr Streeton and Mr Conder, who are the leaders of the movement. The exhibition will be held in early August at an Art Gallery, not as formerly intended in Mr Roberts's studio, for the affair has grown on their hands, and the promoters feel themselves justified in making it an artistic event, seeing that it is the first exhibition of its kind that has ever been held in Australia.' *Table Talk,* 19 July 1889, p. 5: http://trove.nla.gov.au/newspaper article/146022934
2. Canberra 2015, cat. 10, p. 133.
3. The most cogent analysis of the portrait, its role in Russell's career and in Australian art, is Galbally and Slogget 1997, pp. 7–18.
4. Russell's letter to Tom Roberts of December 1887 is quoted in Galbally and Slogget 1997, p. 11.
5. Russell's letter to Vincent van Gogh of Sunday, 22 July 1888. *Vincent van Gogh: The Letters,* no. 647: http://vangoghletters.org/vg/letters/let647/letter.html
6. For a study of the role the French capital played in shaping one group of foreign artists, see K. Adler et al., *Americans in Paris 1860–1900,* exh. cat., London (National Gallery) 2006.
7. The most complete study of the international spread of Impressionist painting remains Broude 1990.
8. See A.R. Josse, 'Akseli Gallen-Kallela: In the Wake of Dream and Reality' in S. Pagé and B. Parent (eds), *Keys to a Passion,* Paris (Fondation Louis Vuitton), 2015, pp. 88–96.
9. D. Jackson and P. Wageman, *Russian Landscape,* exh. cat., Groningen (Groninger Museum) and London (National Gallery) 2003.
10. S. Fraquelli et al., *Radical Light: Italy's Divisionist Painters 1891–1910*, exh. cat., London (National Gallery) 2008.
11. C. Riopelle, *Forests, Rocks, Torrents: Norwegian and Swiss Landscapes in the Lunde Collection,* exh. cat., London (National Gallery) 2011.
12. The National Gallery's early investigations into American painting have been, and continue to be, supported by its on-going collaboration with the Terra Foundation for American Art. The National Gallery acquired Bellows's *Men of the Docks* of 1912 in 2014 (NG 6649).
13. Galbally 1977.
14. Russell and his relations with the French avant-garde are the subject of a major forthcoming exhibition at the Art Gallery of New South Wales, Sydney; O'Conor and his relations with the French avant-garde are the subject of a major forthcoming exhibition at the National Gallery of Ireland, Dublin; Morrice and his relations with the French avant-garde are the subject of a major forthcoming exhibition at the National Gallery of Canada, Ottawa.

## THE SUNNY SOUTH

Tim Bonyhady

1. Galbally and Gray 1989, p. 17.
2. Galbally and Gray 1989, p. 17.
3. Galbally and Gray 1989, p. 17.
4. Eagle 1994, pp. 60–1.
5. Eagle 1994, p. 62.
6. 11 August 1900.
7. *Argus*, 26 July 1890, p. 13.
8. Eagle 1997, p. 23, p. 121.
9. Bonyhady 1985, ch. 2–4.
10. Broomfield 1889, p. 887.
11. 'Art', *Melbourne University Review,* May 1890, p. 83. See also Bonyhady 1985, pp. 148–53.
12. *Australasian,* 12 December 1896, p. 33.
13. *Sydney Morning Herald,* 22 November 1919, p. 8.
14. M. Quick, *American Expatriate Painters of the Late Nineteenth Century,* Dayton (Dayton Art Institute) 1976, pp. 24–5; W.H. Gerdts, *American Impressionism,* Seattle (Henry Art Gallery) 1980, pp. 17–19; W.H. Gerdts, *American Impressionism,* New York 1984, pp. 17–21, 309.
15. McQueen 2009, p. 25.
16. D. Thomas, 'In the Burning Fiery Furnace: Streeton's *Fire's On* 1891', in *Artlink,* vol. 33, 2013, no. 4, p. 51.
17. A remarkable piece of sleuthing by David Hansen. See his 'National Naturalism' in Melbourne 2007, pp. 286, 311, n. 33.
18. Virginia Spate, 'The Sunny South: Australian Impressionism', in Broude 1990, p. 123.
19. *Smike to Bulldog: Letters from Sir Arthur Streeton to Tom Roberts,* ed. R.H. Croll, Sydney 1946, p. 21; Galbally and Gray 1989, pp. 36–41.
20. O. Comettant, *In the Land of the Kangaroos and Gold Mines,* Adelaide 1980, pp. 135–6.
21. Broomfield 1889, p. 883.
22. *Argus,* 3 September 1889, p. 7.
23. Quoted by M. Eagle, 'Friendly Rivalry: Paintings of Waterside Sydney 1888 and 1890', p. 103, in Melbourne 2007.
24. Both quoted by Moore 1934, vol. 1, pp. 93–4.
25. Moore 1934, vol. 1, p. 94.
26. 'The Art of David Davies', *Age*, 13 May 1926, p. 12; A. Streeton, 'Eaglemont in the Eighties', *Argus,* 16 October 1934, p. 49. See also *Advertiser* (Hurstbridge), 2 November 1934, p. 2.
27. *Argus,* Weekend Magazine, 11 August 1945, p. 11; *West Australian,* 1 September 1945, p. 3; *Age,* 2 August 1947, p. 10; *Courier-Mail,* 19 January 1948, p. 4; *News*, 14 May 1948, p. 4.
28. Thomas 1973, p. 28. In 1888, Roberts, McCubbin and Streeton were characterised as the 'Box Hill School'. See *Daily Telegraph,* 1 May 1888, p. 3.
29. McQueen 1996, p. 352.
30. B. Smith, 'New Light on Old Light: Impressionism and the Gold Summers Exhibition', in *Age Monthly Review,* vol. 5, no. 8 (December 1985–January 1986), p. 27.
31. Quoted by Lane, in his 'Introduction', p. 14, in Melbourne 2007.
32. D. Hansen, 'National Naturalism', p. 283, in Melbourne 2007.
33. Quoted by McQueen 1996, p. 235.
34. Galbally and Gray 1989, p. 30.
35. Galbally 2008, p. 224.
36. See T. Bonyhady, 'German Melbourne: Artists, Scientists, Explorers', in *Australische Impressionen: Landschaftsmalerei aus hundert Jahren,* ed. H. Gerke, Heidelberg 1987, pp. 18–33.
37. D. Thomas, 'The Sunny South: Bayside Melbourne Life and Landscape, 1886–1890', p. 87, in Melbourne 2007.
38. A. Mackenzie, *Frederick McCubbin 1855–1917: 'The Proff' and his Art,* Melbourne 1990, pp. 64, 72.
39. Melbourne 1995, p. 94; Thomas 1991, p. 50.
40. Eagle 1997, pp. 58–64.
41. *Evening News,* 15 August 1896, p. 5.
42. Eagle 1994, p. 60.
43. Smith 1945, p. 18.
44. Christie's, London, 26 September 2013, lots 13–18, 22; Christie's, London, 24 September 2015, lots 3–5. See also McQueen 1996, pp. 326, 604.
45. G. Vaughan, 'Earning a Living: Roberts's Patronage and the Australian Art Market', p. 62, in Canberra 2015.

## THE 9 BY 5 IMPRESSION EXHIBITION

Allison Goudie

1. *Melbourne Punch,* 9 May 1889, p. 11.
2. *Table Talk,* 27 April 1888, p. 12. On Grosvenor Chambers, see A. Taylor, *Perils of the Studio: Inside the artistic affairs of bohemian Melbourne*, Melbourne 2007.
3. *Melbourne Punch,* 9 May 1889, p. 11.
4. Canberra 2015, no. 32, p. 157; L. Astbury, 'Around the Studios: Girolamo Nerli "The Sitting"', p. 67, in Brisbane 1998.
5. A. Inglis, 'Aestheticism and Empire: The Grosvenor Gallery Intercolonial Exhibition in Melbourne, 1887', in K. Darian-Smith et al. (eds), *Seize the Day: Exhibitions, Australia and the World*, Melbourne 2008.
6. Astbury 1989, p. 34.
7. *Argus*, 26 April 1888, p. 4.
8. *Melbourne Punch,* 9 May 1889, p. 11.
9. *Argus,* 8 August 1885, p. 5.
10. *National Advocate,* 5 November 1889, p. 3.
11. *National Advocate,* 5 November 1889, p. 3.
12. *Melbourne Punch,* 9 May 1889, p. 11.
13. *Melbourne Punch,* 9 May 1889, p. 11. For further contemporary discussion of this idea, see Spate, 'The Sunny South: Australian Impressionism', p. 120, in Broude 1990.
14. *Melbourne Punch,* 9 May 1889, p. 11.
15. *Sydney Morning Herald,* 20 July 1889, p. 7. See also Broude 1990, especially Spate, pp. 119–20, in Broude 1990; see also G. Vaughan, 'Some Reflections on Defining Australian Impressionism', pp. 16–19, in Melbourne 2007.
16. *First annual exhibition of the Anglo-Australian Society of Artists,* Melbourne 1885, no. 1.
17. C. Dixon, R. Radford and L. Ward, *Turner to Monet: The Triumph of Landscape Painting*, exh. cat., Canberra (National Gallery of Australia) 2008, no. 82, p. 216.
18. See A. Robbins, 'Durand-Ruel's Conquest of London', pp. 182–5, in London, Paris and Philadelphia 2015; A. Gray, 'Harmonic Arrangements: Tom Roberts's Painting', p. 34, in Canberra 2015; and Spate, p. 119, in Broude 1990.
19. *Table Talk,* 1 August 1890, p. 15.
20. *Argus,* 11 June 1889, p. 9.
21. Spate, p. 119, in Broude 1990; Bonyhady 1985, p. 144.
22. *Sydney Morning Herald,* 20 July 1889, p. 7.
23. *Table Talk,* 28 June 1889, p. 3.
24. *Table Talk*, 28 June 1889, p. 3.
25. The 9 by 5 Impression Exhibition catalogue, 1889.
26. G. van Rensselaer, 'Corot', *Century Magazine*, vol. 38, no. 2 (June 1889), p. 265; T. Lane 'The 9 by 5 Impression Exhibition – The Challenge of the Sketch', in Melbourne 2007, p. 304, n. 14.
27. *Table Talk*, 22 June 1888, p. 9.
28. K. Cox, in 'Open Letters: American Artists on Gerome', *Century Magazine*, vol. 37, no. 4 (February 1889), p. 635; Bonyhady 1985, p. 144.
29. *Table Talk*, 16 August 1889, p. 6.
30. *Sydney Mail*, 31 August 1889, p. 491.
31. *Daily Telegraph* (Melbourne), 24 August 1889, p. 10.
32. Lane, p. 159, in Melbourne 2007.
33. *Table Talk*, 16 August 1889, p. 6.
34. *Table Talk*, 19 July 1889, p. 5.
35. *Table Talk*, 23 August 1889, p. 4.
36. A. Montana, 'Arabesques of Beauty: Cullis Hill, the 9 by 5 Impression Exhibition, decorative décor and painting', *La Trobe Journal*, no. 93–4 (September 2014), pp. 82–101; A. Galbally, 'Aestheticism in Australia', pp. 132–3, in Bradley and Smith 1980.
37. Spate, 'Sunny South', p. 117. in Broude 1990, p. 117
38. For example, *Table Talk*, 23 August 1889, p. 4.
39. G. Vaughan, 'Earning a Living: Roberts' Patronage and the Australian Art Market', in Canberra 2015, p. 63.
40. *Table Talk*, 23 August 1889, p. 4.
41. *Sydney Mail*, 31 August 1889, p. 491.
42. *Table Talk*, 23 August 1889, p. 4.
43. *Sydney Morning Herald*, 7 October 1889, p. 6.
44. *Table Talk*, 30 August 1889, p. 7.
45. Letter 79, *Fors Clavigera: Letters to the Workmen and Labourers of Great Britain*, Orpington, 1877, vol. 7, p. 201.
46. *Table Talk*, 23 August 1889, p. 4.
47. *Argus*, 17 August 1889, p. 10.
48. *Argus*, 16 October 1934, p. 49.
49. *Argus*, 17 August 1889, p. 10.
50. *Age*, 17 August 1889, p. 15.
51. *Table Talk*, 23 August 1889, p. 4.
52. *Argus*, 3 September 1889, p. 7.
53. *Argus*, 17 August 1889, p. 10.
54. *Argus*, 3 September 1889, p. 7.
55. *Argus*, 4 September 1889, p. 6.
56. J.P. Russell, Letter to T. Roberts, c.1890/91, transcribed in Galbally 1977, pp. 93–4, pp. 93–4.
57. *Sydney Mail*, 31 August 1889, p. 491.
58. See Spate, p. 125, in Broude 1990.
59. *Table Talk*, 16 August 1889, p. 6.

## CREATING A NATIONAL IDENTITY

Sarah Thomas

1. Broude 1990.
2. R.H. Croll, *Tom Roberts: Father of Australian Landscape Painting,* Melbourne 1935.
3. J. Longstaff, 'The Art Classes at the National Gallery', letter to the editor, *The Age,* 16 September 1886, p. 7. See Astbury, p. 51, in Melbourne 2007.
4. 'Tusque', 'The National Gallery: "On the Line,"' *Australian Magazine,* July 1886, p. 138. Cited in Melbourne 2007, p. 311.
5. S. Dickinson, 'What should Australian artists paint?', *The Australasian Critic*, 1 October 1890, p. 22. Reprinted in Smith 1975, pp. 231–2.
6. Astbury, p. 51, in Melbourne 2007.
7. Roberts, cited by E. Taylor, p. 130, in Canberra 2015.
8. J. Ruskin, 'Letter the Seventy-ninth', *Fors Clavigera,* 2 July 1877, pp. 181–213.
9. M. Eagle, 'Friendly Rivalry: Paintings of Waterside Sydney, 1888 and 1890', p. 106, in Melbourne 2007.
10. D. Thomas, 'The Sunny South: Bayside Melbourne Life and Landscape, 1886–90', p. 91, in Melbourne 2007.
11. *Table Talk*, 30 August 1889, in V. Spate, 'Where the Sun Never Set: Tom Roberts and the British Empire' in Adelaide 1996, p. 76.
12. J. Hylton, 'A Break Away!', p. 183, in Canberra 2015.
13. Streeton, letter to Roberts, 'Saturday night, warm, close rather', early 1891, CY REEL 275 A2478 No. 413, Tom Roberts papers, Mitchell Library, State Library of New South Wales, Sydney. Cited by M. Eagle, 'Seeing Templestowe-Heidelberg', in K. Gellatly and T. Gott, *Heidelberg to Heide: Creating an Australian Landscape 1850–1950,* Melbourne 2001, p. 26.
14. The painting inspired what was arguably Australia's first 'homegrown' blockbuster exhibition in 1985, *Golden Summers: Heidelberg and Beyond,* curated by J. Clark and B. Whitelaw.
15. Editorial, *Argus,* 24 August 1895, p. 6; cited in Canberra 2015, p. 40.
16. The exclusion of Aborigines in these 'national pictures' served to confirm one of colonial Australia's founding myths, that of terra nullius (literally, 'land belonging to no-one'), which was enshrined in the 1901 Constitution. For further information see, for example, H. Reynolds, *Dispossession: Black Australians and White Invaders,* Sydney 1996. On the representation of Aborigines in the colonial

art of Australia, see D. Hansen, 'Seeing Truganini', *Australian Book Review,* no. 321, May 2010, pp. 45–53.

17. B. Anderson, *Imagined Communities: Reflections on the Origin and Spread of Nationalism,* London 1983 (revised edn, London 1991).

## JOHN RUSSELL

Wayne Tunnicliffe

1. John Russell letter to Tom Roberts, Antibes, late 1890 or early 1891, Dredge 2001, letter 7.
2. In writing this essay I am indebted to the in-depth research of Ann Galbally, who curated the touring John Russell retrospective exhibition in 1977–8 and authored Galbally 1977 and more recently Galbally 2008; as well as Ursula Prunster's exhibition and co-authored book, Sydney 2001.
3. Legros exhibited 25 etchings in the second Impressionist exhibition in Paris in 1876. While Russell remained enrolled at the Slade for the next three years he maintained active contact with Australian cultural life, returning to exhibit in Sydney in 1883 with some critical success.
4. Legros apparently did not encourage his students to go to Paris, but Russell had moved in Francophile circles in Sydney in the early 1880s and fellow student friends in London such as the sculptor Harry Bates had already moved to Paris.
5. The portrait is inscribed VINCENT AMITIE. Van Gogh wrote to his brother Theo in 1889: 'take good care of my portrait by Russell, which means a lot to me'. Jansen et al. 2009, p. 79, letter 800. For an account of this friendship and their respective development as artists, see Galbally 2008.
6. See p. 44, Galbally 2008.
7. Inevitably with an influx of artists into traditional communities, a nineteenth-century version of gentrification often occurred as tourists arrived soon after.
8. As recounted in a letter from Monet to Alice Hoschedé, 18 September 1886, quoted Sydney 2001, p. 25, translated from D. Wildenstein, *Claude Monet: biographie et catalogue raisonné,* vol II, 1882–6, La Bibliothéque des Arts, Lausanne-Paris, 1979.
9. Russell is likely to have seen the previous Impressionist exhibition in Paris in 1886 as well as visiting dealer galleries to view works by Impressionist artists.
10. This conflict was experienced by art students and artists in the 1880s when both academic and avant-garde developments were vying for allegiance. Quote from Russell to Roberts, Paris, 26 December 1887, Dredge 2001, letter 8.
11. Quote from Russell to Roberts, Paris, 5 October 1887, Dredge 2001, letter 7. This section of the letter continues with a critique of pointillism which had been developed the previous year by Seurat and Signac, exhibited at the 1886 Impressionist exhibition, and had rapidly gained followers: 'Darn fools spotting canvas with small points of pure colour. Tis as fashionable as gulls wings for hats.'
12. Van Gogh encouraged Russell to leave Paris, writing from Arles on 19 April 1888, Jansen et al. 2009, p. 60, letter 598: 'I heartily hope for you that you will be able to leave Paris for good soon and no doubt leaving Paris will do you a world of good in all respects.'
13. Russell rowed, sailed, swam and boxed.
14. John Russell to Vincent van Gogh, Belle-Île-en-Mer, 22 July 1888, Jansen et al. 2009, p. 194, letter 647.
15. John Russell letter to Tom Roberts, Antibes, late 1890 or early 1891, Dredge 2001, letter 9.
16. In this letter Russell cites a pantheon of contemporary artists he admires including Edouard Manet, Degas, Monet, Auguste Rodin, Pierre-Auguste Renoir, Whistler, Camille Pissarro, Paul Gauguin, Armand Guillaumin, Gustave Caillebotte and Louis Anquetin as well as the hero to all factions at that time, Pierre Puvis de Chavannes.
17. Arthur Streeton to Tom Roberts, around 1891, Dredge 2001, after letter 9.
18. John Russell to Tom Roberts, Antibes, early 1891, Dredge 2001, letter 10.
19. *The Times,* London, 30 November 1891, p. 3.
20. Hilary Spurling discusses the importance of Russell's influence on Matisse in the mid-1890s in H. Spurling, *The Unknown Matisse,* New York 1999, ch. 4 and 5, pp. 99–157.
21. Auguste Rodin to John Russell, Paris, 21 May 1904. A. Beausire and F. Cadouot eds, *Correspondance de Rodin,* vol. II, 1900–7, Paris 1986, p. 126.
22. Russell considered his art collection – which included a painting and drawings by Van Gogh, paintings by Emile Bernard and Armand Guillaumin amongst others, and sculpture by Rodin – to be 'in trust for Australia', something he refers to in letters to Roberts, Van Gogh and his brother Percy Russell.
23. Russell's painting was not hanging in the room with the artists to which Vauxcelles applied his derogatory term.
24. In addition to these exhibitions, Russell participated in the *Exposition de la Société internationale d'aquarellistes* at the Galerie Georges Petit in Paris in 1905, 1906 and 1907, exhibiting 12 individual watercolours and over 67 more in portfolios. For Russell's exhibition history see A. Gérard-Austin, 'The greatest voyage: Australian painters in the Paris Salons 1885–1939', unpublished PHD thesis, University of Sydney and Panthéon-Sorbonne, Paris, 2014.

# Selected Bibliography


**Adelaide 1988**
D. Thomas (ed.), *Creating Australia: 200 Years of Art, 1788–1988*, exh. cat., Adelaide (Art Gallery of South Australia) 1988

**Adelaide 1996**
R. Radford (ed.), *Tom Roberts*, exh. cat., Adelaide (Art Gallery of South Australia) 1996

**Astbury 1985**
L. Astbury, *City Bushmen: The Heidelberg School and the Rural Mythology*, Melbourne 1985

**Astbury 1989**
L. Astbury, *Sunlight and Shadow: Australian Impressionist Painters 1880–1900*, Sydney 1989

**Bonyhady 1985**
T. Bonyhady, *Images in Opposition: Australian Landscape Painting 1801–1890*, Melbourne 1985

**Bonyhady 2000**
T. Bonyhady, *The Colonial Earth*, Melbourne 2000

**Bradley and Smith 1980**
A. Bradley and T. Smith, *Australian Art and Architecture: Essays presented to Bernard Smith*, Melbourne 1980

**Brisbane 1998**
L. Seear and J. Ewington (eds), *Brought to Light: Australian Art 1850–1965 from the Queensland Art Gallery Collection*, Brisbane 1998

**Brisbane 2009**
H.B. Weinberg, *American Impressionism & Realism: A Landmark Exhibition from the Met*, exh. cat., Brisbane (Queensland Art Gallery) 2009

**Broomfield 1889**
F.J. Broomfield, 'Art and Artists in Victoria', *Centennial Magazine*, vol. 1, no. 12, July 1889, pp. 883–9

**Broude 1990**
N. Broude (ed.), *World Impressionism: The International Movement 1860–1920*, New York 1990

**Canberra 2015**
A. Gray (ed.), *Tom Roberts*, exh. cat., Canberra (National Gallery of Australia) 2015

**Dredge 2001**
*The Letters of Tom Roberts, vol. 3, Miscellaneous, 1884–1927, MLA2480, Manuscript Collection, Mitchell Library, State Library of New South Wales*, unpublished transcription by P. Dredge, with L. Prunster and A. Thoms, Sydney 2001

**Eagle 1994**
M. Eagle, *The Oil Paintings of Arthur Streeton in the National Gallery of Australia*, Canberra 1994

**Eagle 1997**
M. Eagle, *The Oil Paintings of Tom Roberts in the National Gallery of Australia*, Canberra 1997

**Eagle 1997a**
M. Eagle, *The Oil Paintings of Charles Conder in the National Gallery of Australia*, Canberra 1997

**Galbally 1977**
A. Galbally, *The Art of John Peter Russell*, Melbourne 1977

**Galbally 2002**
A. Galbally, *Charles Conder: The Last Bohemian*, Melbourne 2002

**Galbally 2008**
A. Galbally, *A Remarkable Friendship: Vincent van Gogh and John Peter Russell*, Melbourne 2008

**Galbally 2011**
A. Galbally, 'National life and landscape: the Heidelberg School as mythmaker 1880–1905', in J. Anderson (ed.), *The Cambridge Companion to Australian Art*, Cambridge 2011, pp. 71–83

**Galbally and Gray 1989**
A. Galbally and A. Gray (eds), *Letters from Smike: The Letters of Arthur Streeton 1890–1943*, Melbourne 1989

**Galbally and Slogget 1997**
A. Galbally and R. Slogget, 'John Peter Russell's *Dr Will Maloney*', *Art Bulletin of Victoria*, vol. 37, 1997

**Grant et al. 2004**
K. Grant et al., *The Joseph Brown Collection at NGV Australia*, Melbourne 2004

**Grishin 2013**
S. Grishin, *Australian Art: A History*, Melbourne 2013

**Hoorn 2007**
J. Hoorn, *Australian Pastoral: The Making of a White Landscape*, Fremantle 2007

**Hughes 1970**
R. Hughes, *The Art of Australia*, Harmondsworth 1970

**James 1999**
B. James, *Art Gallery of New South Wales Handbook*, Sydney 1999.

**Jansen et al. 2009**
L. Jansen, H. Luijten and N. Bakker (eds), *Vincent van Gogh, The Letters*, vol. 5, London 2009

**Lane 2003**
T. Lane, *Nineteenth-Century Australian Art in the National Gallery of Victoria*, Melbourne 2003

**London 2013**
*Australia*, exh. cat., London (Royal Academy) 2013

**London, Paris and Philadelphia 2015**
S. Patry (ed.), *Inventing Impressionism: Paul Durand-Ruel and the Modern Art Market*, exh. cat., London (National Gallery), Paris (Musée de Luxembourg) and Philadelphia (Philadelphia Museum of Art), 2015 (English edition)

**London and Ottawa 1962**
C. Turnbull, E. Young and D. Thomas, *Australian Painting: Colonial, Impressionist, Contemporary*, exh. cat., London (Tate Gallery) and Ottawa (National Gallery of Canada) 1962

**McCaughey 2014**
P. McCaughey, *Strange Country: Why Australian Painting Matters*, Carlton 2014

**McCulloch 1969**
A. McCulloch, *The Golden Age of Australian Painting: Impressionism and the Heidelberg School*, Melbourne 1969

**McDonald 2008**
J. McDonald, *Art of Australia, vol. 1: Exploration to Federation*, Sydney 2008

**McQueen 1996**
H. McQueen, *Tom Roberts*, Sydney 1996

**McQueen 2009**
H. McQueen, *A Framework of Flesh: Builders' Labourers Battle for Health and Safety*, Port Adelaide 2009

**Melbourne 1985**
J. Clark and B. Whitelaw, *Golden Summers: Heidelberg and Beyond*, exh. cat., Melbourne (National Gallery of Victoria) 1985

**Melbourne 1995**
G. Smith, *Arthur Streeton 1867–1943*, exh. cat., Melbourne (National Gallery of Victoria) 1995

**Melbourne 2007**
T. Lane, *Australian Impressionism*, exh. cat., Melbourne (National Gallery of Victoria) 2007

**Melbourne 2013**
E. Taylor, *Australian Impressionists in France*, exh. cat., Melbourne (National Gallery of Victoria) 2013

**Melbourne, Hartford and Washington DC 1998–9**
E. Johns, A. Sayers and E. Mankin Kornhauser, *New Worlds from Old: 19th Century Australian & American Landscapes*, exh. cat., Melbourne (National Gallery of Victoria), Hartford (Wadsworth Atheneum) and Washington DC (The Corcoran Gallery of Art) 1998–9

**Moore 1934**
W. Moore, *The Story of Australian Art*, 2 vols, Sydney 1934

**Radford and Hylton 1995**
R. Radford and J. Hylton, *Australian Colonial Art 1800–1900*, Adelaide 1995

**Rosenblum and Janson 2005**
R. Rosenblum and H.W. Janson, *19th-Century Art*, New York 2005 (revd. edn.)

**Sayers 2001**
A. Sayers, *Australian Art*, Oxford 2001

**Smith 1945**
B. Smith, *Place, Taste and Tradition: A Survey of Australian Art since 1788*, Sydney 1945

**Smith 1962**
B. Smith, *Australian Painting 1788–1960*, London 1962

**Smith 1975**
B. Smith, *Documents on Art and Taste in Australia 1770–1988*, Melbourne 1975, pp. 231–2

**Smith 2002**
T. Smith, *Transformations in Australian Art: The Nineteenth-Century – Landscape, Colony and Nation*, Sydney 2002

**Splatt and Bruce 1981**
W. Splatt and S. Bruce, *Australian Impressionist Painters: A Pictorial History of the Heidelberg School*, Melbourne 1981

**Sydney 2000**
B. Pearce, *Australian art in the Art Gallery of New South Wales*, Sydney 2000

**Sydney 2001**
U. Prunster, *Belle-Île: Monet, Russell & Matisse in Brittany*, exh. cat., Sydney (Art Gallery of New South Wales) 2001

**Sydney 2003**
A. Galbally, B. Pearce et al., *Charles Conder*, exh. cat., Sydney (Art Gallery of New South Wales) 2003

**Sydney 2012**
D. Mimmocchi, *Australian Symbolism: The Art of Dreams*, exh. cat., Sydney (Art Gallery of New South Wales) 2012

**Thomas 1973**
D. Thomas, *Outlines of Australian Art: The Joseph Brown Collection*, Melbourne 1973

**Thoms 1991**
A. Thoms, *Bohemians in the Bush: The Artists Camps of Mosman*, Art Gallery of New South Wales, Sydney 1991

**Topliss 1992**
H. Topliss, *The Artists' Camps: 'Plein air' Painting in Australia*, Melbourne 1992

**Topliss 1985**
H. Topliss, *Tom Roberts, 1856–1931: A Catalogue Raisonné, 2 vols*, Melbourne 1985

# List of Lenders

**Adelaide**
Art Gallery of South Australia

**Canberra**
National Gallery of Australia
The National Library of Australia

**Melbourne**
National Gallery of Victoria

**Perth**
Kerry Stokes Collection

**Switzerland**
Private Collection

**Sydney**
Art Gallery of New South Wales

*And those private collectors who wish to remain anonymous.*

# List of Works

**Charles Conder** (1868–1909)

*Riddells Creek*, 1889
Oil on wood panel on paper on two layers of cardboard, 24.4 × 11.2 cm
National Gallery of Australia, Canberra
Purchased 1972 (Accession No. NGA 72.8) Cat. 7, p. 69

*Dandenongs from Heidelberg*, about 1889
Oil on wood panel, 11.5 × 23.5 cm
Art Gallery of South Australia, Adelaide
M.J.M. Carter AO Collection through the Art Gallery of South Australia Foundation 2012, to mark the 123rd anniversary of the '9 by 5 Impression Exhibition', August 1889. Donated through the Australian Government's Cultural Gifts Program (Accession No. 20124P12) Cat. 8, p. 70

*Departure of the Orient – Circular Quay*, 1888
Oil on canvas, 45.1 × 50.1 cm
Art Gallery of New South Wales, Sydney
Purchased 1888 (Accession No. 829) Cat. 11, p. 74

*On the River Yarra, near Heidelberg, Victoria*, about 1890
Oil on canvas, 30.4 × 40.7 cm
Art Gallery of New South Wales, Sydney
Jean Cameron Gordon Bequest Fund in memory of her mother Mary Gordon 2002 (Accession No. 298.2002) Cat. 18, p. 81

*Coogee Bay*, 1888
Oil on cardboard, 26.8 × 40.7 cm
National Gallery of Victoria, Melbourne
Purchased with the assistance of a special grant from the Government of Victoria, 1979 (Accession No. A41·1980) Cat. 25, p. 89

*A Holiday at Mentone*, 1888
Oil on canvas, 46.2 × 60.8 cm
Art Gallery of South Australia, Adelaide
South Australian Government Grant with the assistance of Bond Corporation Holdings Limited through the Art Gallery of South Australia Foundation to mark the Gallery's Centenary 1981 (Accession No. 815P14) Cat. 31, pp. 96–7

**Tom Roberts** (1856–1931)

*Trafalgar Square*, 1904
Oil on cardboard, 14 × 28 cm
Art Gallery of South Australia, Adelaide
South Australian Government Grant 1988 (Accession No. 8810P45) Cat. 1, p. 64

*Fog, Thames Embankment*, 1884
Oil on paperboard, 13.1 × 21.7 cm
Art Gallery of New South Wales, Sydney
Purchased with funds provided by the Gleeson O'Keefe Foundation 2008 (Accession No. 1.2008) Cat. 2, p. 64

*By the Treasury*, 1889
Oil on wood panel, 23.6 × 14.2 cm
National Gallery of Victoria, Melbourne
Purchased through the NGV Foundation by The Hugh D.T. Williamson Foundation, Founder Benefactor, 2002 (Accession No. 2002.304) Cat. 3, p. 65

*Across the Dandenongs*, 1889
Oil on wood panel, 13.7 × 23.1 cm
National Gallery of Victoria, Melbourne
Purchased, 1962 (Accession No. 1207-5) Cat. 9, p. 71

*Allegro con Brio, Bourke Street West*, about 1885–6, reworked 1890
Oil on canvas mounted on composition board, 51.2 × 76.7 cm
National Gallery of Australia, Canberra and the National Library of Australia, Canberra
Purchased 1920 by the Parliamentary Library Committee. Cat. 14, p. 77

*A Quiet Day on Darebin Creek*, 1885
Oil on wood panel, 26.4 × 34.8 cm
National Gallery of Australia, Canberra
Purchased 1969 (Accession No. NGA 69.4) Cat. 15, p. 78

*Winter Morning after Rain, Gardiner's Creek*, 1885
Oil on canvas, 47 × 66 cm
Art Gallery of South Australia, Adelaide
M.J.M. Carter AO Collection through the Art Gallery of South Australia Foundation to mark the 130th anniversary of the Gallery, 2011 (Accession No. 20111P14) Cat. 16, p. 79

*Saplings*, about 1889
Oil on cedar panel, 34.5 × 14.5 cm
Art Gallery of South Australia, Adelaide
Morgan Thomas Bequest Fund 1927 (Accession No. 0.707) Cat. 17, p. 80

*A Break Away!*, 1891
Oil on canvas, 137.3 × 157.8 cm
Art Gallery of South Australia, Adelaide
Elder Bequest Fund 1899 (Accession No. 0.139) Cat. 22, p. 86

*Holiday Sketch at Coogee*, 1888
Oil on canvas, 40.3 × 55.9 cm
Art Gallery of New South Wales, Sydney
Purchased 1954 (Accession No. 9078) Cat. 24, p. 88

*The Camp, Sirius Cove*, 1899
Oil on canvas on paperboard, 25.4 × 34.6 cm
Art Gallery of New South Wales, Sydney
Purchased 1940 (Accession No. 6928) Cat. 28, p. 92

**John Russell** (1858–1930)

*Madame Sisley on the Banks of the Loing at Moret*, 1887
Oil on canvas, 45.7 × 60.9 cm
Art Gallery of New South Wales, Sydney
Purchased with assistance from the Margaret Hannah Olley Art Trust 1996 (Accession No. 768.1996) Cat. 32, p. 98

*In the Morning, Alpes Maritimes from Antibes*, 1890–1
Oil on canvas, 60.3 × 73.2 cm
National Gallery of Australia, Canberra
Purchased 1965 (Accession No. NGA 65.25) Cat. 33, p. 99

*Les Terrasses de Monte Cassino*, about 1889
Oil on canvas, 65 × 81 cm
Private Collection courtesy of Nevill Keating Pictures
Cat. 34, p. 100

*A Clearing in the Forest*, 1891
Oil on canvas, 61 × 55.9 cm
Art Gallery of South Australia, Adelaide
A.M. & A.R. Ragless Bequest Funds 1968 (Accession No. 6812P17) Cat. 35, p. 101

*Antibes*, about 1890–2
Oil on canvas, 16.5 × 24 cm
Art Gallery of New South Wales, Sydney
Gift of the Margaret Hannah Olley Art Trust 2012 (Accession No. 190.2012) Cat. 36, p. 102

*Aiguille de Coton, Belle Île*, about 1900
Oil on canvas, 60.8 x 50.5 cm
Kerry Stokes Collection, Perth
(Accession No. 1992.043) Cat. 37, p. 103

*Coucher de Soleil sur Morestil*, about 1904
Oil on hessian, 80.6 × 100.3 cm
Private collection, Switzerland
Cat. 38, p. 104

*Rough Sea, Belle-Île*, 1900
Oil on canvas, 63.2 × 63.1 cm
National Gallery of Victoria, Melbourne
The Joseph Brown Collection. Presented through the NGV Foundation by Dr Joseph Brown AO OBE, Honorary Life Benefactor, 2004 (Accession No. 2004.217) Cat. 39, p. 105

*Rough Sea, Morestil*, about 1900
Oil on canvas on hardboard, 66 × 81.8 cm
Art Gallery of New South Wales, Sydney
Purchased 1968 (Accession No. OA14.1968) Cat. 40, p. 106

*Cruach en Mahr, Matin, Belle-Île-en-Mer*, about 1905
Oil on canvas, 60.4 × 73.5 cm
Private Collection courtesy of Nevill Keating Pictures
Cat. 41, p. 107

**Arthur Streeton** (1867–1943)

*Sandridge*, about 1888
Oil on wood panel, 12.8 × 23.3 cm
National Gallery of Australia, Canberra
Purchased 1969 (Accession No. NGA 69.47) Cat. 4, p. 66

*The National Game*, 1889
Oil on cardboard, 11.8 × 22.9 cm
Art Gallery of New South Wales, Sydney
Purchased 1963 (Accession No. OA11.1963) Cat. 5, p. 67

*Hoddle St., 10 pm*, 1889
Oil on cardboard, 7.9 × 23.3 cm
National Gallery of Australia, Canberra
Purchased 1974 (Accession No. NGA 74.138) Cat. 6, p. 68

*Between the Lights – Princes Bridge*, 1888
Oil on canvas, 82 × 152 cm
Private collection, London
Cat. 10, pp. 72–3

*Fireman's Funeral, George Street*, 1894
Oil on canvas, 45.3 × 38.2 cm
Art Gallery of New South Wales, Sydney
Purchased 1980 (Accession No. 43.1980) Cat. 12, p. 75

*The Railway Station, Redfern*, 1893
Oil on canvas, 40.8 × 61 cm
Art Gallery of New South Wales, Sydney
Gift of Lady Denison 1942 (Accession No. 7209) Cat. 13, p. 76

*'Still glides the stream, and shall for ever glide'*, 1890
Oil on canvas, 82.6 × 153 cm
Art Gallery of New South Wales, Sydney
Purchased 1890 (Accession No. 859) Cat. 19, p. 82

*'The purple noon's transparent might'*, 1896
Oil on canvas, 123 × 123 cm
National Gallery of Victoria, Melbourne
Purchased, 1896 (Accession No. 33-2) Cat. 20, p. 83

*Golden Summer, Eaglemont*, 1889
Oil on canvas, 81.3 × 152.6 cm
National Gallery of Australia, Canberra
Purchased 1995 (Accession No. NGA 95.604) Cat. 21, pp. 84–5

*Fire's On*, 1891
Oil on canvas, 183.8 × 122.5 cm
Art Gallery of New South Wales, Sydney
Purchased 1893 (Accession No. 832) Cat. 23, p. 87

*Sirius Cove*, about 1895
Oil on wood panel, 68.8 × 16.8 cm
National Gallery of Australia, Canberra
Purchased 1973 (Accession No. NGA 73.1) Cat. 26, p. 90

*Blue Pacific*, 1890
Oil on canvas, 91.4 × 50.8 cm
On loan to the National Gallery from a private collection
Cat. 27, p. 91

*Ariadne*, 1895
Oil on wood panel, 12.7 × 35.4 cm
National Gallery of Australia, Canberra
Members Acquisition Fund 2016 (Accession No. NGA 2015.1124) Cat. 29, p. 93

*Circular Quay*, 1892
Oil on wood panel, 19.3 × 47.6 cm
National Gallery of Australia, Canberra
Purchased 1959 (Accession No. NGA 59.222) Cat. 30, pp. 94–5

# Index

# Credits

Photographic Credits:

ADELAIDE © Art Gallery of South Australia, Adelaide: cats 1, 8, 16, 17, 22, 31, 35

AMSTERDAM © Van Gogh Museum (Vincent Van Gogh Foundation), Amsterdam: fig. 30

BRISBANE © Queensland Art Gallery, Brisbane: fig. 10

CANBERRA © National Gallery of Australia, Canberra: cats 4, 6, 7, 15, 21, 26, 29, 30, 33 and figs 11, 19, 27; © National Gallery of Australia, Canberra and the National Library of Australia, Canberra: cat. 14

KANSAS CITY, MISSOURI © Nelson-Atkins Museum of Art, Kansas City, USA / Bridgeman Images: fig. 39

LONDON © London Metropolitan Archives: fig. 37; © The National Gallery, London: figs 3, 4, 38; © Tate, London 2015: fig. 24

MELBOURNE © National Gallery of Victoria, Melbourne: cats 3, 9, 20, 25, 39 and figs 2, 8, 12, 14, 20, 23; © State Library of Victoria: fig. 18

MORLAIX © Musée de Morlaix: fig. 29

PERTH Kerry Stokes Collection, Perth © Acorn Photo, Perth: cat. 37; © State Art Collection, Art Gallery of Western Australia: fig. 25

PRIVATE COLLECTION © 2015 Christie's Images Limited: cat. 38; © Photo courtesy of the owner: cats 10, 27 and fig. 7; © Photo Justin Miller Art, Sydney Australia: fig. 5; © Private Collection courtesy of Nevill Keating Pictures: cats 34 and 41

SYDNEY Art Gallery of New South Wales, Sydney © AGNSW: cats 2, 5, 11, 12, 13, 18, 19, 23, 24, 28, 32, 36, 40 and figs 16, 26, 31, 34, 35; © State Library of New South Wales: fig. 15

WASHINGTON, DC © Freer Gallery of Art, Smithsonian Institution, Washington, DC: fig. 17



First published in Great Britain in 2016
by National Gallery Company Limited
St Vincent House, 30 Orange Street
London WC2H 7HH

www.nationalgallery.co.uk

ISBN: 9781857096125
1042732

British Library Cataloguing-in-Publication Data. A catalogue record is available from the British Library.

Library of Congress Control Number: 2016954664

Publisher: Jan Green
Project Editor: Claire Young
Editor: Emily Winter
Picture Researcher: Félix Zorzo
Production: Jane Hyne
Designed by Lawn Creative, Liverpool
Index compiled by Elizabeth Wiggans
Printed in Italy by Verona Libri
All measurements give height before width

Front cover:

**Arthur Streeton**, *Ariadne*, 1895
National Gallery of Australia, Canberra

Members Acquisition Fund 2016
(Accession No. NGA 2015.1124) (Cat. 29, p. 93)

Pages 2–3:
**Tom Roberts**, *Allegro con Brio, Bourke Street West*, about 1885–6, reworked 1890
National Gallery of Australia, Canberra and the National Library of Australia, Canberra

Purchased 1920 by the Parliamentary Library Committee (Cat. 14, p. 77)

Pages 6–7:
**Charles Conder**, *Coogee Bay*, 1888
National Gallery of Victoria, Melbourne

Purchased with the assistance of a special grant from the Government of Victoria, 1979
(Accession No. A41-1980) (Cat. 25, p. 89)

Pages 8–9:
**Tom Roberts**, *A Break Away!*, 1891
Art Gallery of South Australia, Adelaide

Elder Bequest Fund 1899 (Accession No. 0.139)
(Cat. 22, p. 86)

Pages 62–3:
**Arthur Streeton**, *Golden Summer, Eaglemont*, 1889
National Gallery of Australia, Canberra

Purchased 1995 (Accession No. NGA 95.604)
(Cat. 21, pp. 84–5)

Pages 108–9:
**John Russell**, *Les Terrasses de Monte Cassino*, about 1889
Private Collection courtesy of Nevill Keating Pictures (Cat. 34, p. 100)